do it for le$$!

W9-APY-639

How to Create
Your Dream Wedding
Without Breaking the Bank

# weddings

## Denise Vivaldo

SELLERS
PUBLISHING

Published by Sellers Publishing, Inc.
Copyright © 2008 Denise Vivaldo
All rights reserved.

Edited by: Megan Hiller
Cover design: Heather Zschock

ISBN 13: 978-1-4162-0519-7
Library of Congress Control Number: 2008923779

P.O. Box 818, Portland, Maine 04104
For ordering information: (800) 625-3386 toll-free
Visit our Web site: www.rsvp.com • E-mail: rsp@rsvp.com

Web site: www.DIFLWeddings.com

Photo credits:
Front cover photo: Getty Images/George Doyle
Back cover author photo: Victor Boghossian
Interior photos:
Pages 8, 11, 20, 45, 47, 48, 52, 56, 57, 75, 86, 104, 131, 132, 140, 141, 146, 147, 148, 150, 153, 156, 157, 160, 163, 165, 166, 167, 174, 176, 177, 180, 185, 186, 187, 190, 194, 198, 199, 202, 210, and 248 by Matt Armendariz.
Pages 219, 220, 222, 225, 227, 229, 231, 234, 237, 241 and 245 by Hee Youn Kim.
Pages 85, 87, and 249 by Jon Edwards.
Page 84 by Victor Boghossian.
Page 28 and 93, Bristol Farms by Jon Edwards.
Page 79, Contessa Premium Foods by Jon Edwards.
Page 252, Jamie McMonigle and Associates by Jon Edwards.

Illustrations by Cindie Flannigan.
Food Styling by Denise Vivaldo and Cindie Flannigan of Food Fanatics.net.

No portion of this book may be reproduced, stored in a
retrieval system, or transmitted in any form or by any means,
mechanical, electronic, photocopying, recording, or otherwise,
without the written permission of the publisher.

10 9 8 7 6 5 4 3 2 1

Printed in China.

Dedication:
*To my mother, Doris Vivaldo, who gave me two perfect weddings.*
*Bird, you were right about everything.*

# contents

# introduction

Throughout my twenty years as a chef and caterer in Hollywood, I've produced all sorts of weddings from spectacular celebrity events, with yachts, helicopters and 12-tiered wedding cakes, to small, intimate ceremonies on a public beach with receptions of fresh lemonade and popcorn. Without exception, I have enjoyed every sort of wedding, except for one kind. What I hated to see were people who spent a great deal of time, emotions, and money, and yet they still weren't happy on their wedding day. They allowed families, money, expectations, and fantasies to clash horribly around the event, truly spoiling a day that could have been one of the happiest in their lifetime.

So through the years, I've been able to help couples and families struggling with wedding issues to avoid unhappy wedding experiences by asking them the right questions. And with their honest answers, we all worked together to execute their big day. I want weddings to be as painless and as flawless as possible. Most importantly, I want everyone to enjoy the special event — especially the bride and groom.

In fact, I believe that by making the bride and groom confident, secure, and in control, the couple sets the tone together for a successful wedding and, ultimately, a successful partnership and marriage.

In *Do-It-for-Less! Weddings*, I want to help you organize and experience a beautiful wedding that doesn't break either family's bank account or leave you in debt for the first foundational years of marriage. In America today, the national average cost for a wedding is $27,000. That's enough money to use as a down payment on a house, car, or boat! This number is frightening to me, and it should be to you as well.

Now, don't misunderstand; if you want and have the resources to get trained, white doves to coo Barry Manilow hits for your recessional, it can be arranged. Anything can be arranged. But if you're on a budget but would still like to have the wedding of your dreams (and have money for a fabulous honeymoon!) keep reading.

*Do-It-for-Less! Weddings* encourages you to think outside of the box. With some resourcefulness and careful planning, we'll work together to make every dollar count and give you the event of your dreams.

Here's a quiz to help you start thinking about and planning your do-it-for-less wedding. Answer honestly! It will help you decide if you're up to the job of producing your own fabulous wedding. And remember — this book is about your hopes and dreams for your wedding, not someone else's expectations or out-of-scale ideas from the billion-dollar wedding industry.

1. What's the happiest, sweetest, or most important thing you'd like your fiancée to remember about your wedding day together fifty years from now.

2. What's an example of a special or precious element you remember about the last wedding you attended?

3. Without considering other people's expectations, what do you really think is important to a successful wedding?

4. Write a paragraph that visualizes your dream of a perfect wedding — maybe it is a wedding you saw on television or in a magazine or something you remember from childhood. What comes to mind?

5. If this is your second wedding, can you be honest about what you learned from planning the last one?

6. Why do you want to have a wedding? Why not elope?

The true purpose of a wedding ceremony is to announce to the world that two people are joining their lives. Unlike the weddings of yesteryear — orchestrated to help a male inherit the farm, protect a brother's widow, or, my favorite, save women from a life of misery — weddings today celebrate the love, respect, and long-term commitment between two people. Still, wedding fever strikes most all new brides-to-be, and they don't leave much planning for the marriage itself. By budgeting and prioritizing, you'll keep perspective on what's truly important and keep your inner Bridezilla at bay.

In *Do-It-for-Less! Weddings*, I'm going to show you how to plan a perfect wedding in less time, for less money, and with fewer headaches, leaving you more time to enjoy the day, and more important, the relationship itself.

Can you direct your own big day? I know you can. Let's get started!

# chapter 1
# planning your
# dream wedding

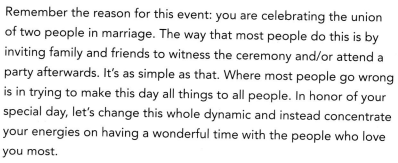

Remember the reason for this event: you are celebrating the union of two people in marriage. The way that most people do this is by inviting family and friends to witness the ceremony and/or attend a party afterwards. It's as simple as that. Where most people go wrong is in trying to make this day all things to all people. In honor of your special day, let's change this whole dynamic and instead concentrate your energies on having a wonderful time with the people who love you most.

Because your wedding is a once-in-a-lifetime event (hopefully!), you will probably feel pressured to make it perfect, particularly if you want your "dream" wedding. If you are feeling any outside pressure, I suggest you tell those responsible for the pressure that it is your wedding and you feel strongly about doing it your way. However, if they would like to foot the bill, you'd be happy to consider their preferences.

If you are the source of your own stress, then this is where we can help. We need to address all the issues that are causing your anxiety, such as wedding deadlines and budget, and place the control firmly back into your hands.

# GET REAL: CAN YOU DO IT YOURSELF?

Of course you can do it yourself, but you must first realize that spending $35,000 on your wedding is not just beyond your means, but it would also be a most unfortunate first step to take in life with your new husband. If you and your families want to avoid a Bridezilla wedding and can't or won't spend an egregious amount of money for a one-day event, this book is for you.

When you do your wedding yourself, you are your own wedding coordinator. Organization and creativity are key requirements for orchestrating your own wedding. If you are not the most creative bride, it's at least helpful to have creative or artistic friends to help plan the decorations and flowers. If you are a bride dedicated to saving money and have friends or family who can help you, planning your own wedding is a great alternative to going into debt for a lot of extraneous extravagances.

If you are willing to be resourceful and creative in regards to location, food and beverage options, cakes, decorations, invitations, and wedding attire, then you can coordinate your own wedding. Take our Do-It-for-Less! Survey to ensure that you have what it takes.

## DO-IT-FOR-LESS SURVEY

1. Are you or someone you know very organized? ❑ Yes ❑ No
2. Are you willing to let go of the "dream" wedding and focus on the memorable event? ❑ Yes ❑ No
3. Do you have someone willing and able to orchestrate the actual event while you are being the bride? ❑ Yes ❑ No
4. Do you have a group of people who you can enlist to help you? ❑ Yes ❑ No
5. Do you have five hours a week to spend on doing it yourself? ❑ Yes ❑ No
6. Are you good at throwing parties? ❑ Yes ❑ No
7. Do you need to have a wedding on a budget? ❑ Yes ❑ No
8. Is there a trusted person to whom you can give control on "the day"? ❑ Yes ❑ No
9. Do you (or someone close to you) love to cook? ❑ Yes ❑ No
10. Are you (or someone close to you) good at crafts? ❑ Yes ❑ No
11. Are you (or someone close to you) good at decorating? ❑ Yes ❑ No

If you answered yes to eight or more questions, you are absolutely the right person to do your wedding yourself! If you didn't, you can still cut costs by carefully choosing one to two wedding components that you can do yourself for less.

## ENLISTING HELP

By enlisting the help of friends and family members to help plan your wedding day, you can guarantee a much smoother wedding experience. Dedicated and reliable people who love you are invaluable in the wedding-planning process. To ensure that your day arrives and plays out just as you wanted it to, you should provide every person helping you with detailed information about his or her responsibilities.

Each assignment, task, or responsibility — from ordering the invitations to picking up the bridesmaid dresses to arranging transportation for the wedding party — needs to come with a specific list of instructions, due dates, and detailed criteria. The less you leave up to their imagination, the more your wedding will be what you want.

For projects that work well with a group, invite friends and family over on a Sunday afternoon to make wedding favors. The following Sunday, invite a few other people over to make invitations and save-the-date cards. Consider these afternoon get-togethers a Do-It-For-Less Mini-Party. Here are a few examples of things you can accomplish at a mini-party.

### Do-It-For-Less Mini-Parties:

- Assemble wedding favors for the wedding guests.

- Assemble birdseed bags or bubble bottles for use during the bride and groom's exit.

- Embellish and hand-address save-the-date cards to remind your friends and family of the event, and mail six months to a year prior to the wedding day.

- Stuff and address invitation envelopes and mail these six weeks prior to the wedding day.

- Embellish your wedding program/order of service.

- Hand-letter and embellish place cards so people will know where to sit during the reception dinner.

- Create a throw-away bouquet from inexpensive silk flowers.

- Mix CDs for the reception.

- Prepare any reception food that can be made in advance and frozen until ready to serve.

- Organize and assemble centerpieces that do not require the use of fresh flowers.

- Iron the tablecloths for the reception.

Do you know someone with an extra freezer? If yes, then go ahead and make as much of the food ahead of time and freeze it. Make that another Sunday get-together! You can make your cake months ahead of time if you wrap it well and keep it frozen. See page 214 for more details.

What if you don't know anyone willing to cook for or with you? Consider hiring a culinary student or two to come to your home and cook. Ask the professors which students stand out as exemplary and test their skills before hiring them. Even if you're not comfortable handing over the entire menu, culinary students can make indispensable sous-chefs. They can prep your "mise en place" and wash the dirty dishes, leaving you enough time (and sanity) to make much of the reception food ahead of time.

What if you are struggling to find a location for your wedding? Consider asking one of your friends with a beautiful house and yard if you could have your wedding there. Not having to pay rental fees for your ceremony or reception location could save you lots of money. Borrowing space, tables, chairs, or flatware from your friends and family will save you money, though not always time or energy. You won't have to spend time negotiating with vendors, but you will have to retrieve and return the borrowed items in good condition.

Still, when you're on a tight budget, there's nothing quite as cheap as free! Just borrow wisely and treat the items with respect. Likewise, always remember that these people are your friends and family and should be treated accordingly. Don't saddle them with too much responsibility, and always be gracious and thankful for their help. They love you and are more than willing to help, just make them feel appreciated.

## THE IMPORTANCE OF LISTS

I mentioned earlier that you need to make lists for your friends so they can handle their wedding responsibilities. By enlisting the help of friends and family members to help plan your wedding day, you can guarantee a much smoother wedding experience. Dedicated and reliable people who love you are invaluable in the wedding planning process. However, just because your friends have a track record for being reliable, doesn't necessarily mean that they will be every time. To ensure that your day arrives and plays out just as you want it to, you should provide each person helping you with detailed information about their responsibility.

This goes for you, too — be sure to create detailed lists for yourself. I don't know about you, but I can't remember what I did yesterday unless I write it down. Being organized is the single most important thing you can do. And being organized means lists, lists, lists! Here are the must-have lists for your wedding:

## Budget List

This is single-most important list of your wedding planning. Doing your wedding yourself requires that you keep track of the money you spend out of your set budget. Do not exceed your budget.

## Master Timeline

This is the second-most important list that you will use. The master timeline keeps you on track of your overall responsibilities for the wedding and includes all your major deadlines. It helps you keep up with appointments, meetings, and deadlines. Keep this list handy so you can add to it as things occur to you

## Guest List

This is where you start your planning and budgeting. The easiest way to figure out how much your wedding is going to cost is by deciding on a head count. Use your guest list to keep track of save-the-date cards, invitations, thank you cards, menu planning, and seating arrangements.

## Reception Lists

### Grocery lists

See the shopping lists for specific menus, which are divided up according to what can be purchased or made ahead of time and what is more last-minute.

### Food prep lists

This includes lists for make-ahead items and lists for all those details that often get overlooked in the rush of the last week.

### Beverages and bar list

This include the costs for all beverages you will serve at your wedding. This is helpful because you can immediately see how it affects your budget.

## List of All Involved Parties

Include on this list the names, addresses, phone numbers, and email addresses of everyone involved in your wedding. This includes everyone from family members, attendants, wedding participants, and the officiate to all of your vendors and the local police and fire departments, nearest hospital, taxi service, and 24-hour plumbers and electricians.

## List of Any Do-It-For-Less Components

Make separate lists for each wedding component for which you are personally responsible. This will ensure that you can keep track of the numerous details.

# GREEN WEDDINGS

Here are a few Do-It-for-Less! tips for making your wedding eco-friendly.

### Buy organic and locally produced.
If you are cooking your own food, buy organic, locally grown or produced ingredients when you can. Local products take less fuel to get to you. Even organic liquor is available. Vodka is made domestically and is the easiest to find but brandy, gin, and rum are also made organically.

### Print on recycled paper.
Print your invitations, save-the-date cards, thank you notes, or any other paper items on 100 percent recycled paper. Unlike twenty years ago, recycled paper now comes in all colors and varieties.

### Use the Internet.
Do announcements concerning your wedding electronically so that no paper is used at all. Set up a wedding Web site to share information and photos with your guests. Include a slide show of your wedding photos after the wedding is over. This is especially nice if you are having your wedding at a distant location or have friends or relatives that can't attend but would love to be part of your wedding without leaving their own homes.

### Consolidate locations.
Have your wedding and reception at the same location; save you and your guests, time, gas, energy, and money. Assuming most of your guests live nearby; have your wedding as close as possible to home.

### Borrow your wedding dress.
Have a friend who just got married and is your size? Why not ask to borrow her dress. Save yourself money, stress, and start a lovely, new tradition. Or buy one that's been worn once. Check online for deals. Web sites like CraigsList.com, WoreItOnce.com, SellYourWeddingDress.com, and UsedWeddingDresses.com are all good sources. Remember, buy slightly larger as you can always have it taken in.

### Planet-friendly gifts.
Ask your friends for presents that help you help the planet like a composting system for your yard, a bicycle built for two, gift certificates to a garden center, re-useable food storage boxes, or organic cotton sheets and towels.

### Shopping tote bags.
Print your Save-the-Date info on a re-usable shopping tote. Or use cloth totes for your wedding favors. Roll each one up and tie with a ribbon or twine with guest name tags and let them double as place cards.

### Honeymoon locally.
Plan a honeymoon close to where you live like a nearby resort or charming bed and breakfast. Destination honeymoons take extra time, money, and fuel.

### Forego disposables.
Use only cloth napkins at your reception. Use real dishes and flatware. Borrow or rent instead of purchasing disposables that will be added to a landfill.

### Eco-smart wedding registry.
Register for wedding gifts you can use at the reception. Ask guests to have these gifts sent to you two weeks early. A pretty chafing dish, flatware, table linens, candles and tea lights, occasional or folding tables, outdoor furniture; anything you will use again.

### Get potted.
Use potted plants, flowers, herbs, or even vegetables for your centerpieces. Use as wedding favors for guests to take home and plant in their garden. Or purchase plants that will end up as part of your own yard.

### Donate.
Second marriage? Have everything you need? Ask your guests to donate to your favorite charity or environmental organization. Word your request in a way that makes it sound like the lovely and appreciated gift that it is. Include an easy way for people to donate like a Web site address or, better yet, a stamped and addressed card that people can slip a check into and mail. You might write something like this: *There isn't a thing in the world they need now that Gail and Wally have each other, although they would greatly appreciate a donation in their name to the Save the Bay Foundation.*

# MASTER TIMELINE

You'll next need to incorporate all your to-do lists into a master timeline. Use these guidelines to help you schedule everything you need to create the perfect day.

## 9 TO 12 MONTHS BEFORE

### Budget
- Establish a wedding budget and set up a wedding bank account.
- Decide how to share expenses between your families.
- Determine the type of wedding you want (size, formality, style, color scheme).
- Determine how many guests may attend.

### Ceremony
- Select several potential wedding dates and times.
- Determine who will officiate at the ceremony.
- Select and secure your ceremony location.

### Reception
- Book a caterer.
- Book your reception location.
- Book your entertainment.
- Begin choosing your wedding cake baker and florist. Sign necessary contracts.

### Photography
- Select and secure a photographer/videographer.

### Miscellaneous
- Announce your engagement in the newspaper.
- Book specialty transportation for the wedding party on the wedding day.
- Shop for wedding rings.

## 6 TO 9 MONTHS BEFORE

### Guests
- Start compiling the guest list.
- Select the attendants for your wedding party.

### Bridesmaids
- Schedule fittings for the bridesmaids.
- Choose bridesmaids' dresses and accessories.
- Schedule delivery dates for all bridesmaid items.

### Wedding Attire
- Shop for the wedding dress, headpiece, veil, etc.

### Miscellaneous
- Start planning for the honeymoon.
- Register with a gift bridal registry.

## 4 TO 6 MONTHS BEFORE

### Invitations and Printing
- Select, order, or make your invitations, stationery, napkins, and wedding favors.
- Design and print the program for the ceremony.
- Prepare all maps and directions for the ceremony and reception.
- Send out Save-the-Date cards.

### Attire and Accessories
- Select and order the mens' attire.
- Double check all bridal attire arrangements.
- Determine wedding hairstyle.

### Miscellaneous
- Make appointments for a physical exam with your doctor/dentist.
- Check requirements for blood test and marriage license in your state.
- Finalize honeymoon details and make the necessary reservations.

## 2 TO 4 MONTHS BEFORE

### Food
- Confirm the menu.
- Confirm the wedding cake details with the baker.
- Plan the bridesmaid's luncheon and any other parties.
- Plan a rehearsal dinner, time, and place.

### Accommodations
- Arrange the necessary accommodations for out-of-town guests.

Miscellaneous

- Finalize the florist details, photographer, videographer, DJ/MC, etc.
- Set the dates and times with the officiate for the rehearsal.
- Buy a wedding guest book.

## 6 TO 8 WEEKS BEFORE

Invitations

- Mail invitations.

Photography

- Set appointment with photographer for your formal bridal portrait.

Gifts

- Select gifts for all your attendants.

Attire and Accessories

- Set appointments with any hairdressers and/or makeup artists.

## 4 TO 6 WEEKS BEFORE

Reception and Ceremony

- Decide what your menu is going to be for the reception.
- Confirm florist details and delivery times.
- Plan the seating for the reception as well as other details for the ceremony and reception. Start writing place cards.
- Purchase (borrow) all wedding accessories such as the ring pillow, goblets, garter belt, candles, etc.

Gifts

- Buy or make a gift for the groom.
- Buy a gift for the bride.
- Wrap and present the wedding party gifts.

Wedding Attire

- Schedule a final fitting for your gown so it can be ready for your formal bridal portrait.
- Pick up your wedding rings.

Bridesmaids

- Make sure all bridesmaids' attire has been fitted.

## 2 WEEKS BEFORE

Reception

- Set up final consultation with your DJ/MC.

Accommodations

- Reconfirm your guests' accommodations.

Wedding Attire

- Make sure all clothing and accessories for you and the bridal party are ready.

Miscellaneous

- Get your marriage license and any blood tests that are needed.
- Handle business and legal details such as name changes, address changes, etc.

## THE WEEK BEFORE

Reception and Ceremony

- Review any seating details with the ushers.
- Finalize the seating arrangements.
- Make sure all wedding attire fits.
- Review all the final details with your photographer, videographer, etc.
- Give a final head count to the caterer.
- Finish all the place cards for the reception.

Guests

- Call any guests who have not responded yet.

Honeymoon

- Reconfirm your honeymoon reservations. Ensure you have any necessary plane tickets.
- Start packing for your honeymoon.

Miscellaneous

- Delegate responsibilities to reliable individuals on your wedding day.
- Finalize your rehearsal dinner arrangements or other plans.

## THE DAY BEFORE

- Review and rehearse the details with your wedding participants.

## THE BIG DAY

- Make sure the best man and maid of honor sign your wedding certificate.

**BENEFITS OF A
WEDDING PLANNER**

Choosing a wedding coordinator to handle the last month of your wedding will save you an immense amount of stress. Picking the flowers and decorations does not stress a bride as much as the final responsibility of making sure that the wedding comes together successfully at the right moment. In the few weeks leading up to the wedding, a bride can experience more stress than she probably felt the entire 12 months of planning. Hiring someone to handle these last few weeks can ease the level of anxiety.

And now that the nuts and bolts are in place, it's time to get creative. Inspiration is all around you. I was in Costco the other day and found a display of wire-edge ribbon. I especially liked a 2-inch-wide striped ribbon in pale pink, lavender, and yellow. A roll of 150 feet costs about $6. I could have bought five or six rolls and used that as my color scheme jumping-off point, using just one of the colors as the main décor color and accenting with the other two colors.

Sometimes it is truly that simple. Remember, people won't care what your inspiration is; they will simply enjoy the mood it creates. It is the framework on which you build your wedding, the foundation that supports everything else. Once you pick a theme, stick with it! It'll cost you too much time and money to change themes. If you just can't choose, then do a bit of pricing on your three favorite themes. You'll find that some directions are easier and less expensive to pull off than others.

Books (we suggest some of our favorites in the Resources Guide on page 260) and magazines are filled with photos to inspire you. Tear out pages in magazines. Collect your favorite images from Web sites. Pick out some color swatches from bridal and stationery stores. Compile all of these elements that you find inspirational into a wedding binder for easy reference.

Do you already have a location in mind? It's easier to fit your theme to an existing location than it is to fit an existing location into your theme. What is your favorite flower? Is it in season when you want to have your wedding? What is your favorite color? Monochromatic looks make for easy elegant planning.

We've supplied you with themes in pages 131 through 209. Each of eight wedding plans has its own theme, menu, decorations and centerpieces, invitations, and suggested locations.

Still need help getting inspired? Take the following test to find out.

## DISCOVER YOUR DREAMS: BASIC INSPIRATION SURVEY

Rank wedding component importance:

Wedding dress _____    Reception music _____
Tuxedo        _____    Reception food _____
Flowers/décor _____    Honeymoon      _____
Photography   _____    Down payment on house _____
Videography   _____
Ceremony music _____

Preferred season:
❑ Spring    ❑ Summer    ❑ Fall    ❑ Winter

Preferred time of day:
❑ Morning    ❑ Afternoon    ❑ Late afternoon
❑ Early evening    ❑ Evening

Favorite color:                Alternate color:

_____        _____


Accent colors:

_____  _____  _____


Favorite flower:                        Alternate flower:

_____        _____


How would you describe your preferred style of wedding?
Check all that apply.
❑ Modern            ❑ Clean        ❑ Zen
❑ Fun               ❑ Retro        ❑ Old-fashioned
❑ Casual/informal   ❑ Glamorous    ❑ Floral/botanical

How would you describe your ideal videography to look?

❑ **Video Journalistic style** that yields edited documentary of the
event to show how the day unfolded.

❑ **Cinematic style** that captures and yields the "meaning" of your
wedding to create an overall dramatic tone and effect reminiscent
of an actual cinematic film.

❑ **Storytelling style** that uses prerecorded sound bites from the bride
and groom that are added in after the wedding to tell a story and
narrate the events.

❑ **Short Form style** that edits the video to fit within an allotted short
time frame and focuses on the highlights of the day.

❑ **Traditional style** that typically looks like a family-shot video and
is the least formal of all.

What would you describe your ideal photography to look like?

❏ **Traditional photography** which includes classical posing and a large amount of photographer and client interaction during the photo shoots.

❏ **Photojournalistic photography** which typically calls for more candid and free shots, with little photographer/client interaction.

❏ **Fashion-based photography** which references the couture-themed photography found in magazines like *Vogue* and *Elle*.

❏ **Contemporary photography** which focuses on capturing the mood, theme, and feel of your wedding event rather than traditional poses.

## CEREMONY INSPIRATION SURVEY:

What type of music do you envision in your ceremony?
Check all that apply.

| | | |
|---|---|---|
| ❏ Choir | ❏ Soloists | ❏ Pre-recorded |
| ❏ Classical | ❏ Country | ❏ Jazz |
| ❏ Big Band | ❏ R&B | ❏ Religious |

Where would you like to have your ceremony?

| | | |
|---|---|---|
| ❏ Small chapel | ❏ Garden | ❏ Lodge |
| ❏ Cathedral | ❏ Beach | ❏ Country club |
| ❏ Hotel banquet hall | | ❏ Backyard/home |

Favorite main décor color?

_____

Favorite accent colors:

_____  _____  _____

What are your feelings about ceremony flowers/décor?

❏ Flowers, flowers everywhere! Large, decorative centerpieces with showy blooms and embellishments.

❏ Several large, eye-catching pieces and small, creative pieces elsewhere.

❏ One or two large arrangements and simple stem pieces elsewhere.

❏ When it comes to flowers and décor, less is more.

## RECEPTION INSPIRATION SURVEY:

What kind of music/entertainment do you envision at your reception?

❏ Swing ❏ Bluegrass ❏ Rock
❏ Rockabilly ❏ Jazz ❏ Big Band
❏ Top Forty ❏ Country ❏ R&B
❏ Classical ❏ Pre-Mixed CDs ❏ CDs
❏ Live Band ❏ DJ

Where would you like to have your reception?

❏ Fellowship hall ❏ Garden ❏ Lodge
❏ Restaurant ❏ Beach ❏ Country club
❏ Hotel banquet hall ❏ Backyard/home

Favorite main décor color?

_____

Favorite accent colors:

_____  _____  _____

What are your feelings about flowers/décor at the reception?

❏ Elaborate floral centerpieces and striking décor pieces to achieve a stunning effect.

❏ Memorable impact arrangements to catch the eye and matching themed décor pieces scattered throughout the reception location.

❏ A limited number of focal floral pieces at the significant tables and smaller, more inexpensive decorative centerpieces.

❏ Pretty, simple floral centerpieces and accent with tasteful decorations.

What type of dining style is more appealing to you?

❏ Elaborate sit-down dinner
❏ Elegant buffet
❏ Brunch
❏ Dessert reception
❏ Cocktails and appetizers
❏ Casual dinner

# chapter 2
# budgeting your
# dream wedding

My goal as you read this book is to help you discover ways that you can plan your wedding for less time, money, and energy. A wedding is ideally supposed to be the happiest day of your life, not the most stressful. By creatively thinking about your wedding and weighing what aspects are most important to you, you can lessen the stress of the day. No matter what your budget looks like, you can plan a beautiful wedding. Cost-cutting techniques can be applied anywhere when you add a little resourcefulness and strategy to your planning. Remember, this is your wedding! Spend money on what matters to you, and cut corners on other things. Make planning your wedding a memorable experience and recognize that beautiful weddings do not have to come with unmanageable price tags.

# THE IMPORTANCE OF HAVING A BUDGET

The average cost of a wedding today rings in at about $27,000 dollars. Most couples cannot afford to spend this much on a wedding without going into major debt. Next to buying a house and raising children, wedding costs will be one of their most expensive endeavors. For a couple still needing a place to live, this expense has the potential to be crippling to their future finances. To boot, most parents don't want to be strapped with such a financial burden, particularly if they are about to enter retirement.

Without a budget, weddings can easily spiral out of control when eager, dreamy-eyed brides begin planning this long-awaited day of their lives. It's time to be realistic. Creating a budget for your wedding day and sticking to it will keep you from veering toward financial irresponsibility while allowing you to be confident in your planning.

Knowing your financial limits will make negotiating with wedding vendors much more simple. Communicating directly with them about the money allotted for their services allows you to be in control of the situation and makes it harder for them to sell you a needlessly expensive floral arrangement, photography package, or wedding dress. Having control over your wedding planning ensures your satisfaction with the wedding and your finances after the big day is over.

Typically close to or more than 50 percent of the wedding budget is allotted to the wedding reception. The rest of the breakdown looks typically like this:

- Photography 10 percent
- Music 10 percent
- Stationery 4 percent
- Flowers 10 percent
- Wedding Attire 10 percent
- Additional Expenses 6 percent

## Who pays for what?

When planning a wedding on a budget, every dollar counts, no matter who gives it to you or how you got it. Things are much different today than they were when your parents got married. Forget clear-cut rules and traditional designation of wedding responsibilities. Today, it is socially acceptable for the bride and groom's families to split the cost of the wedding. Also, with couples marrying later, many have money of their own to put toward the wedding. You can follow traditional wedding etiquette or go your own way. It's up to you.

## STEPS TO PREPARING YOUR WEDDING BUDGET

1. Determine a total, maximum amount you are willing to spend on all aspects of your wedding.

2. Determine the number of guests who will attend your wedding.

3. Use an online wedding budget calculator (see Resources page 260) to see how an "average" wedding would break down based on the "average" percentages for your total budget and guest count.

4. Investigate real costs for the various components of your wedding, especially the element you have decided is your top priority. (Remember: you decide on what aspects of the wedding you would like to splurge and on what elements you are willing to cut back.)

5. Adjust online calculator to allow for your indulgence of choice and see if it leaves adequate money for the remaining components. If not, cut, compromise, or adjust portions of your budget. (But never adjust your top line, overall budget number).

6. Continue tweaking the budget until you have a workable, realistic budget.

7. Print or record your detailed wedding budget and use it when making your choices and negotiating with vendors.

### The bride traditionally pays for:

- Wedding ring for groom
- Wedding gift for groom
- Bridesmaid gifts
- Medical visit for bride
- Bridesmaid luncheon
- Accommodations for out-of-town guests

### The groom traditionally pays for:

- Wedding ring for bride
- Wedding gift for bride
- Groomsmen/usher gifts
- Bride's bouquet
- Mothers' corsages
- Groom's boutonniere
- Groomsmen boutonnieres
- Usher boutonnieres
- Marriage license
- Medical visit for groom
- Gloves/ties/ascots for attendants
- Limousine service
- Honeymoon arrangements
- Clergy/officiate fee

### The bride's family traditionally pays for:

- Wedding gown, headpiece, and accessories
- Bridesmaid bouquets
- Grandmother corsages
- Ceremony/reception flowers
- Altar baskets/arches
- Canopy/carpet
- Kneeling bench/candelabras
- Rented items for wedding
- Rented items for reception
- Invitations/announcements
- Wedding programs
- Napkins/matches/printed items
- Church fee
- Musician/soloist
- Church janitor
- Reception hall fee
- Catered reception/professional services
- Wedding photography
- Video photography
- Orchestra/band/DJ
- Wedding cake
- Wedding favors
- Rice or seed bags
- Wedding breakfast
- Bridal brunch
- Father of bride formal wear

### The groom's family traditionally pays for:

- Groom's cake
- Rehearsal dinner
- Father of groom formal wear

# MASTER BUDGET

As we first mentioned, decide on the dollar amount you want to spend on the wedding and write it at the top of a piece of paper. This is your "desired budget." The next step is to set up a wedding bank account and deposit this budgeted amount into your new account. If you are unable to deposit the money in an account, set up a line of credit with a set amount and use it, and it alone, for your wedding purchases. Whether this money is your and your fiancé's money or money from both of your parents does not matter. The important thing is that once you determine the specific amount, do not alter it.

When you're thinking about a wedding budget, consider all the different aspects of the wedding. What to include and exclude depends upon your specific wedding, but it will most likely include some or all of the following:

- Wedding attire
- Save-the-date cards and postage
- Invitations and postage
- Wedding cake
- Food
- Beverages, possibly including alcohol and bar
- Caterer (unless you enlist help and do it yourself)
- Location rental (unless you use a free location)
- Rentals (tables, chairs, linens, flatware, plates, glasses, etc.)
- Disposable goods (plastic glasses and paper cups, plates, napkins, garbage bags)
- Decorations (for reception and ceremony locations)
- Party favors and attendants' gifts
- Flowers
- Officiate fee
- Photographer (unless you enlist help)
- Videographer (unless you enlist help)
- Music/entertainment (including lighting, generators, and other necessary equipment)
- Wait staff/kitchen help (plus tips, unless you enlist help)
- Bartender (if necessary)
- Valet parking (if necessary)
- Clean up/maid service (if necessary)
- Wedding license
- Wedding coordinator (if necessary)

Don't feel overwhelmed; remember that you have control over your budget and can pick what is most important to you — whether it be the wedding pictures, the reception food, or stunning floral arrangements — and focus your efforts and money there. Once you identify the element you want to enhance most, break down the remaining aspects of your budget.

Use the Initial Budget Worksheet in this chapter to analyze the cost-effectiveness of doing your wedding yourself (Do-It-for-less-style) or purchasing the goods and services from a vendor. You will need to do some research into actual costs of the different components of your wedding choices. Prices of many of the components will vary widely depending on region and your personal choices. See Chapter 3 of this book to learn more about the various options available for different wedding components such as stationery, clothing, flowers and decorations, gifts and favors, music, and photography.

There are several online wedding budget calculators (see listings on page 260 under Wedding Budget Resources) to help you determine how a typical wedding budget breaks down according to the total budget and the number of guests. Most of the on-line wedding budget calculators allow you to adjust percentages as you like, which will enable you to make changes based on what you have determined is the "splurge" component of your wedding.

## INITIAL BUDGET WORKSHEET

Check off all that apply and write in the estimated cost of buying, making, or enlisting help with items. Expand the budget to include the specific line items you want to include in your wedding.

| | Purchased cost | Do-it-for-less cost |
|---|---|---|
| **Invitations and Other Stationery** | | |
| ❑ Save-the-date cards | _____ | _____ |
| ❑ Save-the-date postage | _____ | _____ |
| ❑ Invitations | _____ | _____ |
| ❑ Invitation postage | _____ | _____ |
| ❑ Other stationery | _____ | _____ |
| **Reception** | | |
| ❑ Cake | _____ | _____ |
| ❑ Food | _____ | _____ |
| ❑ Beverages | _____ | _____ |
| ❑ Caterer | _____ | _____ |
| ❑ Wait staff/kitchen help | _____ | _____ |
| ❑ Bartender | _____ | _____ |
| ❑ Disposable goods | _____ | _____ |
| ❑ Entertainment | _____ | _____ |
| **Wedding Attire** | | |
| ❑ Bridal attire | _____ | _____ |
| ❑ Groom's attire | _____ | _____ |
| **Rented Goods** | | |
| ❑ Location rental | _____ | _____ |
| ❑ Rentals | _____ | _____ |
| **Decorations** | | |
| ❑ Decorations | _____ | _____ |
| ❑ Party favors | _____ | _____ |
| ❑ Attendants' gifts | _____ | _____ |
| ❑ Flowers | _____ | _____ |
| **Visual** | | |
| ❑ Photographer | _____ | _____ |
| ❑ Videographer | _____ | _____ |
| **Miscellaneous** | | |
| ❑ Officiate fee | _____ | _____ |
| ❑ Valet parking | _____ | _____ |
| ❑ Clean-up service | _____ | _____ |
| ❑ Wedding license | _____ | _____ |
| ❑ Wedding coordinator | _____ | _____ |

## TWENTY COST-CUTTING TIPS FOR A DO-IT-FOR-LESS! WEDDING

### 1. Start planning early.
Allow yourself plenty of time to research the best and most cost-effective options. Decisions made in haste can end up costing you more money than you want to spend.

### 2. Set up a wedding account.
Before you make any other decisions, decide on the dollar amount you want to spend for the big day. Set up a wedding bank account and deposit this budgeted amount. If you draw only from these funds for the wedding, you'll be sure to stick to your budget. If you must go into debt for your wedding, open a wedding-only credit card with a set limit. Pay it off each month, if at all possible, and do not increase your limit for any reason.

### 3. Enlist help early.
Since weddings can be overly stressful if all of the responsibility falls on one person, enlist the help of friends and family members. Wedding to-do lists don't look quite as overwhelming when the tasks are delegated among your friends and family. Chances are, many of these people would be more than happy to help with your wedding — just don't burden them with too much work. Respect their time, and assign them only one or two tasks. They are your friends, not pro-bono employees.

### 4. Use seasonal products.
Using seasonal fruits, vegetables, or flowers in your wedding will be less expensive than produce or flowers sourced out-of-season or shipped from an exotic location. Let the seasonality charts (page 50 and 109) help you make the best decision for these aspects of your special day.

### 5. Have an off-season wedding.
More weddings occur in the late spring, summer, and early fall months. You'll find better deals on locales and vendors during the "off season" of late fall, winter, and early spring.

### 6. Have an off-day or off-hour wedding.
Most weddings occur on Saturday afternoons and evenings, and pricing for these peak times will likely be nonnegotiable and more expensive. Consider having your wedding on a Friday evening, Saturday morning, or on Sunday.

### 7. Make your own invitations.
Scrapbook and stationery stores carry many beautiful and elaborate papers that you can use for making your own invitations. With a dash of creativity, your own computer, and a printer, you can make invitations that are both beautiful and within your budget. If you don't trust your own skills as a designer, use the creative resources of your friends and family or look at online samples and base your design on one you find.

### 8. Have your ceremony and reception at the same location.
Some ceremony sites also offer fellowship or reception halls. By keeping your guests at the same location for the entire event, you can save on multiple site fees, ease the hassle of transportation for your guests and the wedding party, and, most importantly, simplify the planning process for yourself.

### 9. Have a smaller wedding.
Don't feel obligated to invite your twice removed step-cousin's friend or an acquaintance you haven't spoken with in over a decade. Having fewer guests allows you to focus on quality over quantity. A small wedding on a moderate budget has the potential to be more beautiful and elegant than a large wedding on the same budget.

### 10. Limit the bar.
You don't need to fund a full bar for your guests. Provide them with sparkling and regular water, wine, two or three types of soft drinks, and beer; it is more than enough to offer at the reception. In a pinch, you could even limit your bar further to just water, tea or fruit punch mixed with sparkling water, and champagne for a toast. You could also opt for a dry reception, especially if it takes place earlier in the day.

### 11. Skip the four-course, sit-down meal.
A wedding brunch or lunch is less expensive than providing dinner for your guests. Not only will you save money on the food, but you'll also be spending less on alcohol, as people generally drink less early in the day. If you have an evening wedding, consider a buffet instead of a served meal, or try something different like a dessert-only reception with a variety of decadent treats.

### 12. Use an old caterer's trick and have two wedding cakes.
Showcase a small, but beautiful wedding cake on the dessert table, and serve slices from a sheet cake in the back. The "hero" wedding cake

doesn't even have to be real; it can be made from a Styrofoam base and decorated like a traditional cake.

### 13. Skip the traditional cake in favor of festive cupcakes instead.

A beautiful cupcake display can be a stunning and unconventional option for a wedding dessert that is easier to make than a cake. These cupcakes are simple to decorate, and guests delight in these Lilliputian goodies.

### 14. Embellish your own dress.

The purchase of your wedding dress is one aspect of the wedding budget that can quickly spiral out of control. Consider buying a pretty but simple wedding gown and adding your own simple embellishments to match the décor and theme of your wedding. This is an option only for those with highly-skilled hands. If you are not confident in your own sewing skills, you most likely know someone who can help from the generation when clothes were oftentimes made at home. Embellish a veil with pearls or paillettes onto gloves. For a winter wedding, add a white, fur-trimmed stole to your ensemble.

### 15. Forgo the formal.

Have the groom and his groomsmen wear nice suits or décor-coordinated clothing instead of tuxedos. Most men own or can easily obtain a nice suit for less money than it would cost them to buy or rent a formal tuxedo. This is a great option if your wedding is less formal or set for an outdoor location like a garden or beach.

### 16. Make your own bouquet.

Avoid the elaborate bouquets from florists, which are known to be pricy. Instead, tie several long-stemmed flowers with beautiful blooms together and wrap the stems with a wide satin ribbon that matches the décor of your wedding. This inexpensive and pretty bouquet can be made the day before if kept well-hydrated in a cool place.

### 17. Use potted plants in place of floral arrangements.

Offset the expense of buying all your arrangements from a florist by planting small, flowering shrubs or herbs in decorative pots. Using small squares of wheatgrass is a popular option that imparts a fresh and light feeling. These make beautiful centerpieces for your reception tables, and guests of honor can take them home as favors.

### 18. Add a personal touch to your wedding music.

Enlisting the services of a live band or performer for your wedding can be very expensive, and if your guests want to dance longer than planned, you could get charged an unexpected overtime fee. Save money and make your music more personal by requesting the services of musically inclined friends or family to perform at your wedding. For the reception, borrow or rent a professional CD player and speakers and put a member of your wedding party in charge of managing the CDs.

### 19. Hire a photographer who will provide you with high-resolution images on a disk.

One of the most expensive components of wedding photography is not the photographer's time, but the photographer's charges for individual prints. You can save some money if you choose a photographer who will provide you with high-res files and allow you to make your own prints. You can post them on any number of photo-processing Web sites so friends and family can order their own as well.

### 20. Beg, borrow, and steal.

Search for wedding locations, decorations, or furniture that you can borrow from your friends and family. Does your best friend have a beautiful backyard that would be perfect for your ideal wedding? If so, ask her. All she can do is say no, and she would probably be delighted that you asked. An assortment of folding tables borrowed from different people can be covered with custom-made tablecloths. Chairs, too, can be covered and decorated to match your wedding décor, and they don't have to match perfectly. Consider borrowing flatware, dishes, and glasses if you can. Borrowing these items can help you stay within your budget and leave you with extra cash for other parts of the wedding or, more practically, life after the ceremony. Just make sure that you photograph and label pictures of each borrowed item so that you can return them to their rightful owners! And most importantly, be sure to thank anyone who helps you in writing. Regardless of how small a gesture, they have extended help to you and deserve graciousness and thankfulness from you. See page 33 for some tips on proper thank-you etiquette.

# chapter 3
# do-it-for-less!
# wedding components

This chapter delineates all the line items listed in your wedding budget, including invitations and other printed pieces; clothing for the bride, groom, and attendants; flowers and other decorations; gifts and favors; music and entertainment; and photography and videography. From the do-it-for-less approach to other possibilities, the details offered here will help you determine what will work for you and your budget.

## INVITATIONS AND OTHER STATIONERY

Printed pieces are traditionally your main method of communication for the big day, and often serve to cohesively unite the wedding theme. To this end, some brides have stationery and paper pieces printed in complete packages for every wedding function, with envelopes inside other envelopes and sheets of vellum on top. Other brides pick and choose the elements they want. The latter way, of course, is the option that most easily allows for trimming costs. Here's a list of the most common printed items for a wedding.

### Typical Printed Pieces
1. Save-the-Date cards
2. Invitation Package
   a. Invitation
   b. Interior envelope
   c. Exterior envelope
   d. Location/Reception directions
   e. RSVP
      i. RSVP card
      ii. RSVP return envelope
3. Ceremony program
4. Menu
5. Place cards
6. Thank-you cards

### Invitations
Wedding invitations are the first major item that anyone will see about your wedding. You want them to reflect the tone and theme of your special day. (Save-the-date cards typically come before the invitations, but they are generally simpler and do not have to be as closely tied to your theme.) The invitation should visually communicate the type of affair your guests should anticipate. Informal affairs should have simple invitations, perhaps handwritten. Invitations to formal weddings should reflect formality accordingly. In addition, weddings with a certain theme are best accompanied by themed wedding invitations.

Be sure to send your wedding invitations on time, especially because some guests will need enough time to arrange travel plans. It is customary to send out invitations anywhere from four to eight weeks prior to the ceremony, with six weeks being the ideal time frame.

Wedding invitations should always include the names of the people who are hosting or paying for the event. Other necessary information includes the date, time, and location of the event, as well as any specific information regarding the reception. This reception information is sometimes printed on a separate card. If your wedding requires either very formal or casual dress, make mention of it in the invitation. The last line that typically appears on the invitation is the RSVP.

Traditionally, proper etiquette calls for wedding invitations to include handwritten addresses on envelopes. While this may seem tedious in today's fast-paced society, it shows sincerity and personalization. If you have hundreds of guests at your wedding, make sure to enlist the aid of members of your wedding party (particularly your maid of honor) in addressing the envelopes.

## Save-the-Date Cards

Save-the-date cards are especially helpful if you are planning a destination wedding or your nuptials will be held over a holiday. But, regardless of your wedding location, your guests will appreciate the advance notice. Also, you have the added satisfaction of knowing that your wedding is on their calendars. Many save-the-date cards now include photos and magnets that will provide an even longer lasting impression.

Use simple wording on these cards. Include your names, wedding date, and the location; that's all that is necessary. Save-the-date cards can be mailed up to one year, or more, in advance of your wedding and should mention that an invitation will follow.

## A Word on Envelopes

Make sure that you research your card stock and envelope options early in the design process so that you can match your invitation to an envelope of corresponding size and color. In fact, as counterintuitive as it may seem, it is highly recommendable to find an envelope first. As many DIYers have found, there is nothing worse than spending money to print invitations for which you have no matching envelopes. Use these guides below when ordering envelopes — knowing the proper lingo will make sure you get exactly what you're wanting, especially when shopping online. Before ordering, always confirm the envelope dimensions, as some envelope converters use slightly different measurements than the ones listed here.

Beyond size and availability of envelopes, colors can be difficult to match — particularly whites and creams. Keep in mind that a white or cream card stock from one manufacturer will likely be a different shade, brightness, and texture from another manufacturer. Unless you can buy the same exact stock for your invitations and envelopes, you might want to choose a contrasting color for the envelopes instead. Envelopes with a pearlescent or metallic sheen to their rich color pair beautifully with many white and cream invitations. Check out the Web sites (listed on page 261) as sources of information about cardstock and envelope printing.

# ENVELOPE SIZES AND STYLES

## A-STYLE
A-style envelopes typically have a deep, square flap for a clean, modern look.

| A-STYLE | ENVELOPE SIZE | ENCLOSURE SIZE |
|---|---|---|
| A-2 | 4.375" x 5.75" | 4.25" x 5.5" |
| A-4 | 4.75" x 6.5" | 4.5" x 6.25" |
| A-7 | 5.25" x 7.25" | 5" x 7" |
| A-8 | 5.5" x 8.125" | 5.25" x 7.75" |
| A-10 | 6.25" x 9.625" | 5.75" x 9.25" |
| Slim | 3.875" x 8.875" | 3.625" x 8.625" |

## COMMERICIAL
Standard commercial envelopes have shallow, pointed flaps. For a smarter look, choose a square flap. If using a No. 10, consider the ever-interesting policy envelope, which seals on the end.

| COMMERICIAL | ENVELOPE SIZE | ENCLOSURE SIZE |
|---|---|---|
| #6¼ | 3.5" x 6" | 3.25" x 5.75" |
| #6¾ | 3.625" x 6.5" | 3.5" x 6.25" |
| #8⅝ | 3.625" x 8.625" | 3.5" x 8.375" |
| # 7 | 3.75" x 6.75" | 3.5" x 6.5" |
| #7¾ (Monarch) | 3.875" x 7.5" | 3.75" x 7.25" |
| #9 | 3.875" x 8.875" | 3.75" x 8.675" |
| #9 (policy) | 4" x 9" | 3.75" x 8.5" |
| #10 | 4.125" x 9.5" | 4" x 9.25" |
| DL | 4.313" x 8.625" | 4.125" x 8.375" |

## BARONNIAL
These classic envelopes have a deep-v pointed flap and are frequently used for formal invitations. Some manufacturers now offer an even deeper-v style, sometimes referred to as a European flap. Be very careful that you're ordering a European style, and not a European size, as they differ completely from U.S. envelope sizes.

| BARONNIAL | ENVELOPE SIZE | ENCLOSURE SIZE |
|---|---|---|
| #4 | 3.625" x 5.125" | 3.375" x 4.875" |
| #5 | 4.125" x 5.5" | 3.875" x 5.25" |
| #5½ | 4.375" x 5.625" | 4.125" x 5.375" |
| #6 | 4.75" x 6.5" | 4.25" x 6.25" |

## SQUARE ENVELOPES
Many people love the look of square invitations, they are the most contemporary of your options. Depending on the manufacturer, square envelopes come with both pointed and square flaps. Take note that square envelopes require extra postage.

| SQUARE | ENVELOPE SIZE | ENCLOSURE SIZE |
|---|---|---|
| 5" | 5" x 5" | 4.75" x 4.75" |
| 5½" | 5.5" x 5.5" | 5.25" x 5.25" |
| 6" | 6" x 6" | 5.75" x 5.75" |
| 6½" | 6.5" x 6.5" | 6.25" x 6.25" |
| 7" | 7" x 7" | 6.75" x 6.75" |
| 7½" | 7.5" x 7.5" | 7.25" x 7.25" |

## The RSVP Dilemma

If you've ever planned an event, you know that more and more, guests disregard RSVP requests. What was once considered a common courtesy is now almost completely ignored — regardless of how easy you make the process of responding. Most people either forget to RSVP or feel that it is unnecessary. And sometimes, even those who do RSVP don't show up themselves. This being said, is it time to eliminate the RSVP request altogether?

With the exception of sit-down events, I have dropped RSVP requests from my invitations and assume that about fifty percent of my invited guests will actually attend. This saves money on RSVP cards, but still causes a certain level of anxiety for hosts. And for seated dinners, an accurate count is crucial for the kitchen. In lieu of — or perhaps in addition to — an RSVP card with your invite, you might consider some alternatives like a phone tree, an e-mail-based RSVP network, or a wedding Web site that can help track which guests will be attending.

## Trimming Costs with a Wedding Web Site

Wedding Web sites are an inexpensive and easy way to communicate with the important people in your life about your special day. With so many inexpensive and free Web site templates available, you can save money on many of your printed pieces by developing a wedding Web site. In lieu of printing RSVP cards, maps, and the like, you can print a simple invite that directs guests to your personal wedding Web site for all the details. Some companies even offer templates tailor-made for wedding plans — all you have to do is enter or upload your information to customize the site for your event. Many couples keep the sites updated even after the wedding with pictures from the honeymoon, their new address, and blogs about married life. Check out some of these top-rated companies below to help you get started:

Web site: **www.mywedding.com**
Cost: Free
Available: Wedding Party Information • Upload Photos
Gift Registry • Wedding Story

Web site: **www.wedquarters.com**
Cost: 7-Day Free Trial or $29.95 – Year Long Subscription
Available: Unlimited Pages • Unlimited Photos • Unlimited RSVPs
Unlimited Events • Unlimited Updates

Web site:   **www.weddingwindow.com**
Cost:       7-Day Free Trial or $59.00 – Six Month Subscription
Available:  save-the-date E-Cards • Unlimited Photos • Unlimited
            Pages • Unlimited Entries • Unlimited RSVP Event Entries
            Audio/Video Albums • Elegant Design Selection
            *Rated #1 Wedding Web site Provider Overall by The Wall Street Journal*
            **Featured in Martha Stewart Weddings Magazine Spring 2007 issue,*
            *"Designing a Wedding Web site"*

Web site:   **www.theweddingtracker.com**
Cost:       2-Week Free Trial or $60 – Year Long Subscription
Available:  Online RSVP • News Updates • 200 Photos
            Photo Printing• Events & Accommodation Info.
            Registry • Wedding Party • Visitor Counter

## Thank-You Cards

A personal thank-you note is the only appropriate way to say "Thank You!" Even if you've made a point to thank someone in person for their gift, a personal thank-you note is the only way to express sincere appreciation.

## Thank You Do's and Don'ts

Never send a preprinted thank-you card. When you commit this sin of etiquette, you are telling the person receiving the card that her gift was not important enough to even receive mention in your note. A personalized, handwritten note, even if brief, tells guests how much you appreciated their gift and how it will be cherished for years to come. Handwritten notes express sincerity and warmth.

In addition, be sure to send thank-you notes to friends and relatives who arranged showers and parties for you. It is fine to thank them for the party or shower in the same thank-you card as their gift.

When you receive more than one gift from someone, each gift must be recognized with its own thank-you card. If you receive a shower gift from a friend or relative and then, three weeks later, receive a wedding gift from the same person, it is not appropriate to thank them in one card.

Shower gifts should be acknowledged within ten days of the party and wedding gifts within two weeks after returning from the honeymoon. Wedding gifts arriving before the wedding should be responded to immediately, so that an extended period of time does not pass between receiving the gift and its thank-you card.

- Be sure to put your new return address on all thank-you cards. Your guests will appreciate having your current address.

- Although colored ink is readily available at your favorite stationery store today, it is still better to write your notes in dark blue or black. It is more easily readable.

- When writing thank-you notes, never start the note with "I." Always use "you" more than "I" or "me" in the note.

### More on Thank-You Notes

No matter for what or to whom you are sending these notes, the approach is always the same. Be specific, be honest and express your gratitude in such a way that the receiving party feels appreciated. A thank-you note for a gift is relatively simple and straightforward. Here are a few examples of other occasions that will require a written thank you:

**Gift:** Friend who loaned you several crystal vases

*Dear Amanda,*

*Thank you so much for allowing me to use your grandmother's crystal vases as the centerpieces for my wedding reception. They were stunning and made the entire atmosphere of the room so lovely. The use of your vases was a wonderful gesture of our friendship. I appreciate it more than words. You are such a kind friend, and it was a beautiful way to share my wedding with you. Thank you again so much.*

*With Love,*

*Anne*

**Gift:** Friend who donated her time to help you make wedding cupcakes

*Dear Jocelyn,*

*Thank you so much for taking time out of your busy schedule to help me bake the wedding cupcakes for the dessert table. I know you had your hands full with other things, but your help was invaluable to me. The sincerity of the gift of your time means so much to me. It was a wonderful way to share my wedding experience with you. I appreciate your gift so much.*

*With Love,*

*Anne*

**Gift:** Groom's parents who helped pay for the reception

> *Dear Mr. and Mrs. Smith [or however you typically address your new in-laws],*
>
> *Robert and I could not have dreamed of having such a beautiful wedding experience had you not donated your time and money to the process. I know that it was a heartfelt gift because it was not required, but we would like for you to know how very much it means to us. You are such wonderful people, and I am so glad to be considered part of your family now. We are sincerely grateful for your participation in making our wedding the most memorable day of our lives.*
>
> *With Love,*
>
> *Anne*

## Types of Printing

Wedding invitations can be as simple as a handwritten card and can be as expensive and elaborate as your imagination allows. Most, however, depend on one of these basic forms of printing:

- Laser or ink jet printing
- 4-color digital printing
- Thermography
- Engraving
- Letterpress

Each of these techniques produces a different look for your invitation, and each technique varies in price. Some are more expensive than others. Using one of these techniques for your invitations depends on how you want your invitation to look and how much money you have allotted for it in your wedding budget.

### Do-It-for-Less! Laser and Ink Jet

Elegance is not synonymous with expensive and can be found in the simplest of invitations, if you exercise good taste and creativity. By far, the most inexpensive way to print your invitations is to buy nice card stock, type out the desired text for your invitation, print it on your home laser or ink jet printer, and then make black-and-white copies at a local print shop. Don't forget to have the employees trim your invitations to the perfect size — they can likely do it more accurately and quickly than you for only a few extra dollars.

A generic 8.5 X 11-inch card stock yields two 4.25 X 11-inch pieces, two 5.5 X 8.5-inch pieces, or four 4.25 X 5.5-inch pieces.

| 8.5 X11 | two 4.25 X 11 | two 5.5 X 8.5 | four 4.25 X 5.5 |

Depending on your resourcefulness and style, you can easily get four invitations out of a single sheet of paper. These cards would fit perfectly in an A-2 envelope. (See the charts on page 31 to learn more about envelope styles and sizes.)

If simplicity is what your heart desires, leave these invitations as they are. For more decorative flair, use stamp sets, embellishments, and dusting glitter, available at most scrapbook and stationery stores. This option does require a modicum of creativity and control to keep your invitations from looking like a kindergarten art project, but it works well for brides on a strict budget. Done well, do-it-for-less invitations can be a beautiful technique for the efficient and creative bride.

## DO-IT-FOR-LESS INVITATION PERSONALIZATION

Use paper craft or scrapbook supplies to make your own invitations from purchased card and envelope stock. Stores like Michael's and Target have good selections.

### Rubber stamps:
Use a metallic or light-colored ink to stamp initials, flowers, or hearts onto your invitations.

### Embossers:
Initials or other design elements can be easily embossed onto card and envelope stock to create an elegant and upscale look. Desktop embossers can be special-ordered with design elements or initials, and they make quick work of personalizing note cards and the flaps of envelopes.

### Paper punchers:
Much like very large hole-punches, paper punchers cut a decorative shape in paper.

They also come in shapes specifically designed for corners. Cards that are punched look especially beautiful with a second color paper inside peeking through.

### Decorative scissors:
Similar to pinking shears, decorative scissors cut paper into a variety of different shapes. Use them to cut a pretty edge on your invitation.

### Embellishments:
Add wedding bells, butterflies, flowers, birds, a bouquet, or champagne glasses to the front of your cards. There are hundreds of embellishments to choose from in the scrapbook section of craft stores.

### Ribbon:
Tie a small bow to the front of your cards or tie ribbon around the fold.

## Four-Color Digital Printing

To achieve professional, high-quality printing for your wedding invitations while not completely overspending your budget, consider 4-color digital printing. Assuming you start with a strong file, this type of printing consistently yields vivid and vibrant images because of the digital quality of the information transfer. Invitations requiring many different colors or photographs work best with the 4-color digital printing option. Keep in mind that images and text printed in this way will be flat to the paper, rather than raised off the paper as with engraving and thermography.

Couples who choose this type of printing receive their orders faster than those who choose the more intricate and time-consuming styles like engraving or letterpress. Visit weddingpaperdivas.com to view examples of beautiful invitations printed on a 4-color digital press. For the economical bride, these invitations remain affordable without sacrificing personal style.

## Offset Printing

If working with a graphic designer, you may prefer offset printing over digital printing to take advantage of the large sheet size available with offset presses. These printers are normally used for higher quantity print runs than a small ceremony requires, but they can be an economical choice if you want a large variety of printed pieces for your wedding. With a bit of measuring and calculation, you can conceivably arrange everything — your invitations, place cards, thank-you notes, wedding programs, enclosure cards, maps, and RSVP cards — to all fit on one sheet and print simultaneously.

## Thermography

Thermography, more commonly known as raised ink printing, offers the classic design of engraving for far less money. If you don't want to spend all your wedding cash in one place but still long for a lovely, formal wedding invitation at a very reasonable price, choose thermography. High temperatures fuse a combination of wet ink and a powdered substance together and leave a raised appearance on the paper.

Through this process, you get the look of engraving without the exponential cost, and you also get invitations with increased clarity and high resolution, which works well for small, detailed fonts.

Research and choose a reputable printer that knows specific details about this printing type. Should you enlist the services of one who is less than experienced, you could end up with ruined invitations and a migraine. Experienced printers know to use only cardstock and paper designed specifically to withstand the high temperatures of the fusing process so that your invitations turn out just as beautiful as you imagined them to be.

### Engraving

Brides who are planning ultra-formal ceremonies are ever desirous for engraved invitations. Considered one of the oldest and most formal printing techniques, this style calls for "sandwiching" the invitation paper between a copper plate containing the etched image, design, or text and another inked plate. The process creates a raised or "engraved" image on the front of the paper and leaves a slight indention on the back. Some people spend literally hundreds and even thousands of dollars to ensure that their wedding invitations display this regal and classic look. Choosing this style of printing doesn't make much sense for those couples attempting to plan within the narrow confines of their budget, unless you are prepared to allocate more of your budget to these deluxe paper goods.

### Letterpress

Letterpress printing celebrates a unique and old-fashioned printing style that has regained popularity in the past decade. The cards, when done right, are works of art and are priced accordingly.

Letterpress invitations are printed from metal type and custom engraved plates onto handmade or uniquely textured types of paper. These soft papers are used to best emphasize the sharp contact of the metal type with the paper; in other words, they intensify the design imprint. If your invitations require several colors, letterpress printing has both an advantage and a disadvantage. With letterpress-style color printing, more ink is pressed into the paper, which adds to the luster and vividness of each color. However, with each new color required there is an increase in cost because the printer must run the paper through the press an additional time.

Of the methods discussed, letterpress printing produces one of the most eye-catching and distinctive invitations, but it is neither an efficient nor practical method for couples planning on doing their wedding for less money. But then again, these invitations tend to look absolutely gorgeous and will catch the attention of all your guests.

# CLOTHING AND ACCESSORIES

## Wedding Attire

Wedding attire not only adds to the mood and ambiance of the ceremony and reception, you will also capture the look forever in your wedding photography and videography. And, of course, choosing something tasteful and lovely can absolutely be achieved while being mindful of your budget.

### Bridal Attire

Planning and choosing clothing and accessories for the wedding are often the most exciting part of wedding planning, at least for the women involved. Men usually couldn't care less. This is evidenced by the statistic that even though the bride's clothing and accessories make up about nine percent of the wedding budget, the groom's clothes amount to less than one percent. All of that says, he won't be heartbroken (or probably even notice) if his suit is made from gabardine twill rather than Italian cupro cashmere.

Saving money on your wedding attire can be very easy, if this is a component of the wedding where you do not mind being conservative. Some brides are completely comfortable with purchasing a less expensive dress or having one made. Others have dreamed about the perfect gown since they were little girls and cannot bear to part with that dream for anything. Remember, this wedding is your wedding. If you want to wear a glamorous Priscilla of Boston gown, be prepared to plan a very creatively budgeted ceremony and reception. On the other hand, if your wedding attire is an area of your wedding where you are willing to compromise, this chapter is filled with amazing ideas and resources.

## 10 WEDDING DRESS-COST CUTTING TIPS:

### 1. Start shopping early.
The easiest way to ensure that you find a pretty dress at a good price is to give yourself enough time to shop the sales, resale stores, and less-popular venues.

### 2. Buy a less-expensive, simpler gown.
This might seem to be an obvious solution to your cost-cutting dilemma, but it really does work! An inexpensive, simple white shift or sheath can immediately look glamorous with the addition of stylish accessories.

### 3. Accessorize
And speaking of accessories, this category has the potential to take your dress from okay to gorgeous. If the dress is simple, it's even more reason to make a big statement with your jewels and trinkets. In addition, these are perfect items to borrow, and most people would be thrilled that you would want to wear something of theirs for your big day!

### 4. Wear a white bridesmaid gown.
Bridesmaid dresses are much less expensive than wedding gowns and are affordable options if you want to purchase designer duds. Wear a white bridesmaid dress from Alfred Angelo or David's Bridal for a less expensive, but still pretty wedding dress alternative.

### 5. Consider less expensive fabrics.
Consider using a polyester-based wedding fabric instead of silk. Using silk-based fabrics immediately increases the cost of the dress. Many wedding gowns come in various fabrics. If you fall in love with a certain style of dress, see if you can order the dress in a less expensive fabric.

### 6. Make your own dress.
Make your own dress or consider asking a local seamstress, friend, or family member to craft it for you. Choose a wedding dress pattern and fabric and then embellish the dress on your own with seed pearls, lace, ribbon, or sequins. This is only an option if you feel confident about your inner seamstress. Local tailors generally do not charge high prices for their work. If a friend or family member makes your wedding dress, offer to pay them for their labor and time.

### 7. Rent a dress.
Many formalwear shops rent out their dresses. By renting a dress you can choose something from a high-end designer and have money left over for a wedding. This is a great option if you do not care about saving the dress as memorabilia of your day.

### 8. Choose a dress requiring few alterations.
Alterations can quickly add up. Just because you love the ballroom gown with its seven layers of skirts does not mean your budget will feel the same way. Find the dress that fits you best and requires the fewest alterations.

### 9. Wear an all-white evening gown.
The term "bridal" adds a significant amount to any dress price tag. By wearing a white evening gown, you can achieve a bridal look for less money. Stores like Off-Fifth Sak's Fifth Avenue Outlet and Nordstrom Rack generally sell evening gowns for less. Online shopping can also be a great resource for finding a white evening dress.

### 10. Shop sample sales.
Many upscale department stores sell their wedding dresses from last season at a discount in order to make room for the new styles that come in. Make some phone calls to the different department stores and find out when these sales occur.

### 11. Bid on eBay or search a resale shop.
Often women will sell their once-worn weddings dresses at cheap prices on eBay or at a resale shop. You can guarantee huge savings on these dresses, particularly if you wear an average size, as those are easiest to find. In addition to second-hand dresses, eBay sometimes has going-out-of-business sales from various wedding dress vendors.

## BRIDAL RESOURCE COMPARISON GUIDE

Consider the following bridal gown comparison guide across the pricing range to help you decide where to buy your dress.

### FREE/BORROW

Keep tradition in the family! What could be more special, memorable (and coincidentally, cheap) than wearing your mother's wedding gown from years past? Maybe you are not completely taken with the vintage wedding dress look? Wear an older sister's wedding dress or ask around to any of your recently married friends. Chances are that any of these people will be willing to help you.

### INEXPENSIVE

Target For the purposes of this book, an inexpensive wedding dress falls into the price range of less than $100 to $500. Online shopping at Target.com is one of the best sources for purchasing a brand-new, inexpensive wedding dress. Their dresses are not available in the retail stores, but there are multiple pictures of each dress, as well as a sizing chart at your disposal. Most of the Target wedding dresses range between $90 to $150.

Lane Bryant Lane Bryant offers beautiful and inexpensive wedding dresses for the full-figured bride. Their searchable online bridal boutique offers many different configurations for wedding dress ensembles including dresses, mix and match separates, and wedding accessories. Each dress is offered in a range of sizes from 14-28. The average dress costs about $150, which is easily affordable for the budget-minded bride.

### MODERATE

Jessica McClintock Jessica McClintock has always been known for her beautiful gowns. Her timeless styles range from girl flower frocks to prom dresses to stunning wedding gowns. Enjoy the flexibility of shopping online at the Web site JessicaMcclintock. com and then visit one of the forty-three boutiques across the nation to try on your dress for fittings and alterations. Most Jessica McClintock gowns run at a modestly affordable price between $200 and $800.

David's Bridal As the largest and most successful bridal retail store in the country, David's Bridal is a guaranteed budget pleaser when it comes to wedding attire. Five wedding lines are available at David's Bridal. The in-house lines include David's Bridal Collection and David's Bridal Woman. The other three lines are Galina, Oleg Cassini, and Monique Luo. Each line has dresses that range from $500 to $1300, but David's Bridal often has sales that cut the prices in half. You can find formal, casual, classic, or European-styled gowns here for a relatively modest price.

Group USA Group USA is a largely untapped resource for moderately priced wedding gowns that still maintain their glamour without the exponential cost of couture wedding-wear. Since a limited number of stores are scattered across only fifteen different states, Group USA has made several other shopping options available. You can browse the dress collections online or in their catalogue and then order the dresses online, through the catalogue, or over the phone. Many of their gowns are very modern and fashion-forward, but the best part about Group USA is price range between $200 and $800.

### EXPENSIVE

Priscilla of Boston One of the leading wedding designers, Priscilla of Boston is noted for their unique and glamorous gowns. The couture designs are memorable, eye-catching, and highly sophisticated. The look, however, must be bought at a price. Priscilla of Boston produces five main dress lines including Priscilla of Boston, Platinum, Vineyard, Melissa Sweet, and Us Angels Flower Girls. The prices for the designer wedding gowns range anywhere from $2,000 to $9,000 with the majority of the gowns priced under $6,000. The Vineyard Collection typically includes the least expensive gowns. The Maeve and Bailey dresses retail for $2,600.

Bridesmaid Attire

Bridesmaid dresses can enhance the theme and beauty of the ceremony or they can seriously detract from it. Carefully and tastefully choose the dresses for your bridesmaids to complement the overall theme and décor of your wedding. A beautiful ceremony can easily go awry when tasteless and overdone bridesmaids dresses clash with the altar.

As the bride, it's your responsibility to pick something tasteful and pretty, while not forcing your best friends to take out a loan just to be able to stand with you on your special day. Just as you are working on a budget, so are they. They will be forever grateful to you if the dress you choose is moderately priced.

Simple, clean lines in solid colors make for the best bridesmaid dresses. In fact, the more colors, frills, sashes, and bows that you add to the dress, the more expensive and possibly unattractive the dress will become.

Consider some of our quick and easy ways for your bridesmaids to cut costs on their dresses.

## TOP 7 COST-CUTTING TIPS FOR BRIDESMAIDS

### 1. Shop the discount section.
Be wary of falling in love with the first beautiful dress you see on the rack. Ask the dress consultants if there is a discounted rack. Typically, they will have one but it won't be advertised very well. These dresses are often one or two years behind season, but they are still beautiful and brand-new.

### 2. Shop online.
Take the time to shop for bridesmaid dresses online. You may be hesitant to do so because you feel the selection will be limited. But actually, there are many designers with online galleries for you to view, and you can purchase the bridesmaid dresses online as soon as you find them. This is a great way to expand the selection within the price point you have set.

### 3. Throw out the "bridesmaid" tag.
There is no reason why you can't use an off-the-rack dress from a department store or boutique just because it is not specifically marked as a bridesmaid dress. At the end of summer and winter, especially, stores often have end-of-season sales on their evening wear and regular dresses. These dresses are great because they can be worn again and again to different functions.

### 4. DIY bridesmaid dress.
If you have some time to spare before the wedding, find someone who can make your brides-maid dresses. If your friend or family member can sew, these dresses might only cost as much as you spend on the fabric and pattern.

### 5. Pick a color, but not a style.
Choose a color swatch of fabric that you like and let your bridesmaids pick whatever style of dress they choose. It can be handmade or purchased from a store — as long as it fits with your color scheme. Not all bridesmaids are the same shape and size. This solution allows them to each choose a dress they'll feel happy in.

### 6. Dye your accessories.
Buy inexpensive, basic shoes and accessories that can be dyed to match your dress. There is no reason to buy a pair of high-dollar dove gray shoes from Nordstrom if you can dye a pair of plain white satin shoes to match your outfit. Use Dylon multi-purpose dye and sponge the dye onto the shoes or purse.

### 7. Choose common neutrals.
If you don't like the matchy look of dyed pieces, let your bridesmaids choose neutral shoes out of their closets where slight variations among them will not catch the eye of your guests.

## BRIDESMAID RESOURCE COMPARISON GUIDE

We have compiled a list of excellent bridesmaid dress vendors and designers. Use this resource guide to help you find perfectly priced and beautiful dresses for your bridesmaids.

J. Crew Perfect for a breezy garden or beach wedding, J. Crew bridesmaid dresses are beautiful for their sundress-inspired look and cool easy fabrics. Typically made of taffeta, chiffon, or cotton, these dresses are unique and current in design. Not just for bridesmaids, J. Crew dresses can be worn for many different occasions as they are formal enough for a wedding but able to be dressed down for everyday wear. Ranging in price from $200 to $350 dollars, these dresses might be a little more expensive but since they can be worn again, bridesmaids won't feel like they are wasting money on a one-time event.

Ann Taylor Besides offering three bridal gowns, groomsmen accessories, and flower girl dresses, Ann Taylor has a beautiful selection of bridesmaids dresses. The majority of dresses cost $198 and are made of silk dupioni in saturated pastels to striking effect or silk georgette for flowing looks. Floor length dresses cost more, with prices ranging from $228 to $298. You'll find matching shoes and other accessories to complete the classic Ann Taylor look with one-stop shopping.

Watters and Watters Watters line includes bridesmaid dresses ranging from highly sophisticated and formal dresses to tea-length more casual dresses. Elegant, fashion-forward, and flattering, Watters dresses can be found at most any bridal shop around. An added bonus is that with Watters, you can dress almost your entire wedding party in beautiful gowns with their collections of Junior Bridesmaid dresses, flower girl dresses, and mother-of-the-bride attire. Prices range from about $250 to $400.

Wtoo Wtoo is a branch off Watters and Watters that is primarily styled for the more casual wedding situation. Described as being uptempo, simple, and affordable, these bridesmaid dresses are simply elegant and full of charm. Most of the styles are tea-length, but a few of the dresses maintain the longer, more formal look. Prices range from $200 to $300 and many of the dresses look perfect for outdoor weddings with shorter skirts and brighter colors.

Bill Levkoff Bill Levkoff dresses are sold in many different bridal boutiques across the nation and can also be accessed online through the billlevkoff.com Web site or a variety of others. These dresses are beautiful and elegant, while maintaining a reasonable price tag. These eye-catching designs in rich colors and fabrics range from about $150 to $300 dollars.

David's Bridal The most well-known and accessible bridesmaid dress vendor around, David's Bridal offers a great variety of dresses for all types of weddings, all different sizes of women, and in a multitude of beautiful colors. All David's Bridal bridesmaid gowns are moderately priced, staying between $100 and $200. Both their online and in-store collections are well-stocked and excellent shopping resources. Shop online, find the dresses you like, and then call the nearest boutique to see if they have what you are looking for. From that point, trying on your bridesmaid dress is only a short drive away.

Grooms and Groomsmen Attire

Often considered one of the easiest aspects of the wedding planning process, finding the right outfit for the groom and his groomsman only requires good taste and a few hours of shopping. For the bride and groom who are budget-conscious, there are several things that they can do to defray costs.

First off, decide what the groom and his groomsmen's wedding attire should be by coordinating it with the theme and formality of the wedding.

Basic Rules of Thumb:

- Formal Daytime Wedding: Elegant, dressy suit jacket and trousers typically with a white wing-collared shirt, and a striped tie
- Formal Evening Wedding: Black dinner jacket and matching trousers (white tuxedo shirt and a bow tie optional)
- Semi-formal Evening: Dressy suit or dinner jacket with matching trousers with a white shirt, a vest, and a black bow tie
- Semi-formal Daytime: Day suit (often in a more casual fabric) with a white dress shirt (tie optional)
- Informal Wedding: Nice business suit with a white dress shirt and open collar or simple tie

You do not have to follow these exact rules, but they do serve as a reference point for determining what is an acceptable, tasteful, and budget-conscious style for the wedding.

The next important step is deciding whether or not you want to buy or rent the attire. Renting a tuxedo is infinitely less expensive than purchasing one. Purchasing one is only a good idea if you know that he will have occasions to wear it in the future. Otherwise, renting is the way to go.

From this point, all that is left is choosing what style of tuxedo or suit that you prefer. For more cost-cutting ideas about groom and groomsmen wedding attire, consider our Top 5 List below.

## TOP 5 COST-CUTTING TIPS FOR GROOMS AND GROOMSMEN

**1. Shop early.** Don't wait until a few weeks before the wedding to book all your wedding attire for the groom and his attendants. Shopping early will give you enough time to thoughtfully purchase or rent the clothing at the best possible deal that you can find.

**2. Wear their own shoes** Have the groom and his groomsmen wear their own shoes with their tuxedos or suits. Most men have a nice pair of dress shoes so make this work with the rest of their outfit.

**3. Borrow the tuxedo.** Ask around for friends and family members who have been in weddings or wear tuxedos occasionally to formal work events. If your groom or even one of his attendants is an average size and can borrow

their tuxedo from someone else, you are left with more money to spend elsewhere.

**4. Look for coupons and discounts.** Many formalwear shops and tuxedo rental stores run sales and offer coupons and discounts several times a year. Always negotiate the price of your tuxedo rental and see if they will work with you on a price. Ask about special rates or discount opportunities.

**5. Ask about special package deals.** If you purchase or rent all of your groom and groomsmen attire from the same retailer, they will often give you a special package deal that takes money off your total price. These kinds of savings are excellent ways to cut the costs of the groom and groomsman attire.

# FLOWERS AND DECORATIONS

Flowers are one of the main points of spectacle at many weddings. And because of their traditional importance, this is an area where many brides tend to throw their budgets out the window. In wedding planning, it is easy to feel like vendors are only after your money, not concerned with helping you make your day the most special that it can be. Bearing this in mind, remember that when choosing a florist for your wedding, go with someone who you feel exhibits a strong passion for their work and their clients. Shop around and make sure that your florist has both a passion for their job and the credentials to back them up.

You might find that the person who has the most creativity, flair, and passion for your wedding is not your standard florist but rather a close friend. If you have a friend with a great eye and a personal interest in your wedding, consider letting them handle the creation of your flower arrangements, centerpieces, and decorations. You can even construct a simple bouquet that is fresh, modern, and elegant.

If you like the idea of having a creative friend help you in this department, think about ordering just one or two arrangements from a florist for the most prominent places and making the centerpieces for the guest tables yourself. They can be made the day before if stored in a cool place overnight. Check out several of our "do-it-for-less" tips for successful flower arranging:

## Floral Centerpieces

• **Homegrown options**
Do you have flowers in your garden you can use? If not flowers, do you have a shrub or tree with great leaves that can be used for filler? Autumn leaves in particular make beautiful fillers in wedding centerpieces. Check out the local farmers' market just before closing time for great deals on flowers.

• **Prune and preserve for long-lasting arrangements**
Remove any foliage that will be under the water line and cut the stems on an angle. Use warm water and add a little Sprite or fresh-cut flower food, available from your florist, to prolong the life of the arrangement.

• **Secure arrangements in position**
When trying to arrange and secure branches, grasses, and bamboo stalks, mold a square of chicken wire across the top of the vase to hold the stems in place. You can cover this with parts of the arrangement, itself, or with decorative ribbon.

• **Short and sweet**

It is much easier to make short arrangements than to make tall ones. An easy arranging trick is to hold the flowers tightly together in a small bouquet, then cut all the stems so they are an even length and arrange in the vase. If you're unsure about what flowers will work, take the vase along to a florist and ask for advice.

• **Seasonal advantages**

Cut flowers such as sunflowers or lilies always say "summer." Arrange them in small galvanized vases or buckets for a rustic display. For an alternative, use an empty clean coffee can with the label removed. Tie with a bow of raffia or paint the cans in bright primary colors to complement the flowers. This will also work with empty jam or mason jars.

• **The beauty of monochromatic**

If you are overwhelmed by the sheer choice and variety of flowers, try sticking to one type and color. An all-white arrangement will work with almost any décor and is lovely for a winter wonderland centerpiece.

• **Advantages of potted plants**

Potted herbs and flowering plants also work well for tabletop décor and can be potted a week before the wedding. Hyacinth, azaleas, and chrysanthemums make some popular choices. No need to re-pot them; just place the plant in an inexpensive terracotta pot that is slightly larger than the plastic pot in which it was purchased. Plant the arrangements after the party or give them away as favors.

• **Florist tricks**

Turn back the petals of tulips or roses to give the flowers a more open, airy look.

• **Optimal containers for your arrangements**

Use clear vases or containers that have narrow necks and wide bases. This way you only need a minimum number of stems to fill them. Fill a glass vase with cherries, pebbles, or thick slices of lemons and limes to help keep the flowers in place and add another dimension to the floral arrangement.

## Centerpieces with Other Elements

Don't limit yourself to floral centerpieces. Consider these other components for striking arrangements.

• **Candles**

Use candles as decoration to add soft, mood light to the room. Candles immediately create a romantic, intimate ambiance, which is perfect for a wedding. Float them in water or put them in candlestick holders.

• **Coffee Beans**
Use coffee beans to fill shallow bowls, square vases, or trifle dishes. This dark, luxuriant bean gives off a delicious aroma. Nestle a flower blossom among the beans or a tea light candle. This is a beautiful idea for autumn weddings.

• **Smooth River Rocks**
Fill vases or shallow dishes with river rocks to create an outdoors, marine feel to your wedding. This works well for outdoor-themed weddings.

• **Fruits and vegetables**
The produce aisle carries an amazing assortment of colors, textures, and sizes that you can use to create fabulous centerpieces. You've likely seen lemons and limes in tall, clear column vases before. But think beyond that — whole or halved pomegranates, sliced blood oranges or kiwi, autumnal pears, gourds, apples, and pumpkins, monochromatic green artichokes, asparagus, and herbs. The list is endless! Take advantage of this veritable cornucopia of natural foods to complement your menu and theme.

• **Greenery**
Greenery is less expensive than flowers but can still create a lovely look for your wedding. Since it is not traditionally treated as the main point in a wedding centerpiece, when greenery arrangements are creatively done they are attention grabbing. Winter weddings showcase greenery wonderfully as holly, ivy, and pine needles can be used. Square lucite containers filled with wheatgrass are perfect for spring and summer weddings.

• **Feathers**
Colorful or white feathers and plumes make stunning centerpieces when used to fill tall, slender glass vases. Choose a color to match the décor of your wedding. Light the vase from the bottom with glowing white light to add to the lustrous effect.

• **Organic Materials**
Raid the outdoors for organic materials to use in your centerpieces. Bamboo, reeds, tree branches, acorns, nuts, leaves, and pinecones can all be brushed with glitter and spray painted silver or gold. These make dramatic displays when arranged in tall glass vases. Put the tall pieces in the vase and then fill the remaining space with the glitzy smaller pieces. Or forgo the glitter for a natural, "green" look.

## A Word on Bouquets

Constructing your own bouquet can be a simple task, given a pair of dexterous hands and a few guidelines.

For a simple, yet beautiful bouquet, choose a single type of bloom such as roses, carnations, calla lillies, or peonies. Or, if you prefer a mixed-flower bouquet, choose a variety of types, preferably in the same color family, of all textures and shapes. For instance, if you want a yellow color palette, try sunflowers, daisies, daffodils, and mums.

For an 8-inch bridal bouquet, you'll need 30 to 60 stems. Bridesmaids bouquets will require 20 to 40 stems. Place 5 or 6 attractive stems at an even height and hold securely with one hand. These will form the center or the top of a domed arrangement. Add stems, turning the arrangement in your hand to keep the flowers evenly distributed around the center. Arrange them so that the larger, more prominent blooms are on the outside, anchored by the smaller flowers toward the center.

Secure the stems with floral tape and wire, and use a wide satin ribbon of a contrasting color to finish the look.

## Other Floral Details

You can give leftover materials from centerpieces, bouquets and other arrangements new purpose by putting them to work in other areas of the wedding. Bundles of baby's breath with touches of feathers and greenery will make perfect arrangements for the backs of chairs at the reception. Or take the petals from the remainder of flowers and sprinkle down the aisle and alter. Try and make use of everything left, after all, you paid for it!

## Tips for Working with a Florist

If you do not feel capable of tackling the flowers and decorations for your wedding alone, use a florist but follow some of our helpful tips to maximize your decorating dollars.

### • Don't spread your money out.

Just because you have $1,350 dollars to spend on flowers does not mean that you have to spread that amount throughout the reception and ceremony. Concentrate your money in impact pieces with as much money as you can and use simple, Do-It-For-Less pieces with floating candles and rose petals elsewhere.

• **Days matter. Be flexible.**
The date of your wedding can make it exponentially more expensive to buy flowers for your wedding. Approach your florist early in the planning process to discuss the date for your wedding. Avoid having your wedding around Valentine's Day, Mother's Day, Christmas, or New Years as these days will be more expensive to book a florist and purchase flowers.

• **Be upfront with your vendor.**
Florists want to know your needs and wants immediately. Tell them what specific flowers you have in mind or show them photos of things that you like. The more detailed that you are, the more likely they will be to follow your wishes. Supply them with lists with your exact specifications.

• **Be assured they have adequate inventory.**
Make sure that the vendor you choose is fully stocked with the inventory you will need for your decoration. Make sure that your needs can be met before you sign a contract.

• **Use seasonality to your advantage when planning floral arrangements.**
Use your Flower Seasonality Guide (page 50) to help you make less-expensively in-season choices.

## FLOWER SEASONALITY GUIDE

| spring | | summer | |
|---|---|---|---|
| **Anemone**<br>*White, Pink, Red, Purple* | **Lilac**<br>*White, Violet* | **Alstromeria**<br>*White, Pink, Yellow, Orange* | **Hydrangea**<br>*White, Pink, Purple, Blue* |
| **Baby's Breath**<br>*White* | **Lily of the Valley**<br>*White, Pink* | **Aster**<br>*White, Pink, Purple* | **Iris**<br>*White, Purple, Blue* |
| **Bachelor's Button**<br>*White, Pink, Red, Blue* | **Narcissus**<br>*White* | **Baby's Breath**<br>*White* | **Larkspur**<br>*White, Pink, Purple, Blue* |
| **Bells of Ireland**<br>*Green* | **Orchid**<br>*Most colors* | **Bachelor's Button**<br>*White, Pink, Red, Blue* | **Liatris**<br>*Pink, Purple, White* |
| **Boronia**<br>*Pink* | **Peony**<br>*White, Pink* | **Bells of Ireland**<br>*Green* | **Lily**<br>*White, Pink, Yellow, Orange* |
| **Calla Lily**<br>*White, Yellow* | **Protea**<br>*Pink* | **Calla Lily**<br>*White, Yellow* | **Lily of the Valley**<br>*White, Pink* |
| **Calla Lily, mini**<br>*Most colors* | **Ranunculus**<br>*White, Pink, Orange, Red, Yellow* | **Calla Lily, mini**<br>*Most colors* | **Lisianthus**<br>*White, Pink, Purple* |
| **Carnations**<br>*Most colors* | **Rose**<br>*Most colors* | **Carnations**<br>*Most colors* | **Orchid**<br>*Most colors* |
| **Casa Blanca**<br>*Lily White* | **Scabiosa**<br>*White, Pink, Purple* | **Chrysanthemum**<br>*White, Pink, Yellow, Orange* | **Protea**<br>*Pink* |
| **Daffodil**<br>*Yellow* | **Star Gazer Lily**<br>*White, Pink* | **Cockscomb**<br>*Pink, Yellow, Red, Green* | **Queen Anne's Lace**<br>*White* |
| **Delphinium**<br>*White, Blue* | **Sweetpea**<br>*White, Pink, Red, Peach, Purple* | **Columbine**<br>*White, Pink, Yellow, Orange, Red, Purple* | **Rose**<br>*Most colors* |
| **Gardenia**<br>*White* | **Tulip**<br>*Most colors* | **Delphinium**<br>*White, Purple, Blue* | **Scabiosa**<br>*White, Pink, Purple* |
| **Gladiolus**<br>*Many colors* | **Waxflower**<br>*White, Pink* | **Lavender**<br>*Purple* | **Snapdragons**<br>*White, Pink, Yellow, Orange* |
| **Heather**<br>*Pink* | | **Forget-Me-Not**<br>*Blue* | **Solidaster**<br>*Yellow* |
| **Hyacinth**<br>*White, Pink, Purple* | | **Freesia**<br>*White, Pink, Yellow, Blue, Purple* | **Statice**<br>*Purple* |
| | | **Gardenia**<br>*White* | **Stephanotis**<br>*White* |
| | | **Gladiolus**<br>*Many colors* | **Sunflower**<br>*Yellow* |
| | | **Gerbera Daisy**<br>*White, Pink, Yellow, Orange, Red* | **Tuberose**<br>*White* |
| | | **Heather**<br>*Pink* | **Yarrow**<br>*White, Pink, Yellow* |
| | | | **Zinnia**<br>*Pink, Red, Orange* |

## fall

Aster
*White, Pink*

Baby's Breath
*White*

Bachelor's Button
*White, Pink, Red, Blue*

Cabbage, ornamental
*White, Pink, Purple, Green*

Calla Lily
*White, Yellow*

Calla Lily, mini
*Most colors*

Carnations
*Most colors*

Chrysanthemum
*White, Pink, Yellow, Orange*

Dahlia
*Most colors*

Delphinium
*White, Purple, Blue*

Gardenia
*White*

Gladiolus
*Many colors*

Heather
*Pink*

Lily of the Valley
*White, Pink*

Orchid
*Most colors*

Protea
*Pink*

Marigold
*Yellow, Red, Orange*

Rose
*Most colors*

Scabiosa
*White, Pink, Purple*

Statice
*Purple*

Zinnia
*Pink, Red, Orange*

## winter

Amaryllis
*White, Pink, Red*

Anemone
*White, Pink, Red, Blue*

Baby's Breath
*White*

Bachelor's Button
*White, Pink, Red, Blue*

Bells of Ireland
*Green*

Calla Lily
*White, Yellow*

Calla Lily, mini
*Most colors*

Camellias
*White, Pink*

Carnations
*Most colors*

Casa Blanca Lily
*White*

Cosmos
*White, Pink, Yellow, Orange*

Daffodil
*Yellow*

Delphinium
*White, Purple, Blue*

Dogwood
*White, Yellow*

Forget-Me-Not
*Blue*

Gardenia
*White*

Gladiolus
*Many colors*

Heather
*Pink*

Holly
*Green, Red Berries*

Jasmine
*White*

Lily of the Valley
*White, Pink*

Narcissus
*White, Yellow*

Nurine
*White, Pink, Purple*

Orchid
*Most colors*

Poinsettia
*White, Pink, Red*

Protea
*Pink*

Ranunculus
*White, Pink, Red, Orange, Yellow*

Rose
*Most colors*

Scabiosa
*White, Pink, Purple*

Star Gazer Lily
*White, Pink*

Star of Bethlehem
*White*

Sweetpea
*White, Pink, Red, Purple*

Tulip
*Most colors*

Waxflower
*White, Pink*

# GIFTS AND FAVORS

Let's face it; one of the biggest pieces of the wedding pie is the gift giving and receiving. The bride and groom typically receive many gifts to decorate their new home together, the attendants receive thank-you gifts for their involvement, and the guests receive gifts or favors just for showing up! Gifts and favors can be extravagant and beautiful, extravagant and tacky, inexpensive and tacky, or inexpensive and beautiful. To achieve the latter category of inexpensive and beautiful, you must adjust your mindset to "less is more" and be prepared to "do it yourself." This section is vital for those brides who are looking to give unique and memorable gifts and favors while still staying within their allotted budget. It is easy for a bride to forget her budget when she sees the personalized tote bags, jewelry, and bottles of fragrance available to buy for her bridesmaids. If you are apt to over-spend on these necessary but peripheral frivolities, read this chapter carefully! It is perfectly easy to buy or assemble lovely gifts for all of the people involved in your wedding day for a modest price.

## Bridesmaid Gifts

Your bridesmaids play an important role in your wedding. They keep you sane during the planning process, help you make wise decisions, assist you with the party planning, and come to your aid for the successful and smooth execution of your big day. Their efforts absolutely deserve recognition. Luckily, there are many different ways to go about planning, buying, and/or making the gifts to show your appreciation to these women. Here are some traditional gifts to purchase and some unique gifts that you can make yourself. What all of these gifts have in common is their price tag; each gift in this section costs less than $30.

### Traditional Gifts

**• Spa Day gift certificates**
What woman does not enjoy pampering herself at a spa? Find out what aspect of pampering each of your bridesmaids likes the most and treat them with a gift certificate towards a spa treatment. Better yet, give these gifts before the wedding and have a girls' spa day a few days before your wedding. You can all relax and enjoy the day together.

**• Manicure sets**
Sometimes all it takes is a little primping to make a woman feel her best. A manicure set housed in a cute bag or case is a perfect gift to show your bridesmaids how much you appreciate their work in your wedding. Not only can they use this before the wedding, but also for every ordinary day as well.

• **Makeup bags**

All your bridesmaids will enjoy new makeup bags. Perfect for travelling and home use, choose a bright pattern or have them personalized with each girl's name or initials. These are typically inexpensive but appreciated, practical, and adorable gifts.

• **Game sets**

Buy each of your bridesmaids a board game and set a date for a girl's game night. Games like Pink Poker Night, Unveiled, Dream Phone, Pictionary, and Twister are excellent ideas for this ladies' night and most of them are under $30. Your bridesmaids will enjoy the gift and the laughter that will accompany it.

• **Tote bags/slippers**

Giving personalized tote bags and/or slippers to your bridesmaids has become all the rage with weddings today. Your bridesmaids can take these handy and cute accessories to the beach, the spa, and the gym. They can also substitute as overnight bags for short trips. Mix and match bags/slippers with each girl's favorite color or personality for a sincere and personalized touch. Instead of buying them from a gift shop, try online stores like American Apparel to get a basic shape that can be embellished and personalized.

• **Netflix subscription**

Wait, does this gift reiterate the fact that you're the one getting married and she's the one staying home watching rented movies? Actually, no, it's a fabulous gift for bridesmaids scattered across the country. You can even have a long-distance movie club for your friends, where you stay in touch over the latest chick flicks. Include a bag of gourmet popping corn and instructions for a homemade bucket of buttery goodness.

## Unique and Handmade Gift Ideas

• **Candles**

Make or buy candles for your bridesmaids. Women tend to love candles because they have the ability to make any home warmer and more aromatic. Buy or make plain, scented candles using standard instructions and embellish them. Choose from many different styles. Create faux rock candles, glitzy beaded candles, simple and elegant candles, or personalized candles. Give your bridesmaids something beautiful to match their bedrooms and remind them of your special day.

• **Photo albums**

Put together mini scrapbooks or photo albums for each of your bridesmaids. Decorate and embellish the albums yourself to save money and make the gift more intimate. Begin each album with pictures of you and your friend to capture special moments of your friendship. Leave some blank pages at the back so that each bridesmaid can fill it up with photographs from the bachelorette party, the ceremony, and the reception.

• Handmade jewelry

Use semi-precious stones, pearls, beads, smooth stones, or exotic rocks to make jewelry for your bridesmaids. You can either make it to match their dresses for your wedding or for everyday wear. Brilliant jade and turquoise make stunning necklaces and earring sets that look lovely with informal dresses for outdoor or casual weddings. Or, buy gift certificates toward a beading store and have a jewelry-making bridesmaid event.

• Personalized music CDs

Mix CDs for your attendants. Compile the love songs from your wedding with meaningful or fun songs that remind you of your bridesmaids. Maybe there was a theme song for you and girlfriends the weekend that you spent at the lakehouse after graduation. Maybe you and your friend from high school made up a dance to one of those one-hit-wonders during freshman year. Find the songs that captured special moments like these and put them together for your bridesmaids. It will certainly take more time, but these CDs will forever remind them of your special day and your close friendship.

• Monogrammed stationery

Who doesn't love monogrammed stationery? Bridesmaids will adore this thoughtful gift because it is perfect for thank-you and get-well notes, sympathy cards, and everyday letters. You can choose different styles based on each bridesmaid's personality: modern for the city girl, cute for the girly girl, swirly and formal for the traditionalist in the group. Even if you have bridesmaids who are not avid letter writers, most everyone can appreciate good stationery and will need it at some point.

## Groomsman Gifts

Shopping for your fiancé's groomsmen is one of the easiest parts of the wedding. Since groomsman typically do not have a multitude of responsibilities or input in planning your wedding, you don't have to feel as compelled to buy or make unique or creative gifts to display your heartfelt appreciation. Since gifts and favors do not generally mean as much to men as it does women, traditional gift ideas work like a charm. Unless you want to go all out and personalize a gift to match each groomsman's interests, choose from this list of inexpensive and customary gifts to save yourself time and money. If none of these strike the groom's fancy, he can always turn to the ever-popular silver flask.

## Traditional Gifts

### • Engraved money clips

Simple and useful, money clips will help your groomsmen keep track of their money — well, what is left of it after the bachelor's party anyway. Every man can use one of these. Have them engraved with each person's initials for a customized look.

### • Gift Cards

Most every guy will appreciate (and feel appreciated) if given a little money to blow at the nearest electronics and gadget shop. Guys don't think as much about receiving a "personal" gift, and it is easy, already packaged, and compact.

### • Engraved glass coasters

For many men, dark colors, clean lines, and modern accessories define their ideal bachelor pad. Square glass coasters for the coffee table add an element of sophistication to this living room atmosphere. Engrave the coasters with their first name initial to make the gift more personal. These are gifts that you can be sure they will use. If you need encouragement, just think of Monday Night Football.

### • Personalized playing cards

Playing cards seem to go hand-in-hand with masculinity. Poker, the quintessential gambling game that men love requires playing cards. Give the groomsmen another deck of cards for their Friday night poker tournaments and they will love you. Personalize them with their names or with a wedding theme. Also, consider making the card decks unique to each person. If one groomsman loves to fish, go with a fisherman theme for his card deck. If one man enjoys classic cars, decorate the cards with different vintage, American cars.

## Wedding Guest Gifts and Favors

Wedding favors for your guests do not have to end up breaking your bank. The main purpose for giving away favors at your wedding is to thank your guests for sharing with you in the biggest day of your life. They serve as a token of appreciation and as a physical reminder of your wedding. As long as your gifts come from the heart, they do not have to be expensive. People want to know that you value their presence at your wedding, not that you spent an extravagant amount of money on each of their take-home treats.

Try to match your favors with the overall theme and décor of your wedding. It will help narrow your options. Also try to reflect your personality in the gift. You can certainly use the season of your wedding to guide you in your selection of a gift. If your wedding is taking place in December, it might not be a good idea to give away flip-flops. However, you could get away with filling small, sheer bags with creamy seashells as a favor for a Northeastern, Cape Cod-infused wedding.

You are virtually unlimited when it comes to ideas for wedding favors. Keep in mind that you can typically recreate even seemingly expensive ideas for a less money using a little ingenuity and hard work. Get together with some of your bridesmaids and your family to brainstorm ideas for wedding favors. If you need a little help getting started, consider some of our fabulous, tried-and-true ideas below.

### • Organza gift bags
Find these beautiful and sheer fabric bags at craft and gift stores. Inexpensive and versatile, you can fill these pretty bags with unique materials that correspond to your wedding theme or with candy, sugared almonds, or bath salts for a sweet gift.

### • Frosted take-out boxes
Typically available in a host of pastel colors these favor boxes are perfect for spring and summer weddings. Use them just as would use the organza gift bags discussed previously. Fill these adorable take-out boxes with cookies, candies, or other small gifts that your guests will love.

### • Sachets
Depending on the size of sachet you desire, cut 6″, 8″, or 12″ pieces of tulle from a fabric role and fill center of the fabric with dried lavender, rose petals, or other potpourri. Buy these filling materials in bulk to save on cost. Gather up the edges of the fabric around the potpourri filing and tie with a décor themed ribbon.

### • Mulling spices
Cut a 10 by 5-inch rectangle of cotton cheesecloth and fold it in half to create a 5-inch square. Place a small bay leaf, a stick of cinnamon broken into small pieces, four whole cloves, three whole allspice, a strip of dried lemon peel, and two strips of dried orange peel in the center of the cheesecloth. Gather the corners together and tie with cotton twine. This is a great party favor for fall and winter weddings. Include a hand-made tag with the person's name and directions for using the spices.

### • Framed photographs
For small weddings where you can call each guest a close friend, a small photo of the bride and groom in a simple frame is perfectly appropriate and likely appreciated by your guests. You could even write a short note thanking them for joining you on this special day and slip into the back of the frame. It'll be happy surprise should they ever open the frame to exchange photographs.

### • Heart cookie cutters
Give each of your guests a three-piece set of heart-shaped, metal cookie cutters. This simple idea has long-lasting significance because

every time your guests use the cookie cutters they will remember your wedding day.

**• Candles**

Give each guest a small votive candle wrapped in a piece of tulle. Secure with a piece of ribbon for an inexpensive, yet elegant favor. Match the candle color to the overall color of your wedding. Include with this gift a small, personalized matchbook as a reminder of your special day.

**• Color-coordinated jellybeans**

Buy silver heart-shaped tins or small glass jars and fill with an appropriate color of jellybeans. Alternatively, create a jellybean stand where guests can pack goodie bags on their own. Fill large glass containers with different flavors and a scoop for dipping. Everyone loves this bright, edible treat, and it is a great way to incorporate color and a youthful mood into your wedding reception. Red, yellow, blue, and pink jellybean colors correspond best with typical wedding colors.

**• Edible name cards**

For a unique and light-hearted favor, write each guest's name on a big sugar cookie with cake decorating gel. Prop the cookie next to each guest's water glass for a delicious seating guide. For an Asian-themed wedding, write each guest's name on a small strip of paper and slip the end of the paper in a chocolate-covered fortune cookie. Handmade truffles also make for a special gift, dessert, or party favor. When making the truffles, slightly flatten the bottom and make a slit in the top to use as a place card holder.

**• Centerpieces**

Make your party favors into centerpieces. If you have eight guests at one table, have eight bud vases with a single-stemmed flower or individual flowerpots planted with herbs. Tie a décor-themed satin or organza ribbon around each pot. Arrange the flowerpots in a circular pattern in the center of the table with the centermost arrangement slightly elevated on an inverted saucer. Rest the place cards up against the planted flowers in front of each guest's place setting.
Be sure to reference each menu for more gift and favor ideas.

# MUSIC AND ENTERTAINMENT

Music and entertainment go hand in hand at a wedding. Your music choice sets the mood and ambiance for the entire event; it also entertains your guests throughout the experience. Music can be a very important and beautiful aspect of your wedding.

For some couples, music says it all; ceremony music tells the story of their romance, it expressively moves the ceremony through the actions, and it adds a final, personalized touch to the day. These couples typically want music and dancing to play a large part in their reception.

Other brides and grooms find themselves at the opposite end of the spectrum. Music does not yield the same magical effect for them. Fortunately (or unfortunately, depending on which side of the spectrum you belong), these couples will find it much easier to shave costs on their wedding music and entertainment because they aren't fighting a desire for the stringed orchestra and live performer. In order to figure out how best you can save money on your wedding music and entertainment, you have to determine what priority music will have in your wedding, which often goes back to how important it is to you personally. Once you establish this, the next steps are easy.

You can choose from several different options for wedding music, depending on your budget and the formality of your wedding. The most common options include a solo wedding musician, a classical wedding ensemble, a live band, or a DJ. Each of these has its own advantages and drawbacks, as well as some alternatives that might save you some time, trouble, and money.

## Solo Wedding Musician

You can add a beautiful and unforgettable touch to your wedding ceremony or reception with performances by solo wedding musicians. Consider scheduling special music in the ceremony and having a soloist sing "your song." The wedding march sounds fabulous on an organ or piano, but other more unexpected instruments can work just as well. Bagpipes resonate with an earthy, unmistakeable sound, while harps and flutes set a peaceful, calm spirit for the ceremony. Music by a classical guitarist provides an intimate backdrop for smaller weddings, and an oboe offers rich, smooth tones. Check the local yellow pages or search online for wedding musicians, local conservatories, and music performance schools. And, of course, if you have musically-inclined friends or family members, consider their participation as their wedding gift to you.

## Classical Wedding Ensemble

The wedding ensemble provides an element of classical sophistication to any wedding. If you love classical music and instruments, having a live wedding ensemble perform at your wedding can transform the entire event. Woodwind ensembles can play chamber music that is particularly light and delicate, overlaying your wedding with simple elegance. A string quartet is an ensemble consisting of four string instruments, usually two violins, a viola, and cello, that creates a rich and classic backdrop to the ceremony or reception. Either of these musical ensembles is an appropriate accompaniment for both the ceremony and the reception, with the potential to memorialize your wedding through music in a special way.

## Live Band

There is nothing like having a live band at your wedding. There is also nothing like having a bad live band at your wedding. You can select a band from information passed along by word of mouth or from a booking agent easily found in your local yellow pages. Try to see the band play live if you can. You will be able to judge if their music is compatible with your taste, vision, and guests, and how the band members interact with the audience. If that is not possible, then ask for a demo tape. Any professional band should have a demo tape, a photo, and press kit available. For most live bands, the larger the number of musicians and the longer they play, the greater the cost.

## Things to Keep in Mind:

• Holidays are typically billed at higher rates than non-holidays.

• Musicians traditionally break up the evening into sets with a short intermission in between. If you want continuous music you must inform the musicians beforehand. There may be an extra charge if you want the band to play continuously. An alternative is to have recorded music playing during the breaks.

• Decide exactly how long you want the band to play for. If your wedding ceremony and reception are scheduled to last for three hours, agree that the musicians play for this amount of time only. Negotiate some form of overtime payment should the reception extend beyond the originally specified time. Typically, the band should be paid overtime in half hour increments.

• The band will need time to set up the equipment and run possible sound check before the guests arrive. If you are renting a location, prior arrangements should be made to accommodate this.

• It is customary to feed and tip the band members, but it is totally up to you. If you are not providing them with dinner you should let them know ahead of time so they can make other arrangements.

**LIVE BAND GENRES:**

• Country Band
• Cover Band
• Dance Band
• Jazz Band
• Latin Band
• Motown Band
• Oldies Band
• Reggae Band
• Rock Band
• Steel Drum Band
• Swing Band
• Top 40 Band
• 50's Band
• 60's Band
• 70's Band
• 80's Band
• 90's Band
• Wedding Band

## DJ

The most popular and contemporary choice for wedding music and entertainment (and by far the easiest of solutions) is to hire a DJ. With a good DJ you don't have to worry about listening to an out-of-tune, would-be lounge singer. You are typically guaranteed compact equipment set-up and a variety of enjoyable music. You can find DJs easily by word of mouth or through the yellow pages. Another excellent resource is The American Disc Jockey Association. This non-profit organization will help you find an approved DJ in your area. Most all the DJs in this association are experienced, versatile, and punctual. They are also fully insured and carry back-up equipment in case of technical difficulties. Some DJs only play music with a little chitchat in between songs, while others can emcee and provide complete entertainment with games, light shows, and props to accompany different songs. Whatever your specifications, you can easily find a DJ to accommodate the particular style and formality of your wedding.

Consider letting the DJ serve as the Master of Ceremonies throughout the reception. They tend to have a good grasp of wedding time and flow due to their responsibility of timing the music throughout the event. Many also have the right personality type to entertain an audience. Let him announce the bride and groom when they arrive at the reception, alert the guests to important events such as the cutting of the cake, and organize the dedications and dances.

### Things to Keep in Mind:

- It's your responsibility to dictate how the DJ should interact with your guests. Discuss his role in the wedding before the big day to ensure a reception that moves along smoothly without hiccups.

- Suggest a playlist, give guidelines as to what you want and do not want to hear, and require the DJ to stay within these boundaries. There's no need to upset Grandma and Grandpa on your wedding day with some explicit song lyrics.

- Ask to see his inventory list so that you can select CDs from it.

- Make sure to tell him that he will be working at a wedding so that he can dress accordingly and appropriately.

- Allow him enough time to set up and breakdown his equipment.

Now that you have some information about the most standard music and entertainment options for weddings, consider some of our tried and true money-saving techniques. These options are highly reliable as well as cost-effective. If you are a bride on a budget who has her money concentrated in other areas but still wants to provide entertainment for her guests, here are a few easy ways to do so.

## Saving Money on Ceremony Music

• Hire amateur singers.

You don't have to spend an exorbitant amount of money on a profes-sional singer for your wedding. Oftentimes an amateur singer or a vo-cal student from a nearby university will be glad to showcase his or her budding talent for little or no money. They could use the performance experience and you could use the help.

• Ask a friend or family member to perform.

Having the people closest to you involved in the intimacy of your wed-ding day makes for the most special of weddings. If you have musically inclined friends or family who love you and who love to perform, ask them to help you by singing or playing an instrument at your wedding. If you have an aunt who plays the piano, have her play selected pieces for the processional, during the unity ceremony, and to set the overall ambiance and mood of the ceremony.

• Play prerecorded music.

Create a list of the songs you want played during your ceremony. Find a friend who is technologically savvy and reliable and ask them to help you purchase the different songs and burn a wedding playlist that is specific to your order of service and ceremony. Work out the timing of each musical piece with the different ceremony elements and hand the responsibility for playing the CD over to a very responsible friend. Make sure that you have several copies of this CD on hand on your wedding day and be sure to have a sound check before the ceremony begins. This cost-effective option works best in wedding chapels or churches that have good sound equipment and speakers.

## Cutting Costs on Reception Music

• Have a do-it-for-less DJ.

The cheapest and most simple form of entertainment is playing mix CDs on your own audio system. For a formal dinner reception, soft classi-cal or jazz is always a great choice, as guests do not have to compete with the lyrics of a song when trying to hold a conversation. If you have space for a dance floor reserved, make sure to compile a list of songs that people know and enjoy dancing to. Also select appropriate songs for the first dance, the father/daughter dance, etc. A quick and easy way to make your playlists is to have a bridal party or sleepover at which you and your attendants get together with CDs, iPods, and a computer to burn the CDs. Just be careful to burn the songs in the order that you want them played so that you can ensure a seamless flow of music throughout the reception.

Ask a groomsman to monitor the music and be responsible for inter-changing the CDs, pausing for appropriate toasts and speeches, and orchestrating the events of the day. In essence, this lucky guy gets to be your Master of Ceremonies, and you can make sure he is up to the task by being as detailed as possible when delegating the day's responsibilities to him.

### • Shorten the reception.

If you want to have a DJ play your dance music, try to shorten the reception so that you can trim costs a little bit. Since DJs charge by the hour, shorten the reception to an hour and a half or two hours maximum. You could also consider having a longer reception but only hiring the DJ for the hour of time set aside for dancing.

### • Forgo the dancing.

While most brides feel that dancing is a required part of the wedding reception, this just simply is not the case. Many weddings, particularly those with receptions held in church fellowship halls, do not have dancing at the reception. Some traditional religious groups hold dancing to be inappropriate for the sacred event of a wedding. In addition, if the wedding is held somewhere rustic or unusual and pumping dance music through tower speakers is either not an option or doesn't fit the mood, don't feel pressured to provide that for your guests.

## Other Entertainment

Entertainment does not have to be limited to music. Couples can make the wedding both fun and meaningful for their guests with innovative twists on the traditional.

### • Show a bride and groom slideshow.

For a uniquely personal touch to your wedding, consider putting together a slideshow or video to show during the reception while your guests mingle or eat dinner. This could include photographs and video clips from your dating years, the photos from your engagement photo shoot, lyrics from your favorite songs, and any memento that holds a particular place in your heart. You could also record narration for the slideshow in which you share your love story with the guests.

### • Get back to your roots.

Try researching the wedding traditions and rituals of your respective ethnic backgrounds. Even if you are a mixed bag of cultures and nationalities or have never participated in your culture's practices, this is a great way to broaden and enrich yourself as well as your guests.

### • Prepare for the kids.

If you expect a fair number of children at your wedding, consider reserving an additional room wherever your reception takes place. Have someone in your wedding party set up a television with dvds and/or a videogame console. You will have to designate someone to watch them, but it might be the difference between a calm, elegant affair and a stressful, hair-pulling extravaganza.

## PHOTOGRAPHY AND VIDEOGRAPHY

Photography and videography memorialize your wedding in the most tangible way possible. They preserve the visual and audio elements as it happened, for you, your family, and friends to cherish for the rest of your lives together. It's certainly hard to quantify — you can't exactly put a price tag on your memories. But you can make smart choices so that the pictures and videos themselves leave the best, most lasting impression, instead of memories of the frenzy and planning leading up to the big day.

First, decide how important photography and videography are to you. If you like to keep the memories intimately in your heart and know that the most important people saw you on your big day, it can be as easy as requesting copies of the candid pictures taken by your guests and having a friend bring along their camcorder. But if you are among the vast majority of brides, you are considering making the wedding photography one of your higher priorities. And this can be a daunting task, given that any couple can go through several series of portraits and pictures, even before the wedding takes place.

Before you decide that your budget does not allow for a professional photographer and multiple sessions of portraits, remember that you don't have to choose all the options and that there is great value to peace of mind, and a true comfort in knowing that your wedding will be memorialized the way you want.

### Photography

Let's first define some photography terminology that you might find handy when interviewing photographers and preparing for the different portraits and shoots. There's no need to try and commit this all to memory, just put them on your mental shelf and pull down as needed.

#### Types of Film

- **35mm.** Most cameras use this type of film. It describes the size of the negative.

- **Medium format.** A camera or film type that uses a negative larger than 35mm such as 2 ¼ and 4 x 5. These cameras tend to be slower and heavier than 35mm, but they offer greater clarity, smoother tonality, more detail, and a superior final print. Their slow speed lends them particularly well to portrait photography.

### Types of Photography

- **Documentary.** An unstaged, unposed, candid method of capturing photographs.

- **Portrait.** A posed, generally formal photograph.

### Types of Treatments

- **Fisheye.** An extreme version of the wide-angle, which distorts the picture to impart a "looking out of the fishbowl" effect.

- **Multiple exposure.** A process in which a frame is exposed to light multiple times.

- **Panorama.** A special camera function that allows a substantially wider view than normal.

- **Sepia.** A brownish tint that is sometimes applied to black and white photos to give the picture a vintage or antique feel.

- **Selective focus.** Adjusting the focus to emphasize one portion of the photograph while the rest remains blurry.

- **Soft focus.** A lens or attachment that allows all of the edges within a photograph to be softened. This technique is used often in portrait photography.

- **Telephoto.** A lens that allows a photographer to capture things far away.

### Types of Editing/Post-Production

- **Prints.** The final photographs that are presented for purchase.

- **Proofs.** Photographs that are used for approval purposes. These are not retouched.

- **Retouch.** A process in which the photographer removes imperfections in the photo, which include anything from blemishes to dust that was on the lens at the time of the photo.

### Other

- **Shot List**
  A list created by the couple of shots that are required during the wedding. It includes the names and locations of shots to be taken. See the sample photography shot list on page 67, and be sure to explain the styles of shots you like, such as formal, serious, casual, friendly, elegant, posed, or candid.

- **Internegative**
  A negative created from an existing photograph. This is helpful for events like slideshows when you want to use pictures from the pre-digital era.

## Choosing a Photographer

You only have one chance to get the pictures right. Rather than hoping that Uncle Arnold remembers how to operate a camera from his college photography class, budget in a professional photographer for the very important times like the ceremony, formals, and some of the reception. Here are some tips for choosing a photographer who's right for you:

• **Ask around for recommendations.**
As with many things in life, hearing good things about a photographer from people you know and trust can be a much more reliable indicator than a fancy Web site or brochure.

• **Find someone who specializes in weddings.**
This will assure that he or she is ready for all the expected and unexpected events that happen in the process of tying the knot.

• **Be able to verbalize your personal taste.**
Knowing and being able to say what you like and don't like will assure that your personal tastes are reflected in the style and quality of photography that you want. Tear out images from magazines or borrow wedding albums from friends to showcase what you like and, just as importantly, what you don't like.

• **Go with your gut.**
The photographer you want to go with is the one with whom you share a connection. This will lead to a level of comfort and confidence that you want conveyed in every shot.

• **Perform a background check.**
Ask for references, ask to see a couple of finished albums, and familiarize yourself with the packages the studio offers. Ask every question that comes to mind. Do they have reliable transportation? Do they own or rent the equipment? If they rent, who pays? Does the fee cover an assistant or possibly two shooters? Who owns the rights to the images? Will they provide you with a high-res disk of all the images? If not, how does their proofing and purchasing system work? What sort of back-up do they have for digital images? Making sure that you have a comprehensive picture of the photographer you choose will mitigate surprises.

## Photography Options

Conceivably, you could document every detail from the ceremony to your bachelorette party to Sunday afternoon gatherings wrapping tulle around birdseed. But lest it needs to be said again, you're on a budget. So, in a nutshell, here is a list of the standard photography options you'll want to consider. Know which options you want before you approach a photographer.

- **Engagement Photos**

  This is your first real experience with the photographer. You will get to see how he communicates and works, in addition to his style and pace. Whether you choose to take posed portraits in a studio or have a more candid, fun, and trendy shoot at a meaningful location, be creative and have fun. This is a sure-fire way to get the most for your money. Also remember that if you plan to have photos put on correspondence such as save-the-date cards or the wedding program, these photos can be shot at the same time.

- **Bridal Portraits**

  These are pictures of the bride in her wedding gown before the wedding day. They are shot in a variety of places like churches, hotels, and outdoors. Consider this shoot a dress rehearsal — an ideal time to test your hair and makeup and to know what to expect come your wedding day.

- **Pre-Ceremony Shots**

  This includes formal shots of the bride and her bridesmaids, the groom with his groomsmen, and the bride getting ready with the bridal party. It can even include the behind-the-scenes people like florists, caterers, and other helpers.

- **Ceremony**

  If you only book your photographer for one event, the ceremony is the one to choose. These shots will consist of the bride walking down the aisle, snapshots of the guests, the exchanging of vows, any special performances, and the kiss.

- **Formal Pictures**

  These will be the shots after the ceremony, including the bride and groom with extended family, the entire wedding party, the bride with groomsmen, vice versa, and some candid shots.

- **Reception Photos**

  This will capture the cake cutting, the first dance (if there is one), bouquet toss, the toast, the bride and groom leaving, and a range of other pertinent events.

# SAMPLE WEDDING PHOTOGRAPHY SHOT LIST

## PRE-CEREMONY

Panorama of wedding site

Inside shot of wedding site

Bride Dressing

  Mother fastening jewelry clasps

  Bridesmaids helping button/zip gown

  Chatting with bridesmaids

  Shot of veil/garter

  Makeup

  Standing alone in dress

  Leaving for ceremony

Groom Dressing

  Hanging out with groomsmen

  Looking in mirror

  Having his boutonniere pinned

  Tying tie/bowtie

  Talking to his father

## PRE-CEREMONY PORTRAITS

Bride

Bride/maid of honor

Bride/bridesmaids

Bride with sisters

Groom/groomsmen

Groom with best man

Groom with brothers

## CEREMONY

Guests entering

Close-up of guest book

Grandparents/parents being seated

Maid of honor/bridesmaids walking down aisle

Flower girl/ring bearer walking down aisle

Close-up of floral arrangements

Close-up of ring on pillow

Groom waiting for bride

Close-up of groom's face when bride enters

Bride

Back of bride walking down aisle

Shot of father of the bride

Officiant

Bride and groom saying vows

Unity ceremony

Close-up of candles

Exchanging rings

The kiss

Shot of guests from stage

Bride and groom exit

Bride and groom outside

Bride and groom in car

Guests congratulating the couple

## POST-CEREMONY PORTRAITS

Bride and Groom

Bride with groomsmen

Groom with bridesmaids

Bride with parents

Groom with parents

Couple with both families

Couple with both sets of parents

Entire wedding party

Repeat some groupings in outside shots

## RECEPTION

Outside view of reception site

Guests mingling

Bride and groom arriving

Floral arrangements

Centerpieces

Musicians

Wedding cake/groom's cake

Gift table

Couple mingling with guests

Food

Couple's first dance

Bride dancing with father

Groom dancing with mother

Wedding party dancing

Flower girl/ring bearer dancing

Cutting of the cake

Feeding each other

Bouquet toss

Garter toss

Toasts

Decorated car

Couple leaving

Throwing of confetti/petals/rice

Couple driving away

## OTHER PHOTOGRAPHER SHOT LIST TIPS

• Be sure and get candid shots to contrast the posed ones.

• Don't take too many pictures of people eating.

• Make a list of people whose photos must be taken and give to photographer.

### Do-It-for-Less Photography

Fabulous, memorable pictures of your wedding are at your fingertips. It takes a little bit of finesse and a little resourcefulness, but you can do it, especially with our help. Just remember that you'll have these images forever, so be careful as you trim away costs.

• First, let's talk a little more about the professional photographer. Shopping around is obviously recommendable, but you also want to remember that sometimes, you get what you pay for. Meaning, there might be a reason why his rates are so low. As long as his references and "background check" come up clean and tidy, you have made a good first step to pictures you'll want.

• Set up an online account where guests can donate money for your wedding pictures. It is easy to set up a Paypal account, especially if you set up your own wedding Web site. With each guest donating five to twenty dollars, it may be much less expensive than you initially planned.

• Book the photographer for his time, not the album, and try, if possible, to get the rights to your pictures. In the past, it was understandable for photographers wanting to hold on to their negatives, but in the age of digital technology, the photographer is not losing anything by giving you the rights to keep these photos (other than the mark-up he charges for prints, of course.) Get your agreement in writing.

• And speaking of the photographer's time, book him for the essentials, like the pre-ceremony, ceremony, formals, and part of the reception. You certainly don't need a professional photographer for the duration of a six-hour reception — after all, only about eight percent of reception photos make the cut. Because the reception tends to be more casual, candid shots by guests will provide more than enough material.

• Find someone who isn't quite professional. This can include a photography student from the local university, an up and coming photographer, or someone who has a moderate amount of experience as a photographer's assistant.

• Wait until the last minute. This may seem counterintuitive and is certainly not an option for the faint of heart. Two weeks before the wedding, call the top ten photographers in your area that you like and ask to see if they've booked that weekend. More than likely, if they're still open at that late date, they might cut you an amazing deal. Be sure that the family member or friend who you enlisted to shoot your big day is still in reserves; this plan is not guaranteed.

## Other Tips

Even though the bulk of your photography budget will most likely be devoted to the professional taking and printing of your pictures, there are certainly other ways that you can cut costs.

- **Make your own album.**
  Cameras, high-quality printers, and even acid-free paper are becoming more accessible for consumers. In addition, there are several online sources to create wedding albums that will charge substantially less to put together your book of memories. If you do choose to have the photographer put the album together, don't opt for the leather version. A less flashy, inexpensive version will preserve your memories just the same.

- **Set up a photo booth.**
  Upon entering the reception hall, have guests pose in front of a digital or Polaroid camera and write a special message to the bride and groom. A member of the house party can be in charge of putting this album together.

- **Have a photography-savvy friend fill in.**
  A photographer can charge from around one hundred dollars per hour to several hundreds, and the more pictures he takes, the more costly it becomes. Having a friend or family member who is deft with the camera and loves you enough to work for food, gifts, or love can be one of the best money-saving decisions that you make. Here are some professional tips for a non-professional photographer.

  - Buy or rent a nice SLR (single lens reflex) camera and let him or her use it to shoot the wedding. Be sure to give it to him or her beforehand so he or she can practice with the equipment before your big day.

  - Always use an off-camera flash. Anything to soften the on-camera flash will do wonders for the photos.

  - Don't forget the small details like flowers, cakes, a curly lock of the flower girls' hair. These are the small moments that make weddings seem truly intimate.

  - Be extroverted and energetic. Your energy will transfer to guests and ultimately the pictures you take. Don't be afraid to ask someone to turn and look or to have a little fun.

  - Don't overuse the zoom function. The best pictures and stories have details and context outside of the object you are focusing on. When in doubt, walk closer to your subject. You'll capture more detail that way, and when it comes time for printing, you'll be grateful you have the data you need to create large size, high-res prints.

- Use the programmed modes. A person's wedding is not a time to experiment or to try and be creative with the camera's functions. That should be done beforehand.

- Put an ad in the classifieds or on Craigslist to barter services. Trade lessons from a photographer for a skill that you have to offer, whether it's a foreign language, gardening, or even scrapbooking.

## Videography

Video is a powerful and elegant medium to capture the emotion, details, and moments of your wedding. It captures on film all of the moments you don't remember.

In its most primitive day, it was a privilege only afforded by wealth or celebrity. The labor and amount of tape used created an exorbitant expense. But, it has become increasingly popular recently, especially with the growing popularity and accessibility of digital video cameras and film editing software.

There is a lot that you can do to make sure that the videography in your wedding is executed in a way that expresses your personality and tastes, and that it is done within the guidelines of your budget.

Unlike photography, videography is an area in which most people are unfamiliar. So to start, a few key things that you should know:

### Styles of Wedding Videography

- **Journalistic.** This is a documentary style of video that will capture and relay things in the order that they happen. With this style, there are no pre-scripted interviews or posed scenes.

- **Cinematic.** This feels more like a movie or film. The purpose is to capture the emotion and drama of the day rather than each specific event.

- **Traditional.** This is anything that doesn't fit into the other two categories. Most of the time, this style is longer than the other two and resembles a home video, as it is less edited than either the journalistic or cinematic types.

### Types of Wedding Videography

- **Engagement Video.** A video that documents the proposal. It is often shot without the bride's knowledge and is incorporated into the Video Scrapbook.

- **Video Scrapbook.** Includes pictures choreographed to music, usually shown at the rehearsal dinner. This can incorporate video and other sound bites as well. Also called a "photo montage."

• **Bridal Elegance.** A video of the bride in her wedding gown, shot in the style of a fashion shoot.

• **Love Story.** A video on how the couple met, the ins and outs of the relationship and what they envision their future together to be like. This involves interviews with the bride and groom separately and also together. For an example of this, check out the weekly "Vows: Wedding and Celebrations" video on the *New York Times* Web site.

• **Same-Day Edit.** A short recap of the wedding day, itself, presented at the reception. This incorporates footage from pre-ceremony, ceremony, and post-ceremony.

## How to Choose a Videographer

Your wedding day will only happen once, and in the frenzy of the day, you are guaranteed to miss many details, people, and small sub-plots that you will want to revisit once life calms down. Whether you are willing to entrust an amateur to take on this task is clearly up to you and where videography ranks on your list of priorities. If you do decide to use a professional (even if you go with a friend, family member or amateur videographer), here is a list of questions and considerations before you sign on the dotted line.

• What sort of format will be employed? High-definition is the most current technology, and it allows for a much higher quality picture. That said, a Brownie or Super 8 can yield fabulously quirky results that look like a crackly 1950s home movie.

• How many cameras will be used? In an ideal world, the very minimum should be two.

• Ask to see three finished examples of work. If these resonate with you, you are on the right track. If they don't, however, there is no use in trying to bend the videographer into seeing your vision. Their product is representative of how they see the world.

• Are they open to editing and what program will they use to edit? If they aren't willing to edit, you have to be prepared to take whatever is presented. Final Cut Pro is the industry standard. If the software is something different or the answer is ambiguous, be sure and keep digging.

• Will you own the rights to the video? If not, you will have to pay for each copy to be reproduced.

• Will the finished product (dvd) be furnished with chapter titles? If not, how will you navigate around the video?

• Be somewhat wary of referrals from your photographer. Oftentimes, the photographer will get a cut.

## Money-Saving Tips

A professional videographer will charge anywhere from $2,000 to $10,000, and up depending on how much time and how many products you are looking for. As mentioned before, there are many ways to save money in this area, given the accessibility and relative inexpensiveness of technological equipment. Here are some tips for having your videography done for less.

- Have the videographer employ just two cameras, and have him cover the wedding and reception only.

- Pick and choose the things that you would like to see done professionally. Many brides like for their slideshow/video to be done by a professional. An experienced professional will be able to incorporate even old 8mm footage into the montage and be sure that the music is perfectly synchronized with the pictures.

- Edit your own video: It takes a videographer anywhere between 18 and 30 hours to edit a video, and accordingly, that is where most of the investment is spent. Many computers (especially Macs) now come with consumer friendly video editing programs, so it might be worth your while to learn the program and do it yourself. Take a look at Apple's iMovie to start your research.

- You can do the opposite as well: Have friends and family film the wedding and hand it over to a professional to edit.

- Depending on how important videography is to you, concentrate your money in the filming of the wedding and have friends take pictures.

## VOLUNTEER VIDEOGRAPHER
## GUIDELINES FOR STRESS-FREE DAY

If you choose to have a close friend or relative film the wedding, be sure to provide clear expectations of what you want, and provide a detailed photography list as a guide for the event. Share this photography list of pointers with your volunteer photographer.

Always have extras.
Microphones, lights, lenses and batteries. If one component quits working, you'll have no time to find another, so be sure to have a back-up.

Keep shooting.
The more footage you have, the more you will have to work with.

Get an order of events.
You can always anticipate what to expect next.

Visit the location prior to the big day.
To assess the environment for lighting, weather conditions (especially humidity — camera lenses can fog up in areas of high humidity), sound issues (are you a flight path or next to a railroad), exits, parking, and outlets you can use.

Use a tripod.

Wear dark, unnoticeable clothing.
As not to distract guests.

Experiment before the wedding.
It is not acceptable for you to try new things on the big day.

# chapter 4
# reception locations

There are thousands of wonderful wedding locations to choose from, but there are several things you will want to determine about any location you are considering:

- Guest capacity
- Parking facilities
- Handicap accessibility
- Catering facilities / hire a caterer or bring your own food?
- Location fees
- Any necessary permits
- Available electrical / for entertainment / backup generators
- Restroom facilities
- Rules on alcoholic beverages
- Necessary rentals
- Early set-up
- Clean-up arrangements

Weddings and receptions can be held at many different types of sites:

- Aquariums
- Athletic fields and stadiums
- Beaches and lakes
- Boats and yachts
- Churches
- City and state parks
- Clubs
- Convention centers
- Golf courses
- Historic buildings and landmarks
- Hotels, small inns, and B&Bs
- Museums and galleries
- Private mansions
- Race tracks
- Ranches and farms
- Restaurants
- Schools and libraries
- Small airports
- Stores and shopping centers
- Theaters, auditoriums, and concert halls
- Trains and train stations
- Vineyards

# SUCCESSFUL OUTDOOR RECEPTIONS

Having your reception outdoors will require special equipment and arrangements. Some things to keep in mind:

• **Focal point**
The informal charm of a garden wedding is one of its advantages. You can save money on the cost of flowers and decorations. Gardens provide atmosphere and beauty. But all gardens are different and you may want to supplement the garden you choose with flowering potted plants or shrubs around the ceremony and/or reception area. You may want to add a focal point like a gazebo, trellis or arbor.

• **Restrooms**
Find out if the available restroom facilities will work for the number of guests you are inviting. Stock it up with paper napkins, tissues, and plenty of toilet paper. Make sure you have a plunger handy, especially if you have only one or two restrooms to service all your guests. Provide a trashcan and have someone check on it every hour to make sure it doesn't get too full. If the facilities aren't going to be adequate, you might want to choose a discreet location for the porta-potty. The other option is to rent a "honey wagon," which is a much fancier restroom option as it is housed in a trailer and can be air conditioned.

• **Protection from the elements**
You may need a tent if the weather is hot or if there is a chance of rain. Small events might require a few pop-ups that you can decorate as you like, while larger events will require renting something. Tents can be expensive so look around and see what your options are. You can also rent stand-alone umbrellas or tables with umbrellas.

• **Tables and chairs**
You will need tables and chairs unless you're having a picnic. Make sure the location has enough room for the number of tables and chairs you'll need.

• **Dancing**
If your guests are the dancing types, make sure there's plenty of space for them to boogie — or rent a dance floor — and that the music allows for all of your friends and family who TiVo Dancing with the Stars to comfortably dance the night away. Too much decorating can be prohibitive, as can loose cords, unsteady cocktail tables, and precariously placed sound equipment. If you're using a space that contains full rooms of furniture, make arrangements to move it to a safe place, or have it moved before you arrive to prepare for the event.

## ELECTRICAL ALERT

For home venues, do not underestimate the strain additional equipment can put on your electrical system. At one outdoor wedding recently, the father miscalculated what his circuitry could handle. Not only did the swanky outdoor lighting blow a circuit at his house, it fried the lines of the entire block 15 minutes before the reception started. They were able to borrow generators from several friends, but still had to make do with less electricity than they needed.

• **Electrical outlets**

Musicians and DJs need power, as do caterers. Some caterers and party planners will bring their own truck with a generator because the power needed for a party will overload most standard household outlets. Will you be plugging in extra lighting? Coffee makers? Refrigeration? Grills? DJs and musicians will be able to tell you what they require in the way of power.

• **Food**

Food needs special consideration. If food is to be prepared off-site, how will it be transported to the reception site? If food is being prepared at the site, you may need to rent equipment or hire a caterer who has the equipment to do this (power generator, portable refrigeration, etc). Find out what equipment, if any, is available at the site. You will also want to make your food choices carefully to make food preparation and transportation as simple as possible and to minimize the possibility of spoilage.

• **Uneven terrain**

The more remote the location the greater the possibility of uneven terrain. Make sure guests know what type of terrain there will be so they can wear appropriate shoes and clothing. High heals aerate the soil, but your female guests may not appreciate their Jimmy Choos acting as a tiller. Any elderly guests or not very mobile guests may need wheelchairs or other assistance so that they can get around the area safely. Additionally, uneven ground will present a challenge when setting up tables, chairs and tents.

• **Dirt plus water equals mud**

Take a good look at your potential location. What will happen if it rains the night before your party? Will you be saying your vows in a puddle of mud? Look to see if there is adequate drainage or room for water run-off.

• **Planning for inclement weather**

If you can choose a site that has an indoor space available as an alternative, you will have the security of knowing that whatever the weather does, your wedding will go on.

# HOME WEDDINGS: PERCEPTION VERSUS REALITY

Ah, the perfect vision of your wedding reception … the décor looks like it came out of a chic magazine, the champagne is chilling, the weather is warm — but not too hot — the aroma of warm canapés wafts through the air, and your guests are mingling and chatting about the beautiful ceremony, waiting for the bride and groom to arrive at what will be the wedding of the year.

And the not-so perfect vision … 1 a.m. the night before the wedding, you and your family are screeching about the tablecloths, and the place cards have yet to be completed, there's a terrible stench from the scorched bruschetta, and the wine glasses arrived from the caterer with water spots and another bride's lipstick still on the rims. The zeroes are multiplying in your head and you get dizzy thinking about your long-since-forgotten budget. The DJ you hired over the phone bears a striking resemblance to Adam Sandler's character in *The Wedding Singer*, and he seems to have mixed your song list up with that of a couple who spends weekends with a traveling Renaissance fair and weekdays playing *World of Warcraft* at home in a darkened gaming room.

Okay, maybe it's not *that* bad, but there are certain hazards that come with planning any wedding.

Taking a few easy precautions can save a lot of stress and money. You'll be turning a home into an entertaining venue, so don't neglect to consider all of the questions you'd ask at any potential reception site (see page 83 for ideas). Try to anticipate everything you'd need to keep your guests, whether the number is large or small, comfortable, safe, and well-fed.

As you plan a home wedding, keep these tips in mind:

- Party-proof as necessary. It would be embarrassing for your guests and stressful for you if valuables were damaged during the joyous event.

- Have the telephone number of a reliable cab company on hand in case someone needs a taxi.

- Make sure you have space for caterers, DJs, rented equipment, and the first dance. It might be a good idea to have the caterer and DJ come over before committing to a contract to make sure the space is amendable to their needs.

- Consider the toll a home wedding would take on the rest of the family. If you are planning to use a parent's home, decide whether hosting the event would send Mom over the edge, and if her declarations to the contrary are sincere.

- Free is not always cheap. If the modifications will outweigh any convenience or money saved, try to cut back elsewhere, change your expectations for the wedding, or find another venue that might work better. If you have large shelves of hazardous knick-knacks, irreplaceable furniture in every room, a finicky plumbing system, or unreliable wiring, perhaps you should reconsider having the wedding at home. If you need convincing, rent the movie *Father of the Bride* with Steve Martin.

## FREE LOCATIONS

If you are considering another free location and happen to find one that fits your needs, consider yourself lucky! However, keep in mind the trade-offs you'll need to make with a location that may need many adaptations to make it suitable for your event. If you will need to bring in tables, chairs, restroom facilities, generators, decorations, shelters, and food preparation space, you may not be saving yourself any money. Consider, too, whether it will preserve your peace of mind in having to make the space more accommodating. Again, if the trouble won't be worth the money saved, consider another location. But if all these considerations do not dissuade you from using your free space, your thriftiness will pay off.

### Friend's Home

Maybe you have a close friend or relative who has a fabulous home or yard and would be only too happy to let you throw your party on her property. As an incentive, offer to pay for a maid service to come to the house the day after for a professional clean-up. A wedding is an enormous undertaking, even if it is small, so thank the person with a thoughtful gift: a day of pampering at a spa or a gift certificate to a favorite store would be wonderful gestures.

### Local Park

Another popular freebie is a local park. Usually in a convenient location, parks have all the basic necessities: picnic tables and benches, bathrooms, plenty of space, trash cans, and lots of trees for shade. Some even have barbecue grills, so all you need to bring is the charcoal. See page 156 for menus that require only grills for some reheating.

If you can't reserve a specific park area, absolutely send out a scout several hours ahead — or even the day before — to stake out a plot. You may be able to use the decorations and flowers to create a natural-looking self-contained space, or use a nook of the park that would lend itself well to a garden-wedding feel. Please be considerate of other park users. Don't cordon off the whole park, and leave the "keep out" signs at home.

## Beach

The beach has always been the wedding locale of sun-kissed romantics. Many brides have portraits made at the beach, even if the wedding itself is nowhere near the shore! Plenty of shade is a must. If your budget doesn't stretch to include a canopy, ask family members to bring beach umbrellas, and set up a picnic-style reception. The different colors and sizes will make your party look very festive, and you won't need to guild the lily by over-decorating in such a natural, beautiful setting.

You can incorporate swimming, boogie boarding, Frisbee throwing, kite flying, sand-castle building, and even limbo dancing into the reception, if you wish. Provide a good footpath for your guests to use; some guests, especially elders, may find it difficult to walk on sand. You can place dried grass to serve as walkways.

The best time of the day to tie the knot is early in the morning or late afternoon. Noon is the worst because of high temperature and too much light for photography. Stock up on plenty of sunscreen, water, and towels for your guests, and urge them to apply sunscreen regularly, especially after swimming. Check with your local fire department for rules and regulations, as some states prohibit alcohol, barbecues, bonfires, and fireworks on their beaches. Also, check with the lifeguard station for surf conditions and high tide times.

## Rooftop

If you live in a city, consider throwing a rooftop reception post-ceremony. Some apartment buildings have rooftop garden areas designated specifically for residents' use. Of course, consideration for neighbors and permission from the resident committee, landlord, or owner is a must.

# RENTAL LOCATIONS

## Inns, Bed and Breakfasts, and Gardens

A small inn can be a beautiful and classic location for a small wedding. Many inns and B&Bs have hosted numerous weddings and often have a wedding coordinator on staff to help you plan the event and to make sure the day goes smoothly. They may even own tents, tables, or other equipment that you would otherwise rent.

Consider the size of the venue and the size of your guest list; parking space could be a problem in some cases.

Be sure to make arrangements with the owner of the property, and perhaps also the neighbors to comply with local regulations.

## State Parks and Summer Camps

You may not have considered a state park or campground, but if easy, natural, and low-maintenance describe you and your intended, you may want to do so. Some parks have shelters that can accommodate large groups for a meal or a party. There are usually great facilities for games, swimming, hiking, and other pre- and post-wedding fun.

Many summer camps will rent out their dining hall or other indoor space for receptions. Availability may be restricted to fall and spring, when it's not in use for other overnight groups. These locations lend themselves well to a "weekend wedding," as guests can stay overnight at the facility and activities can be offered all weekend long. This is a true "do-it-for-less" alternative that could provide some great memories of your unconventional and memorable wedding.

## Public Parks and Gardens

Contact the local city hall or chamber of commerce for information about public parks, botanical gardens, and arboretums. Find out if there is a maximum number of people allowed, and whether it will be open to the public while your wedding is going on. Will there be a shelter, a kitchen for food preparation, and adequate wiring for your electrical needs? Some parks may not charge a usage fee, but you may not be able to reserve the space in advance. See the section on Local Parks on page 78 for more information.

Botanical gardens make a great location for off-season parties. Even during the fall or winter months when many plants and flowers are out of bloom, you'll still find lots of color and textures. Some gardens have special event areas with waterfalls, lanais, or gazebos. Also, check for after-hours deals during the spring and summer.

## National Parks

Go to the National Park Service Web site at www.nps.gov/parks.html to find a list of all the national parks.

Check individual parks for each one's policy on weddings. Often, they will list popular wedding venues within the park. If permitted, you could get married in a silent grove of redwoods and have a reception on the bluffs overlooking the Pacific Ocean, or you could say your vows next to a pristine lake, with a picnic set up nearby.

Take care to apply for any special-use permits that may be required. Forms can often be downloaded from the Web site.

Find a qualified person to officiate at your wedding; each state's laws are different, so be sure you know what is required of you before you go. This goes for the marriage license, too.

## Art Galleries

If you plan on having a small ceremony in the courthouse but want to meet friends and loved ones for a reception after, an art gallery could be a relaxing and low-preparation space. Many gallery owners are very open to holding events, as it brings in potential customers. At most galleries, seating is at a minimum, so this location works well for cocktail receptions where guests will be standing only for an hour or so.

## Historical Sites

If you are a history buff, or just like the idea of being married in a building centuries old, check out the local historic registry of homes and structures.

Space can be a particular challenge because many now-historic sites were not designed to accommodate large, free-flowing celebrations like a wedding reception. Limitations can include a lack of overall floor space; rooms too small for dancing; and not enough restrooms, parking spaces, or handicap-accessible entrances. There may very well be restrictions on decorating, as the location you're using is extremely valuable in its preserved state. If you run into a problem of this nature, be slow to demand accommodation. Your ideas of décor may dilute the old-fashioned feel.

Ask if musicians are allowed, and where. Ask what sorts of events have worked before, and how they were set up. Have they had trouble accommodating electrical needs in the past?

There may be limitations on food or beverages; many historical sites do not allow red wine because of the risk of stains. Others do not allow food in certain rooms. Ask whether a special liquor permit is required for your event. Also, confirm there is enough kitchen space and equipment for your needs. If not, a caterer or rental company must supply it at extra cost to you. Ask whether lit candles are allowed.

Despite your best efforts, accidents can happen, whether to one of your guests or to the property. And, for a historic setting, such mishaps can be costly. You may have to take out a single-event insurance policy to protect the site and your bank account. But check your own homeowner's policy, if you have one, to see if it extends coverage for any such problems.

## On the Water

If you live near water, you can rent a boat — not an ocean liner and not an inflatable dinghy, but a riverboat, small or large yacht, pontoon, barge, ferry, or something big enough to accommodate your guests comfortably. Some of these boats may or may not be seaworthy, but you will be surprised by how many dry-docked vessels are for rent at reasonable prices. Check with the dock masters at local marinas for information.

## Wineries

A winery can be a dreamy, romantic, naturally landscaped venue for a wedding. While Napa Valley is most famous for its vineyards, Central California and several other regions across the country also have many fine wineries that are just as beautiful. Before you choose one, check the rental, food, and beverage policies; some wineries allow only their wine to be served. Not all wineries host weddings. Do some research to find the perfect spot.

## Places of Worship

A church or synagogue is a lovely, traditional setting, and figures into many brides' dream weddings. Most religious institutions welcome the extra income or donation, especially if the building is empty on the day you plan to hold your wedding. Many church halls have tables, chairs, and sometimes kitchen and parking facilities. Having both the wedding and ceremony at the same location is extremely convenient. But if you are considering serving alcoholic beverages, remember that many churches do not allow them on their premises. Factor in the importance of your choices from the beginning; you may find other ways to celebrate, like with a brunch or dessert reception, or you could have the reception at a nearby hotel or garden.

## Private Clubs and Mansions

Clubs are well-maintained spaces that often have excellent grounds and facilities for weddings and larger events. They may conveniently provide everything from parking and professional event planners to party favors, but often all for a hefty expense. Be aware that most of these locations insist that you use their catering facilities and staff as part of the deal. If you have your eye on a local historic mansion make sure the locale has ample space for the guests and their cars, umbrellas, coats, and children.

In the colder months, you may be able to find a beautiful place that turns into a winter wonderland with snow drifts, fireplaces, and holiday decorations. However, unless you're getting married in a state that will have guaranteed snow during your wedding date, avoid using a room that has a large picture window for the ceremony. You may imagine drifts of beautiful snow, and end up with a gray rainy day. Be sure to ask what seasonal decorations they use; you may be able to save money, as many sites are already heavily decorated.

Make sure your site will be adequately heated during the winter months; old churches can be especially drafty.

## Restaurants

If you're a foodie and love the convenience of meeting a group in a restaurant, this may be just the idea for you. Often you can get a package deal that is comparable to the cost of a rental location, caterers, equipment, and labor for set-up. It may still be pricey, but the things left to purchase or arrange will be few.

Work out a deal with the special events or catering manager. An 18-20% service charge may be applied to your total bill. You may think this is a little high, but this is cheaper and a big savings, for example, on the rental of equipment that would have to be delivered if the event were elsewhere.

Plan a menu that is cost-effective to the restaurant. If necessary, speak with the chef to find out about upcoming seasonal specials. If the menu has eaten up most of your budget, propose bringing your own wine and bottled water. There might be a small corkage fee for the waiter to open and serve your wine, but as you're likely to be buying it by the case, you'll save a little bit of money. Bring your own centerpieces, party favors, and after dinner chocolates. A nice touch is to arrange pre-paid valet parking for guests if the budget allows.

## A FEW FINAL WORDS ABOUT WEDDING LOCATIONS

Make sure your location will accommodate what you want. Is the location large enough to accommodate all your guests? Are dressing rooms available for you to use before the ceremony and after? Is the location easily accessible, especially for those with special needs? Can you find someone to officiate at the location?

The amount you'll pay will vary from location to location. When you're finding out the costs, be sure to ask what is included with the price. Ask for a contract or agreement, and make sure the items included are written out on the contract. Ensure, too, that you know who to contact with any questions; if the venue is a place of worship, do you call the minister or the church secretary? You'll likely be asked to provide a deposit to reserve the date for any location. This needs to be reflected on the contract, as does the balance due and date due. Selecting the location of the ceremony should happen well in advance of the wedding date, up to 12 months ahead if possible. If you wait too long to reserve the location, you may find it's already booked. Plus, there is a lot more to consider beyond the ceremony location.

You'll want to consider the ceremony style well in advance, also, especially if you wish not to follow the more traditional route. Many couples choose to write their own vows, and others prefer older vows with personalized readings. If you're using a venue that hosts a lot of weddings, the music may be included with the location. For example, a church will often suggest its own organist or pianist. If your budget allows, you may wish to personalize the musical program and hire a soloist and accompanist to perform songs significant to you and your beloved. Or you can hire musicians to match the theme of your wedding. Reserve the talent far in advance, right after you've secured the wedding ceremony location.

Whatever you decide is right for your wedding location, find your sticking points and stick to them. If food, photography, and exquisite flowers are most important, do not allow yourself to be talked into splurging on something less important to you. If you find that your wants don't fit in with your budget, reevaluate some facet of your plan. Wedding planning is too often all about money and less about the marriage itself. Plan a few things that send you over the moon, like a vintage wine and an award-winning photographer, arrange thrifty solutions for other things, like cupcakes instead of a grand wedding cake and a borrowed wedding dress, and you'll be off to a great start.

# chapter 5
# reception
# logistics

In tandem with choosing the location of the wedding reception (see chapter 4), you'll need to consider what style of reception you will have. The size of the venue will also dictate the number of guests to invite and the most suitable and practical style of food service. Be careful that the placement of the food, bar, and seating will ensure a free-flowing event with no overcrowding. It is important to review the four styles of food service — buffet, sit-down service, family style, and cocktail party — alongside your choice location, your budget, and your personal vision for your wedding day.

# BUFFET

Many a headache has been saved by opting for buffet-style service. A buffet can be set up in one room with the tables and chairs set up in a different room, and there are no tableside wait staff to pay. If you're in a cramped location, choose the setup carefully, maximizing utility and safety. Try not to set up close to any area that you anticipate will be busy — next to the bar or near frequently used doors — to avoid congestion. Never block exterior doors or a potential fire exit. If space permits, allow the buffet to be free-standing and away from a wall to allow access from both sides and to create a smooth flow of guest traffic. A single 6 to 8-foot buffet should be large enough to accommodate up to fifty guests. If food styling isn't your strength, you can still plan and pull off a beautiful and practical presentation with a few tips.

## Choosing Linens

Make sure the tablecloth is the correct size — not only for the top surface, but also for the drop if you need it to drape all the way to the floor. Don't lessen the ambience of an elegant event with unsightly metal table legs peeking out from under a too-short tablecloth. Once the tablecloth is in place, box it for a tailored look. (See page 102 for more information on tablecloth sizes and boxing instructions.) Many caterers also rent linens or work closely with other local vendors who can supply them.

## Building a Buffet

For a multi-dimensional look, create height on the buffet by elevating the food. Place a riser or pedestal on the tablecloth, and then cover it with another piece of cloth or fabric. The riser should be something sturdy like bricks, small crates, empty boxes, upturned baking pans, chafing dish inserts, even telephone books. Decorative risers need not be covered. Glass bricks, available from building supply stores, create both height and ambiance when illuminated from behind with votive candles. For safety's sake, elevate cool or room-temperature food only and resist the temptation to build too high. Keep in mind the food that will be served, and elevate specific dishes accordingly. A soup tureen or gravy boat placed out of easy reach or in a precarious position is an accident waiting to happen.

## Eye-Catching Centerpieces

A classic buffet may have a centerpiece of flowers or an ice sculpture. This works if you have plenty of space on your table. If space is tight at the venue, consider simply making an ice bowl — you can do it yourself with no previous experience in ice-carving! Ice bowls make particularly attractive and practical serving dishes for ice creams and sorbets. (See photo on opposite page.) You will need flowers, leaves, a lemon, a half-gallon of distilled water, and two bowls. One bowl should be small enough to fit inside the other bowl, with about an inch of space all around.

Use glass bowls if you have them, as it will be easier to see the arrangement as you work. To make the ice bowl, place a 1/2-inch slice of lemon on the bottom of the larger bowl and set the smaller bowl inside. Wedge the flowers and leaves in the space between the two bowls, turning the petals so that they press against the outside bowl. Fill the space between the bowls with distilled water, which freezes clearer than regular tap water, and place in the freezer. Place a dinner plate on top to weigh down the smaller bowl. Flowers will float to the top if not wedged in, so be sure to check the bowl after 40 minutes and push any slipped flowers down with a wooden skewer or add more flowers before the water freezes completely. Let it sit in the freezer until completely frozen, at least four hours or up to a week.

To unmold, fill a sink with very warm water. Lower the bowl into water so that the entire outside (but none of the inside) of the larger bowl is immersed. Hold the bowl in the hot water for 20 seconds. Remove from the water and push the ice until it slides out of the bowl. If it doesn't slide out, return to the water for 10 seconds longer, and then try again. When the outside bowl is removed, fill the inside bowl with hot water and let it sit for 20 seconds. Pour the water out and slide the inner bowl out. Repeat as necessary to remove the small bowl.

To even out the rim of the ice bowl, run hot water over a large knife for 10 seconds. Rub the flat of the knife over the uneven rim of the ice bowl. Repeat until any large lumps are smoothed out. Place the ice bowl in the freezer until ready to serve. Expect the ice bowl to last from 45 minutes to 2 hours, depending upon the room temperature.

Using several smaller flower arrangements and staggering them at different heights using risers is another way to add variety to the buffet. Or have the florist make a garland-style arrangement and snake it through the buffet. Flowers can also be placed behind the buffet, on stands, or even suspended, if space permits. Use lemon greens, clumps of delicate grapes, small apples and pears, twinkle lights, ribbon that matches the bridesmaids' dresses, fabric in the colors of your wedding — anything that fits the theme of your wedding. For a thrifty alternative to flowers, use baskets of beautifully arranged bread, fruit, or vegetables. Send the centerpieces home with friends and family.

Fill a clear glass bowl with water and float three gardenias or dahlias for a simple centerpiece. Gardenias will stand out best against a dark-colored or black tablecloth. Pillar candles or candelabras set at different levels will add a sense of drama to your table and are beautiful and functional at an evening reception. Group different types of candlesticks: short with tall, crystal with brass, silver with ceramic. Use similarly colored candles to tie them together. Allow enough space for the guests to serve themselves safely. Check local fire codes and use fire-retardant cloths when using candles. Inquire at the venue about a small fire extinguisher — or invest in one yourself — and keep it under the table in case of emergencies.

If your buffet looks bare, fill in any spaces with something that can be scattered such as rose petals, loose flowers, or bunches of fresh herbs. But don't junk it up — simple is usually better.

Make sure the music you are using at the reception can be heard all over the space — but not too loudly. If the buffet is in one room, and the guests are seated and the band is playing elsewhere, play music of a similar genre with speakers hidden under the floor-length tablecloths on the buffet table.

## Highlighting the Food

Try using plates and bowls that complement the color of the food and continue in the style of your wedding. White will work with almost anything, so invest in a few basic platters, cake stands, plates, and bowls, or have a caterer or party rental store supply them. You'll find that these basic pieces become mainstays in your repertoire. Register for serving ware that will not only last a lifetime of events and parties, but that will serve a special purpose at the reception. A few personal touches in an expanse of plain white, rented dishes can go a long way.

Display a creative, multi-colored salad in a large glass or crystal salad bowl. Use cutting boards or large tiles lined with clean leaves from lemon trees or rose bushes. Marble, used in counter tops and available at hardware and tile stores, can be used for a number of great food presentations. Look for damaged or broken pieces and ask the store to break them into different sizes for you. Because the surface of marble stays reasonably cool, and stays cool even longer if you chill it first, it is perfect for a cheese and chocolate display. You can incorporate these marble pieces into the centerpieces of your tables if you are serving a sit-down cheese course. Use longer pieces, supported by risers, to create a series of dramatic-looking shelves for the food. Beveled mirrors or mirror tiles can also be used for cheese. Place mirrors under bowls of food to give a suggestion of depth to the buffet.

## The Cheese Course

Caterers frequently depend on cheese trays to supplement more time-consuming dishes. Cheese and crackers work as well for an early brunch as they do for an evening reception. Group several cheeses together, mixing colors, shapes, and textures. Choose at least one semi-hard cheese, one blue cheese (such as Gorgonzola, Roquefort, or Stilton), and one soft cheese. See the menu on page 174 for great suggestions for a cheese course at the reception.

Cheese displays can be built on any clean surface. Use clean pieces of marble, wood cutting boards, or large tiles. Serve the cheese and crackers with bunches of different fruits and whole nuts. Allow six to ten crackers per person, depending on what else you're serving; if the cheese course precedes a large meal, allow three to four per person. If your cheese display surface is large enough, arrange the fruit and crackers around the cheese. If you don't have enough space on the cheese board, then put the fruit and crackers in separate bowls, or scatter the crackers directly onto the tablecloth itself.

Baskets are a must for any party thrower, but you may not have thought to use them at a wedding reception. They are inexpensive, come in all different shapes, and are available everywhere. They can be altered to fit the occasion by spray painting or wrapping the handles with fabric, silk ivy, and flowers. Line your basket with a linen napkin or aromatic herbs before adding food. If you are building crudités, you can line the basket with non-toxic leaves. Try Savoy cabbage, ornamental purple or green kale, lemon leaves, banana leaves, bok choy, or curly green lettuce.

## Assembling Crudités

Crudités is French for "mixed salad." It is commonly used to describe a tray of carrots, celery, and other vegetables. Serving your guests a colorful vegetable crudités platter or a beautiful display of fresh fruit is the easiest way to stretch your food budget. (If you are short of time, buy a prepared crudités tray from your grocery store, and give it class by arranging the vegetables in a decorative serving dish or large shallow bowl with the dip served in a small bowl or cup placed in the center.) Place a crudités station near the entrance of your reception, accessible to guests as they walk in. Depending upon the size of your area you may want to place another crudités station near the beverage area. Have these stations set up before guests arrive so that they have something to nibble on before the main meal is served.

Choose large serving trays, platters, or baskets 14-22 inches wide. If using baskets more than 2 inches deep, crumple up brown paper shopping bags and press into the bottom of the baskets. In catering lingo this is called "false bottoming" the basket. The goal is to build your display close to the rim of the basket. To hide the brown paper, place a layer of greens like parsley, Napa cabbage, frissee, spinach, or other hearty green on top of the paper. If using flat or nearly flat platters or trays there is no need to line the bottom with greens unless you want to.

For vegetable crudités, make a space in the center of your platter for a small bowl of dip. For a natural look you can hollow out half a red cabbage or make a bowl out of several leaves of radicchio or ornamental cabbage to use as a dip bowl. Place vegetables on serving pieces, fanning them out from the center. Place a ring of cherry tomatoes around the dip container to hide the ends of the vegetables. Or, stand vegetables upright instead of laying them flat — try standing them up in several colorful ramekins grouped together. These will be easy to refill, as you can just have the servers bring out full ramekins to fill in any gaps.

The key to a pretty display is in choosing vegetables or fruit in a variety of colors, shapes and sizes. Use the diagram at left as a general guideline. The same design will also work with fruit. Or try it with dried fruit and nuts if that goes better with the food you are serving.

## SERVING AMOUNTS FOR VEGETABLE AND FRUIT DISPLAYS

| number of guests | total amount of assorted vegetables or fruit |
| --- | --- |
| 12 | 3 pounds |
| 25 | 6 pounds |
| 50 | 12 pounds |
| 75 | 18 pounds |

Choose between six and twelve of the vegetables or fruits listed below for your trays. The appearance and flavor of some vegetables are enhanced by simple blanching, the process of plunging vegetables into boiling water for 30 seconds or just until they change color, then rinsing under cold running water or placing in a bowl of ice water to stop the cooking process. The vegetables marked with an asterisk (*) below are improved by blanching.

### VEGETABLES

| | |
| --- | --- |
| Asparagus* | Green beans* |
| Bell Peppers | Green onions |
| Broccoli* | Endive |
| Carrots* | Mushrooms |
| Cauliflower | Radicchio |
| Celery | Radishes |
| Cherry tomatoes | Snow peas |
| Cucumbers | Soybean pods |
| Endive | Sugar snap peas |
| Fennel bulb | Zucchini |

### FRUIT

| | |
| --- | --- |
| Apples | Oranges |
| Blackberries | Papaya |
| Blueberries | Peaches |
| Cantaloupe | Pears |
| Cherries | Pineapple |
| Figs | Raspberries |
| Grapes | Star fruit |
| Honeydew | Strawberries |
| Kiwi | Tangerines |
| Mangoes | Watermelon |

Cut large fruit like pineapple or melons and serve them in their own rinds for a pretty look. To cut a pineapple for display, cut entire pineapple including green top in half lengthwise. Cut each half again so that you have four quarters. Cut pineapple flesh from rind and then cut into ½-inch pieces. See diagram below.

The same procedure is used for honeydew melon, cantaloupe, and watermelon.

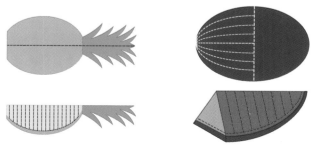

Try serving dried fruit and nuts as an alternative or in addition to fruit and vegetables displays. Buy some nuts spiced and some simply roasted for variety.

| DRIED FRUIT | NUTS |
|---|---|
| Apricots | Almonds |
| Bananas | Cashews |
| Cherries | Hazelnuts |
| Dates | Macadamia nuts |
| Figs | Peanuts |
| Kiwis | Pecans |
| Mangoes | Pistachios |
| Papayas | Walnuts |
| Pineapples | |

## 20 QUICK DIPS

Dress up your fruit and veggies with a delicious tasting dip. The amounts below are suitable for 25 guests. Recipes can easily be doubled or tripled for serving more people.

For great dips to go with your vegetable crudités put two 8-ounce packages of cream cheese or sour cream in the work bowl of a food processor along with 8 ounces of one of the following:

- Marinated artichoke hearts, drained
- Roasted red bell pepper, drained
- Garbanzo beans, drained
- Black beans, drained
- Sun dried tomato tapanade
- Olive tapanade
- Basil pesto
- Caramelized onions
- Chutney

You can also use one of these:

- 4 ounces smoked salmon
- A teaspoon each of coarsely ground black pepper and sea salt
- A quarter cup of fresh herbs
- French onion soup mix

It isn't necessary to serve dips with fruit trays unless you want to. Here are some easy ideas using 16 ounces of yogurt:

- Lime yogurt mixed with $1/3$ cup shredded coconut
- Vanilla yogurt with $1/3$ cup honey swirled in
- Mango yogurt with $1/3$ cup raspberry or strawberry jam swirled in

Or use 16 ounces crème fraiche mixed with one of the following:

- A third cup of honey
- 2 teaspoons ground cinnamon
- ½ cup lemon or lime curd
- $1/3$ cup orange marmalade

## Avoiding Lukewarm Food

If hot food is being served on a buffet, you will almost certainly need a chafing dish. To avoid the usual industrial look of multiple chafing dishes, use different shapes or mix copper with silver and place dishes at different angles. If your event is casual, make your own rustic-looking chafing dish by stacking red bricks to form a base and place a cast-iron griddle or skillet on top. For the heat source, use a canned or gel fuel like Sterno, or votive candles set on a terracotta plant saucer and placed underneath.

Alternatively, if you're having an outdoor event, make use of a grill, gas or charcoal, for warming up food just before serving. See the menu on page 156 for grill-friendly hors d'oeuvres.

## Keep It Moving

For the buffet to flow smoothly, food placement is important. See our buffet flow diagrams below and on page 92. You can also save money by displaying the food to your advantage. Place the most expensive food (or the item of which you have the least) at the end of the buffet line. That way, your guests will have already filled their plates and will have less space left for the pricier item. It may seem sneaky, but it will help you keep your costs down!

## Maintaining the Buffet

Provide your guests with the correct serving utensils. Tongs are the most guest-friendly utensils for a buffet. They can be used for every-thing from salad and rolls to sliced pork and fruit. Select utensils that are the correct size for the serving dish. Too short can be very messy; too long is unwieldy. Provide a spoon rest or small saucer for the uten-sils that may drip and ruin the tablecloth. A 3-inch-wide offset spatula is a must for easy maneuvering of any baked dish, like lasagna. Score the surface of the lasagna into portion sizes to act as a guide.

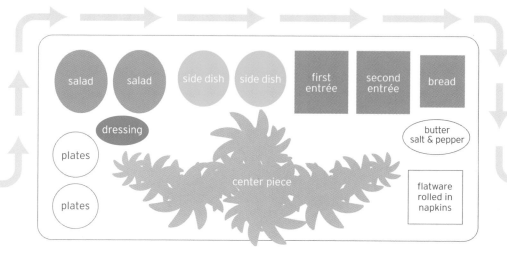

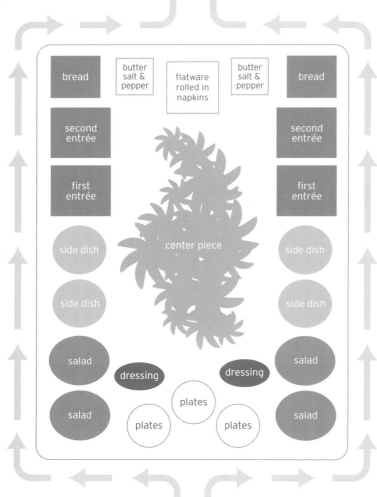

| bread | butter salt & pepper | flatware rolled in napkins | butter salt & pepper | bread |

second entrée · first entrée · side dish · side dish · center piece · side dish · side dish · salad · dressing · dressing · salad · plates · plates · plates · salad · salad

The food should be in manageable-size pieces that will fit the plates and make it from the buffet to the table. For example, if you are serving a roasted pork loin, consider slicing it into medallions first before adding to the chafing dish. Trim cauliflower into florets and other vegetables into bite-sized pieces before serving. Avoid round foods such as beans that may roll off the plate.

If soup is on the menu, use deep bowls or mugs and provide a ladle that gives the correct portion. Have your servers check on the buffet occasionally to monitor the food. Are you going to run out of roasted chicken? If you are expecting a rush of guests who may have been held up at the bar, instruct the hired help to keep an extra pan or two of the hot chicken in a cooler under the buffet. Because coolers are insulated, they will keep hot food hot for limited periods of time. Having the hot food this close will ensure a quick change-out when one pan becomes low. This method of storing food should only be a 15 to 20-minute temporary measure when you expect a quick turnaround, so have the food reheated after you have finished up with the ceremony and are mingling with your guests. If you do run out of something, have the servers simply remove the plate or tray. Fill the space with an extra breadbasket or another tray of potatoes.

## SIT-DOWN SERVICE

For your truly special, all-out event of a lifetime, nothing seems quite as elegant as sit-down service. But plated service does require a lot of planning. Besides preparing the menu, you will also have to set the table. This includes choosing linens, name cards, flatware, glasses, and china, as well as folding the napkins, arranging the seating, and placing the centerpieces.

On the positive side, pre-plating food not only gives you or the caterer the artistic freedom to create stunning presentations but also gives you control over food portion sizes. This can be essential when serving an expensive entrée. Sit-down dinners also allow you to set the pace of the event. If the guests are still dancing and you and the groom have a plane to catch, cut that wedding cake and have the coffee served promptly.

If you are the chef, be prepared to spend time in the kitchen before the wedding, but make sure to completely turn over the reins to reliable friends, family, or hired staff well before the big day. The idea is to enjoy yourself and be carefree at your own party. If you do feel overwhelmed, consider hiring a waiter to help out if your budget allows. Better to hire a server than appear overworked at your own wedding. (See page 128 for hiring tips.) With careful planning, you can design a make-ahead menu that takes a minimum of effort on the wedding day. For example, place trays of cold or room-temperature hors d'oeuvres throughout the venue. Then start the meal with a salad or appetizer that can be plated before guests arrive. Dress the salad or assemble the appetizer just before serving — a cluster of bruschetta would be ideal. Choose a casserole- or stew-style main course such as Boeuf Bourguignon that can be held in a warm oven. Accompany it with glazed carrots, which can also be made ahead and kept warm in the oven. Brown the pan under the broiler just before serving. Don't worry about dessert; there will be plenty of wedding cake!

## COCKTAIL PARTY

One of the most overlooked party styles is the classic cocktail. If a reception lasting several hours isn't appealing to you — or you have a plane to catch — a simple hour-and-a-half to two-hour-long occasion to mingle with guests may fit the bill. And cocktail parties can be a glamorous, easy way to keep your expenses way, way down. Cocktail parties are very space-efficient, and all you need to serve are hors d'oeuvres and drinks. The hors d'oeuvres can either be passed on trays or placed in different stationary locations.

By using a few stand-up cocktail tables, you'll give your guests some places to congregate, while giving yourself more surface space for serving hors d'oeuvres. Cover with a small tablecloth or place mat and use for your placed hors d'oeuvres, an ice-filled tub of drinks, or a tray of pre-poured wine glasses. Provide your guests with small, sturdy plates and plenty of cocktail napkins.

Avoid food that is awkward or too big to eat. Finger food should be small enough to be eaten within one or two bites. People will be balancing a drink in one hand and possibly a plate in the other, so select food that isn't going to roll off the plate. Whenever possible, serve food that can be eaten easily without a plate. See the menu on page 156 for lots of hearty appetizers that are adaptable to any style of cocktail party.

# FESTIVE WEDDING COCKTAILS

## spring

### Raspberry-orange champagne cocktail
*Sunrise Brunch menu (see page 132)*

This cocktail is a big hit with anyone fortunate enough to be on the receiving end. If you suspect that your guests will be similarly enamored, increase the number of servings by 50 percent — or even double it!

    1 raspberry

    1 tablespoon Grand Marnier

    1 medium orange, cut in half and sliced in ¼-inch-thick half moons

    3 ounces champagne, chilled

*Place a raspberry in the bottom of a champagne flute. Add a tablespoon of Grand Marnier to glass. Place half a slice of orange on the rim of the glass. Fill flute three-quarters full of chilled Champagne and serve.*

### Bellini
*Sunrise Brunch menu (see page 132)*

The classic bellini is a beautiful and delicious cocktail to serve with the Sunrise Brunch menu. The pale peach color mimics the color of the sunrise. If fresh peaches are difficult to find use frozen peaches to make the peach puree. You can make this easily in large batches by combining the peach puree, peach schnapps, and vodka in correct proportions in pitchers, increased by the number of servings, and then pouring a measured amount into each flute before adding the just-uncorked champagne.

    1 tablespoon peach puree

    ½ ounce peach schnapps, chilled

    ½ ounce vodka, chilled

    3 ounces champagne, chilled

*Pour into a champagne flute the peach puree, the schnapps, and the vodka. Pour the champagne over the top and serve.*

### Mimosa
*In Full Bloom menu (see page 140)*

A Mimosa with Grand Mariner added for a special twist is a lovely addition to the In Full Bloom spring menu. Decorate the rim with a lime slice, too, if desired. You can make this easily in large batches by combining the orange juice and Grand Marnier ahead of time in pitchers in correct proportions, increased by the number of servings, and then pouring a measured amount into each flute before adding the just-uncorked champagne.

    1 ounce orange juice, chilled

    3 ounces champagne, chilled

    ½ ounce Grand Marnier, chilled

    Oranges slices, cut into quarters, for garnish

*Pour the orange juice and Grand Marnier into a champagne flute. Top with the champagne and serve.*

## summer

### Limoncello Iced Tea
*Waterside Jewels Picnic menu (see page 148)*

The perfect cocktail for an outdoor wedding on a warm day. For an easier serving method, combine the ingredients ahead of time in correct proportions increased by the number of servings, and pour into pitchers for serving.

    ½ ounce Limoncello

    ½ ounce vodka

    4 ounces sweetened brewed tea, iced

    Lemon slices for garnish

*Pour Limoncello, vodka, and iced tea over ice in tall glasses. Garnish with lemon slices and serve with straws.*

### Mango Tequila Sunset
*Sunset Cocktail Party menu (see page 156)*

This is the perfect cocktail to serve as the sun goes down on a warm summer evening. Purchase decorative bamboo cocktail picks for skewering the mango and watermelon. Buy firm mangos and scoop them with a small melon baller. Use a slightly larger melon baller for the watermelon.

    ½ ounce tequila

    1 ounce pomegranate liqueur

    4 ounces mango juice

    Ice cubes

    Mango and watermelon balls for garnish

*Fill a 10-ounce highball glass halfway with ice, and pour tequila and pomegranate liqueur over the ice. Slowly top with mango juice for a layered drink. Place a piece of mango and a watermelon ball on a skewer for garnish.*

## autumn

### Calvados Martini
*French Countryside menu (see page 166)*

Serve this great fall cocktail in martini glasses with a thin slice of apple floating in it. To make beautiful, thin slices of apple, use a mandolin or the slicer attachment on a food processor. Putting sliced apples in acidulated water (water with lemon juice) will keep the flesh from browning.

> 1 ounce Calvados apple brandy
>
> 2 ounces vodka or gin
>
> Thinly slice apple for garnish

*Pour Calvados and vodka into a cocktail shaker filled with ice. Shake vigorously for 10 seconds. Strain into martini glasses and garnish with a slice of apple.*

### Prosecco Cocktail
*Amber Nights menu (see page 176)*

Use rough-cut sugar cubes for a unique look. To make an orange twist, use a citrus zester or a channel knife to cut a long, curling strip of orange zest 2-3 inches long. You can get about 10 orange twists from one large orange.

> 1 dash bitters
>
> 1 sugar cube
>
> 1 ounce Amaretto liqueur
>
> 3 ounces Prosecco, chilled
>
> Orange twist for garnish

*Place the sugar cube in the bottom of a champagne flute and pour the dash of bitters over it. Top with amaretto and Prosecco, and garnish with an orange twist.*

## winter

### Hot Coffee Cocktail
*Winter Wonderland menu (see page 186)*

You must, of course, have champagne with this elegant menu. But serve our hot coffee cocktail as an after-dinner drink. Use glasses that have handles, such as Irish coffee glasses.

> 1 ounce Kahlúa
>
> 1 ounce bourbon
>
> 4 ounces hot brewed coffee
>
> ½ ounce heavy whipping cream
>
> Whipped cream for garnish
>
> Ground cinnamon for garnish, optional

*Add Kahlúa and bourbon to the glass, and top with coffee. Stir in cream. Top with a dollop of whipped cream and sprinkle with cinnamon.*

### Caribbean Champagne Cocktail
*Island Spice menu (see page 198)*

Warm up your winter wedding with flavors from the Caribbean. Moisten the rim of the glass with a little water and press the rim into gold or white sanding sugar to add sparkle to your drinks. You can make this easily in large batches by combining rum and pineapple liqueur ahead of time in correct proportions, increased by the number of servings, in pitchers, and then pouring a measured amount into each glass before adding the just-uncorked champagne.

> 1 ounce light rum, chilled
>
> ½ ounce pineapple liqueur, chilled
>
> 3 ounces champagne, chilled

*Pour rum and pineapple liqueur into champagne glasses. Top with champagne and serve.*

## CHAMPAGNE AND CAVIAR

For the ultimate in simple entertaining, you can indulge your guests with bubbly and caviar. This classic combination says elegance and opulence with each little burst of caviar on the tongue. Served alongside chilled champagne and followed with a slice of richly decadent wedding cake, this unexpected treat can make for a complete reception for those on a budget.

### Champagne

Champagne is a sparkling wine with high levels of carbon dioxide that make it fizz and bubble. Real champagne comes only from the Champagne region of France, even though many other sparkling wines are made in exactly the same way. They are no less delicious than champagne and usually cost less. Look also for sparkling wines from Spain known as Cava, or from Italy known as Spumante and Prosecco.

Champagnes come in a variety of styles: from very, very dry to very sweet. The difference is the percentage of sugar it contains.

- **Extra Brut** is extremely dry and contains up to 0.6% sugar
- **Brut** is very dry and contains less than 1.5% sugar
- **Extra Dry** contains anywhere from 1.2-2% sugar
- **Sec** is lightly sweet and contains 1.7-3.5% sugar
- **Demi-Sec** is sweet with 3.3-5% sugar
- **Doux** is very sweet with more than 5% sugar

To purchase a champagne that will please most of your guests, stay in the mid-range with Brut, Extra Dry, Sec and Demi-Sec. Dry champagnes like Brut and Extra Dry are best served before or with a meal, while Sec and Demi-Sec are more suited to drink after a meal.

A Blanc de Blanc champagne is a white champagne made from white chardonnay grapes. Blanc de Noirs are made from red grapes and result in a pink-gold colored champagne. Rose champagnes are considered the finest, mostly since they are the most difficult to produce. Rose usually has a richer, fuller taste than the blanc de noirs.

Many high-quality champagnes and sparkling wines are available at membership stores like Costco and BevMo at great discounts. Always buy a bottle to sample before purchasing them for your wedding.

### Champagne Suggestions

Price range:  $  $8-$14
  $$  $15-$24
  $$$  $24+

Mumm Napa Brut Prestige ($$)
Roederer Estate Brut ($$)
Argyle 2000 Brut ($$)
Roederer Estate Rose ($$$)
Perrier Jouet Brute ($$$)
Veuve Clicquot Brut Yellow Label ($$$)

**Sparkling Wine**
Segura Viudas Cava ($)
Bodegas Jaume Serra Cristalino Cava ($)
Bouvet Brut Signature ($)
Domaine St. Michelle Cuvee Brut ($)
Zardetto Prosecco ($)
Freixenet Brut Nature Cava ($)
Martini & Rossi Prosecco ($)
Nino Franco Prosecco ($)
Mionetto Prosecco ($)
Mumm Napa Blanc de Noirs ($$)
Carpene Malvolti Prosecco ($$)
Chandon Blanc de Noirs ($$)
Mumm Cuvee Napa ($$)
Chandon Brut Classic ($$)

### Why do caviar and champagne go so well together?

Caviar is salty, rich, and dark, champagne is light and fresh; they complement each other's taste. (As in marriage, opposites often attract!)

Years ago, I was introduced to this taste combination from a Russian couple asking me to cater their wedding. They also included very cold, vodka shots, and the guests had fun.

If caviar isn't your thing, champagne works wonderfully with most seafoods. Try chilled shrimp, slipper lobsters, or ceviche cups in lieu of caviar. You might want to offer an ice-cold shot of lemon vodka instead of (or in addition to) the champagne.

## Caviar

Caviar is the roe, or eggs, of fish and savored the world over for its unique texture and flavor. The most highly prized caviar comes from the sturgeon, but you'll find many other types of delicious roe on the market at more reasonable prices. Take a look at the wide variety available:

### Beluga

Beluga is the largest caviar and the most sought after. Beluga comes from sturgeon, which has become so rare that prices have more than doubled in a very short time. The finest beluga is caught by Russian and Iranian fishermen in the Caspian Sea. While Russian caviar has been considered the best, Iranian caviar is also highly praised.

### Lumpfish Caviar

Available in red or black, lumpfish caviar is a very good value for the money (about $2 an ounce) and has a pleasing, salty "pop" on the tongue. It works well as an elegant garnish for appetizers. It comes from lumpfish caught in the North Sea, between Iceland and Denmark. As lumpfish caviar is dyed, it should be used cold to prevent any color bleed.

### Osetera

Osetera caviar comes from the sturgeon and is usually small pearl sized. Osetera's color ranges from jet black to light gold and has a smooth buttery flavor. Osetera comes from Russia, Iran, and Uruguay.

### Sevruga

Sevruga is the smallest-sized and most abundant caviars and so is less pricey. Sevruga has the strongest flavor of all sturgeon caviars.

### American Blackfish Caviar

Blackfish caviar comes from the bowfin. Also known as "Chourpique," it is best when served with crème fraîche and a squeeze of lemon juice. This caviar is firm and shiny and comes in brown and black.

### Paddlefish Caviar

Paddlefish caviar is rich and complex with a smooth aftertaste. It comes in either dark gray or golden colors. It comes from paddlefish that are found in Alabama and Missouri rivers.

### American Hackleback Caviar

Hackleback is a sturgeon indigenous to the Missouri and Mississippi river systems. It has an intense, nutty, sweet taste.

### Avruga Caviar

This caviar is from the roe of the common herring found in Spain and has a smoky, lemony flavor, with less of a fishy taste. It is fairly inexpensive and does not bleed as some cheap caviars do.

### Tobico Caviar

Tobico caviar comes from the flying fish of Iceland. It ranges in color from black to bright red. Tobico caviar can be bought already flavored with ingredients like wasabi.

### Salmon Caviar

From the waters off North America, salmon caviar varies in color from orange-gold to vibrant red. The eggs are large and succulent and are very mild tasting. It is the caviar of choice when color is important.

### Whitefish Caviar

Whitefish caviar has a slightly crunchy texture and can vary in color from gold to orange to black. It is mild, non-fishy, and non-bitter with a bit of a fruity taste. Produced in Canada, the Great Lakes, and in Montana.

### Tarama

Tarama is the salted and cured roe of carp, cod, or tuna and is often sold smoked. Cured and aged for over one year, Tarama can be blended with oil, lemon juice and chopped onions to make the caviar spread Taramosalata.

### Botarga Caviar

Botarga is called the poor man's caviar. It is made from roe of the grey mullet. It is pressed, cured and wrapped in a layer of beeswax to keep it fresh, resulting in a dry slab, which is sliced or grated. The taste is more "ocean" than fishy and slightly salty from the curing process.

### Trout Caviar

Smaller than salmon roe and orange in color, the flavor is less salty than sturgeon and mildly sweet in flavor. It one of the least expensive caviar options, but has great flavor.

## FAMILY STYLE

A wedding, no matter how large or elaborate, still retains a definite sense of intimacy. Family from all over, and friends from far, far back will travel to witness the union of a loved one, and the group affirmation of a wedding is symbolic and tangible. If buffet-style service isn't for you, and sit-down service is out of reach, consider family-style service. You can serve the food on large platters, each platter holding enough to feed the table, and let your guests get to know each other as they pass the food.

This is yet another great way to make use of serving pieces that came as wedding gifts, which will give an individual feel to each guest table. If you think your guests will enjoy the close quarters, and you want them to have plenty of opportunity to talk, family-style service could work for you. Consider how easy platters of food will be to pass around the table, and divide them up into smaller servings as necessary. Provide mitts and trivets as necessary for very hot foods. No matter how great a hostess you may be in your own home, you do not want to flit from table to table to right a spilled plate of vegetables, or refill a pitcher of sauce; you can hire a few servers to transport the platters to and from the food preparation area, and to deal with any issues that may arise at your guests' tables.

## COMBINING SERVICE STYLES

Remember that this is your day. You can serve whatever you want, however you want. If you met over burgers and a shake, you can serve dressed-up sliders and miniature malts in shot glasses for appetizers. Your guests might even prefer that to some of the more traditional wedding fare.

In the end, you may find the most practical and successful idea involves mixing and matching a variety of serving styles. Choose that combination that best meets your time and budget restrictions. You could start by passing the hors d'oeuvres on trays or placing them on a buffet while the wedding party finishes with pictures after the ceremony or the bride and groom greet guests. Then, you could seat your guests for a sit-down, pre-plated dinner. For dessert, serve cake and coffee around the bride and groom, while they cut the cake, toss the bouquet, and toss the garter. Whatever you choose, enjoy yourself! The more fun you have, the more fun your guests will have. And don't forget to eat all this delicious food you've planned for months!

## SEATING DIAGRAMS AND GUIDES

| round tables | | |
|---|---|---|
| diameter | guests | maximum |
| 24 inches | 2 | 2 |
| 30 inches | 2 | 4 |
| 36 inches | 4 | 5 |
| 48 inches | 6 | 8 |
| 54 inches | 7 | 9 |
| 60 inches | 8 | 10 |
| 72 inches | 10 | 12 |

| square, rectangular, or oblong tables | | |
|---|---|---|
| length and width | guests | maximum |
| 36 x 36 inches | 4 | 4 |
| 48 x 48 inches | 6 | 8 |
| 60 x 60 inches | 8 | 10 |
| 60 x 30 inches | 6 | 8 |
| 72 x 30 inches | 6 | 8 |
| 96 x 30 inches | 8 | 10 |

## UTILIZING YOUR RECEPTION SPACE

Let's say you want to have your closest friends and family members, about forty guests, for a sit-down dinner reception at a historic inn. You may have to rent tables, but how many should you rent? And will there be enough space in the dining room for them? First make a rough floor plan of the room, including length and width measurements. Use the seating diagrams and guides included here to plan how many guests can fit around certain sizes and shapes of tables.

If you choose eight 36-inch round tables that can seat five people each, draw eight circles on your floor plan to represent the tables. Add about 2 to 3 feet to the diameter of each table to represent space taken up by chairs. Keep 2 to 4 feet between chair backs, and try to allow easy access to the kitchen and restroom areas. Try different configurations until the tables fit with the necessary amount of space between each one.

What can you do if, no matter how hard you try, you just can't fit all the tables in unless you take out a load-bearing wall? Try using a table of a different shape so that you can make use of more floor space. Instead of round tables, you could use three 96 by 30-inch buffet tables that can seat up to ten guests each if separated, or twenty-six guests total if placed end to end to form one long banquet-style table.

Alternatively, you could place three 60 by 30-inch tables in a "U" shape in one half of the room, allowing for a head table for the bride, groom, and wedding party. This will leave room for dancing or a dessert and coffee buffet.

If you decide to rent tables and chairs, many rental companies will draw a free computer layout for you. If your venue owns tables and chairs and is including them in the rental, the manager can certainly advise you about the best arrangements, and may even have pictures of other weddings and receptions they've hosted in the past.

seating for 30
(each 36-inch table seats 5 guests)

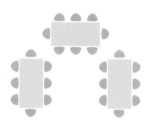

seating for 24
(8 guests per 60 x 30-inch table)

seating for 20
(10 guests per 96 x 30-inch table)

A crucial part of seating arrangements that is sometimes overlooked is the receiving line. Every guest wants to personally give the bride and groom best wishes, and you may not encounter each and every one in the buffet line. Find a place and time where you can allow whoever so wishes to line up for hugs and handshakes. You may want to include the whole wedding party in the receiving line, or just your families or parents, or simply you and your spouse. The room may be cramped with tables and chairs, so find a place where the traffic will flow. The beginning of the reception is a good time for the receiving line, or maybe in between dinner and cake. The whole day can seem a blur, and remembering that you took the time to speak to your friends and family will leave happy memories for you and them.

If the innkeeper or venue manager says that your 40 guests won't fit comfortably in a room or with the arrangement you're imagining, trust her. She's probably been there and done that already. Take advantage of her experiences. Schedule a meeting to talk about the floor plan and run all of your ideas for moving furniture and arranging seating past the staff first.

How have you envisioned your reception while planning the wedding? Do you picture the traditional head table with the bride and groom flanked by the wedding party? A romantic table for you and your newly wedded spouse? Tables by family or age? Whatever your dream arrangement, be sure to plan the logistics before your wedding day.

The traditional head table is a tradition for a reason: it gives you and the attendants a chance to relax and survey the happy crowd while enjoying the meal you planned so carefully. Guests can come up to greet you and wish you well, but you have at least a short time to rest without feeling like you must mingle. The sweetheart table, for the happy couple only, builds in some one-on-one time during what may be the most intense day of your entire relationship! Again, your guests can drop by the table to tell you how beautiful they found the ceremony, and you can greet them as a couple. There are endless combinations for seating your guests; pick the one that works for you. You may spend hours considering who will get along with whom, or you may scatter the place cards at random, and hope for the best! The day is sure to bring some new friendships when your family and friends meet his.

## EVENT RENTALS

You may find that your venue doesn't have enough seating available for all of your guests, or maybe you want to take advantage of some outdoor space and need appropriate accommodations to do so. Renting equipment will inevitably play a part in your wedding planning, unless your family business happens to be a party planning and rental operation.

For a sit-down dinner with rented tables, chairs, linens, china, flatware, and glasses, expect to pay at least $15 and up per person for rentals, depending on what part of the country you live in and how luxurious your choices are. Of course, depending on your needs, you could require more or less.

Not sure where to start? Look in the yellow pages under "party rentals." Call a nearby company first because the closer they are, the less expensive the delivery charge. Explain the basics of your reception to the representative, who will ask you a host of questions so he can give you a quote. A trained representative should be able to determine if you need anything other than the obvious, such as tenting or a dance floor. If your space does require a tent, then the rental representative should inspect the party site to accurately measure the area and ascertain the need for any fire department permits. Always check that the company has liability insurance.

Ask them to mail, fax, or e-mail the quote to you. Look it over and see if there are any places to save some money: Plain white chairs are less expensive than the gold ones they suggested. Do you really need five patio heaters? You or even your caterer may be able to provide some of the items for cheaper than the price quoted.

## Linens and things

If you're having a relatively small wedding, it might be a good idea to invest in a couple of neutral, machine-washable tablecloths that can be used at the wedding, and also at other events in the future. A standard black tablecloth can be used for evening and formal events or as a base on which to add more tablecloths.

Overlay different colors and textures of cloth on top of a basic tablecloth. Look in the bargain bins at fabric stores for remnants that can be used to add layers. Another great alternative to buying tablecloths is to use bed sheets in different patterns and colors.

## Table sizes

First, you will need to measure your tabletop. Measure the length and width for rectangular and oval tables; the diameter for round tables; and one side for square tables. If you will be using the leaves on your table, remember to include their lengths in with your measurements. For the overhang or drop, add an extra 20 inches to the length and to the width for oval, rectangular, and square tables. For round tables, add 20 inches to the diameter. This will give you the minimum of a 10-inch drop for the tablecloth. For a longer drop of about 14 inches, add 28 inches instead of 20 inches to your measurements. For a fold-up table, be sure to use a floor-length tablecloth to hide the legs. The chart allows for a minimum of a 12-inch drop; use it as a starting point for finding the perfect tablecloth for your party.

# TABLECLOTH SIZING

### ○ round tables

| diameter of table | guests | tablecloth size |
|---|---|---|
| 36 to 48 inches | 4 | 60 inches |
| 46 to 58 inches | 6 | 70 inches |
| 64 to 76 inches | 8 to 10 | 90 inches |

### ▭ rectangular tables

| length and width of table | guests | tablecloth size |
|---|---|---|
| 36 x 78 inches to 48 x 90 inches | 6 to 10 | 60 x 102 inches |
| 36 x 96 inches to 48 x 108 inches | 8 to 12 | 60 x 120 inches |

### □ square tables

| dimensions of table | guests | tablecloth size |
|---|---|---|
| 28 x 28 inches to 40 x 40 inches | 4 | 60 x 60 inches |

### ○ oval tables

| length and width | guests | tablecloth size |
|---|---|---|
| 28 x 46 inches to 40 x 58 inches | 4 to 6 | 52 x 70 inches |
| 36 x 58 inches to 48 x 70 inches | 6 to 8 | 60 x 84 inches |
| 36 x 78 inches to 48 x 90 inches | 8 to 10 | 60 x 102 inches |
| 36 x 96 inches to 48 x 108 inches | 12 to 14 | 60 x 120 inches |

## TABLECLOTH BOXING

1. Place table-cloth on top of table so that it hangs down evenly on all sides.

2. Grab the right front corner of the tablecloth and pull it up off the floor.

3. Fold the right front corner diagonally across the top of the table so that the front and side of the tablecloth hang smoothly to the floor.

4. Fold the right front corner halfway back, smoothing folds underneath, to create a clean edge.

5. Secure with T-pins at the back. Repeat with the left front corner.

## Table settings

As our food has simplified over time, so has the flatware. Gone is the arsenal of flatware such as celery forks, knife rests, and finger bowls. You'll need to consider your needs when deciding whether to rent, purchase, or go disposable. Consider how difficult the food will be to eat without the proper utensils, and then ask the caterer's advice. This is another area where he or she might be able to provide for your needs less expensively than would a party rental company.

Regardless of how many forks you use, the same rules still apply: Start from the outside, using the first knife and fork for the salad, and work your way inward. The knife and fork closest to the dinner plate is for the main course. When setting the table for your reception, refer to the diagrams below for the correct placement of flatware and glasses. If you're not serving a salad course, don't bother providing salad forks. Make sure that equally obvious non-necessities don't wreak havoc on your budget. Absolutely set the table and decorate with non-perishables the day before the wedding to save time and energy.

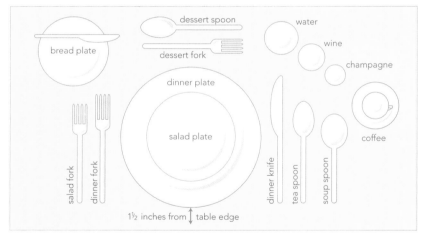

## Tucked-in tables

If you're planning to go all the way with your sit-down meal, or you just want to add a formal touch to a less formal presentation, don't leave out the classic cloth napkins. You can easily rent these from the same vendor who is supplying tablecloths, or you can buy cheap cloth napkins. No need to have dozens of napkins in the same color or pattern; mix and match for an eclectic look. This is a great way to reinforce a color scheme if you are using plain white table linens, plates, and serve ware. For formal parties, mix solid black and white napkins or add one color to the black and white that complements your décor or flowers. Folding napkins into decorative shapes (see the illustrated instructions below for some ideas) will add a special touch to any party without adding cost; fold them a week before your party.

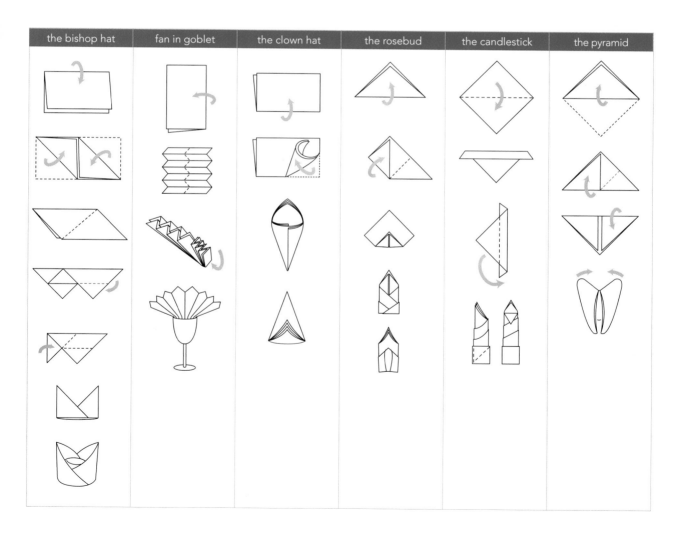

| the bishop hat | fan in goblet | the clown hat | the rosebud | the candlestick | the pyramid |

# chapter 6
# planning your wedding menu and catering the meal

The date is set, the invitations have been mailed, and you've written your beautiful, personal vows months in advance. Now, what are you going to serve at the reception? In Chapter 5, we discussed what kind of service — buffet, cocktail, or sit-down — would be most suitable for your reception. Armed with that information, you can now build a fantastic menu. If you consider yourself a gourmet chef, then you can build the whole menu around your famous coq au vin recipe. But not everyone is kitchen-savvy. If you're more comfortable making reservations than dinner, planning a menu and preparing food for a party can be quite daunting.

With a few guidelines and thoughtful food selections, you can easily put together delicious and memorable menus that will wow your guests.

This chapter breaks down the logistics of catering for a crowd. Large-scale cooking requires different skills than cooking an intimate dinner for two (which you may have mastered during this blissful dating period!). Take the time to read this chapter thoroughly before you chop carrot one. Even the most experienced party-givers will find some words of wisdom here to improve their processes for cooking for a crowd.

## THE CATERING BRIDE

The first and most important question to ask yourself is: are you planning on providing food for your own wedding? If your answer is "yes," then consider how confident a cook you are. Do you know just how you'd like everything to look and taste? Are you, truth be told, just a little bit particular about the minute details of your wedding? If you truly feel that you and only you can pull off the event of your dreams, make it happen! But consider a few things. You can cook for your own wedding in advance — but come wedding day, you should be far, far away from the kitchen and instead, dancing with your new spouse. If you plan to do most of the food preparation yourself, plan on hiring help or calling in favors from your friends and family to take over at least a few days before the wedding. You will have enough to do at the last minute and no time for kitchen patrol.

## HIRING A PROFESSIONAL CATERER

On the other hand, it may be worth the larger chunk of your budget to hire a caterer, and do the rest yourself. The peace of mind brought by professional help cannot be underestimated. If it's all you can do to wrangle the family and friends long enough to say, "I do," you don't need the headache of cooking the food.

I recently saw an editor of a wedding magazine on a morning television show talking about tips for working with a caterer for a wedding. Her suggestion was to not tell the caterer that the event was a wedding, because the caterer would inevitably charge more! This is not recommended; honesty is still the best policy when working with any vendor. Your caterer is present to make your life easier, and to make your wedding day delightful. They do more than just cook! Many caterers are also event planners, meaning they supply more than just the food. They usually buy their supplies wholesale and have industry contacts, which can result in some great deals for you on other wedding needs. They may be able to offer you a package that includes food, alcohol, rented items, wait staff, flowers — the whole shebang.

## TEN TIPS FOR A SUCCESSFUL RELATIONSHIP WITH YOUR CATERER

**1. Look for a caterer that is licensed and insured in your city.**

They should have a city-permitted kitchen for you to visit and inspect upon request.

**2. Ask them if they have catered weddings before.**

There are special nuanced methods that go into planning a wedding that an experienced pro can help provide. Many caterers provide wedding planning inclusive of their service. You buy the menu; they help with the entire production as a planner. They can act as your wedding hosts.

**3. Preview an event portfolio or DVD.**

Pictures speak a thousand words about style and execution. Do their pictures look like the event you imagine?

**4. Never be afraid to ask a caterer for a list of previous clients or references and phone them.**

Your questions might include: Was the caterer on time? Were you happy with the service? Would you hire this caterer again? Was the food as wonderful as they promised? Was the final bill what you agreed upon?

**5. Request a tasting of the caterer's menu or recommendations.**

If they ask for a tasting fee, it could be money well spent. Decide now if their food meets your expectations, and don't wait for the big day to receive an unpleasant surprise. If you like what you see and taste, ask about customizing a package to fit your needs. If the menu you love comes with side dishes that aren't quite what you had in mind, or you don't think you'll need the caterers to act as servers, ask (nicely!). Many caterers will provide a drop-off, customized food service. All the food should arrive fully or partially cooked with reheating instructions.

**6. Be honest with the caterer about your budget from day one.**

Most caterers will work to meet their clients in the middle. If you want to ask for a discount on a particularly pricey item, do so, or ask the caterer's opinion on ways to cut back. Ask the caterer for a breakdown of each item; then, if you feel you can supply the flowers cheaper, do so.

**7. If the budget seems an insurmountable problem, ask your caterer if you may supply some of the food items.**

Their concern will be product liability insurance, meaning they can't be held responsible for food they didn't make. If it's important to you, offer to sign a waiver, or agree that you will provide your own insurance. It can be that easy. Your mom provides her fabulous cheese puffs and stuffed mushrooms, and your caterer handles the entrée. Anything can be settled with the right attitude.

**8. Ask for a contract, and make sure you understand it.**

There may be a per-slice cake-cutting fee and overtime for wait staff if they stay beyond a prearranged time. Some caterers specify that a guest count can go up but not down. This means that if you told the caterer that one hundred guests are coming but only seventy-five show up, then you are still going to be charged for the full hundred. If, on the other hand, you tell the caterer that you are expecting another ten guests the day before the party, you will be charged for these extra guests. These fees are usually not applied until your final invoice.

**9. Plan on bringing the caterer any necessary phone numbers or contacts.**

Like the baker who is responsible for the cake or the party rental company that will be delivering the tables and chairs. If there are any last-minute problems, it's best to let the caterer handle them if possible; your caterer likely knows every vendor in town, and can smooth out the typical snags much more efficiently that you can. Make sure your caterer is aware of everything that will be going on: deliveries, decorations, and friends and family who have volunteered to help.

**10. Remember the guest count is what will drive up the cost of your wedding.**

Is it more important to you to have 150 people for cheese and crackers, or 50 for a sit-down dinner of steak and champagne? You decide. Whatever you decide, an experienced caterer has done it all before, and can likely offer you some of the best of both.

## OTHER OPTIONS FOR HELP

If food and service from catering companies prove to be pricier than you can afford, seek out culinary schools, and contact students who might welcome the practice under pressure. See page 129 for tips on hiring.

If hiring is out of the question, have a food preparation party in lieu of yet another shower or bachelorette party! Buy all the groceries, set up an assembly line, and have your friends come over for cocktails and food prep. Have plenty of refrigerator and freezer space clear, or enlist some of the friends to carry home pans of food to store. If your friends are the type who would love to help you with the wedding, but don't know how to begin, this could be a great option for you. Be sure to have a post-wedding thank-you party for the same group, but this time, leave the cutting boards at home, and pass out personalized gift bags instead.

If your budget is stretched to the limit, you don't think you can afford to hire help, and you're obviously going to be busy doing other things, think carefully about relying solely on friends and family to orchestrate the food service before and during the wedding. If your parents are the first to volunteer to help, decide whether the food responsibilities will keep them so busy that they'll be unable to enjoy your wedding. If you have aunts, cousins, or close family friends who offer assistance, consider yourself lucky, and don't ask so much of them that your wedding becomes a burden. Express your thanks for their help with thoughtful gifts: spa certificates, a homemade dinner, or a night out at a nice restaurant.

If you're relying on the help of friends and family, you may find that very complicated dishes, no matter how experienced they are, might be stressful for everyone. See the suggested menus beginning on page 132 for help in planning manageable, affordable, and memorable dishes.

If you'll be counting on some combination of your own culinary prowess, your mother's help, and the wedding-day services of two longtime neighbors, make sure everyone is aware of exactly what you want. If you'll need them to purchase groceries, make sure they have a way to do so by supplying cash beforehand. If you want the food plated a certain way, sit down and go over the details before the big day. If you want the buffet arranged in a particular way, draw a picture or leave detailed instructions. But once the day breaks on your wedding day, leave things in the hands of a few trusted friends or family members and enjoy yourself. Repeat: leave the kitchen and do not return! Even if the salmon isn't quite perched at the angle you envisioned on the bed of mashed potatoes, be grateful for the people who are excited about your new life, and are willing to pitch in to start it off beautifully.

## BUDGETING FOR THE MENU

A major factor in menu-planning is budget. You may not be aware of how much this is all going to cost, so make several trips to the grocery stores, wholesale clubs, produce markets, and specialty stores to price out the ingredients ahead of time. Alcohol is probably going to be the high-ticket item of the party. (See the Beverage Consumption Guides starting on page 250.)

Take a trip to the liquor section of your grocery or club store, and ask the manager about discounts for buying wine by the case. Remember to take a note pad and write down the prices of all the alcohol you will be serving. And don't forget disposable or rental glasses, and also napkins, ice, lemons, limes, and olives. You may decide that to keep things simple, you want to serve only one mixed drink, like sangria, and buy champagne or sparking wine for toasting.

With the bar expense figured, you can now calculate your food cost. Do you know how much those racks of lamb are going to cost? Unlike clothing, groceries cannot be returned in most circumstances, not even for store credit, so careful shopping is a must.

### Seasonality

One of the best do-it-for-less tips we can give you is to shop with seasonality in mind. For example, do not get your heart set on peaches for a New Year's wedding unless you have your own hothouse in the backyard. If you don't know what fruit and vegetables are in season, ask the produce manager of your local grocery store or take a look at our seasonality guide on page 109. Berries that might cost $2.00 a carton in the height of summer may ring in at $4.00 a carton in the dead of winter. If you buy produce in season, it will taste better, be cheaper, and be more readily available. If you decide you have to have berries in the middle of winter, you are going to pay extra for shipping them from wherever they are grown — and they won't taste as good because they had to be picked while unripe to survive their journey.

### Simplicity

Do you really need six courses? Simplifying the menu should save you some money. Look at the menu ingredients: Can you make a substitution for an expensive piece of meat or fish? Can the veal in the main course be replaced with a chicken breast? Sure it can. For a very casual wedding, try serving a one-course meal such as a substantial salad with seafood or a pasta dish. Served with crusty bread just warmed in the oven, this menu is sure to please everyone. Or, change the style of the party. Instead of an evening event, make it a breakfast, brunch, or afternoon event, where most people will expect less fancy fare. Or, have a dessert and coffee party as a do-it-for-less alternative. Have the ceremony begin around 8:00 p.m., and specify in the invite that the ceremony is followed by a "light reception" or "dessert and coffee" so that your guests don't anticipate a full meal.

## SEASONAL PRODUCE GUIDE

| spring | | summer | | fall | | winter | |
|--------|--|--------|--|------|--|--------|--|
| fruit | vegetables | fruit | vegetables | fruit | vegetables | fruit | vegetables |
| berries | asparagus | apricots | basil | apples | broccoli | grapefruit | avocados |
| mangoes | avocados | berries | beans | cranberries | brussels sprouts | oranges | broccoli |
| oranges | basil | cherries | beets | dates | cabbage | pears | brussels sprouts |
| papayas | beans | dates | chile peppers | grapes | cauliflower | tangerines | cabbage |
| | beets | figs | corn | nuts | celery root | | cauliflower |
| | broccoli | grapes | cucumbers | oranges | chile peppers | | celery root |
| | cabbage | mangoes | summer squash | pears | cucumbers | | chicory |
| | chile peppers | melons | sweet peppers | persimmons | fennel | | fennel |
| | cucumbers | peaches | tomatoes | | greens | | greens |
| | head lettuces | plums | | | leaf lettuces | | mushrooms |
| | peas | watermelon | | | mushrooms | | spinach |
| | radishes | | | | spinach | | sweet potatoes |
| | shallots | | | | sweet peppers | | |
| | spinach | | | | sweet potatoes | | |
| | sweet peppers | | | | winter squash | | |
| | turnips | | | | | | |

### Big Ticket Foods

Know that leaner cuts of meat are usually more expensive than the fattier cuts, as are trimmed and pre-portioned steaks. It is typically cheaper to buy a whole beef tenderloin from a club store and trim and cut it into steaks yourself than it is to buy prepared steaks. You can do this several weeks in advance if you wrap them well to protect from freezer burn. But you have to decide whether the extra cost is worth the convenience and time you save by buying prepared foods.

Less commonly consumed meats, such as lamb and veal, are usually more expensive than chicken or beef. Chicken can be substituted for veal in many recipes. Seafood as a whole can be pricey, so careful selection is essential. (See page 120 for tips on selecting seafood.)

If a recipe calls for cooked shrimp, look in the freezer case for deveined and pre-cooked shrimp. You'll find prepared shrimp very cost-effective in the time saved in shelling, deveining, and cooking. These only need to be thawed according to package instructions and refreshed with a squeeze of fresh lemon juice to be recipe-ready.

# ESTIMATING FOOD QUANTITIES

The length of your reception plays a big part in determining food quantities. For a reception beginning with a cocktail hour, followed by a dinner, you should calculate seven pieces of canapés and hors d'oeuvres for each guest.

If a reception starts earlier in the day, around 4:00 or 5:00 p.m. on a Saturday, people tend to be hungrier, so plan for ten to twelve pieces of canapés and hors d'oeuvres per guest. Receptions are expected to last until the usual time for dinner, say 6:30 to 7:00 p.m.

If your reception starts at about 6:00 p.m. and is not followed by dinner, much more food is needed. Estimate twelve to fourteen canapés and hors d'oeuvres per guest, and choose recipes that seem more filling and substantial on an empty stomach — bacon-wrapped shrimp, for instance, instead of carrot sticks with curry dressing.

Accurately estimating quantities can be difficult, particularly with buffet or cocktail receptions. You could either run out of food too early or have food left over. It helps if you assign someone to monitor the food intake of your guests. For your peace of mind, have some extra food in reserve for unexpected demand. When service is butler-style — that is, plated and served by wait staff — you have much more control over the flow of food. When the budget is tight, butler-style service can actually end up being cheaper because you can control portions and timing. In contrast, buffets can be picked clean in a very short time and, when not replenished, quickly reveal that there was not enough food.

How much food people will eat on any given occasion is, for the novice entertainer, difficult to estimate, but it helps to take the following issues into consideration:

• Age of guests
Older people tend to eat less than younger people, and certainly less than hungry teenagers. Figure out how many guests you'll have and their approximate ages.

• Type of food
Light foods go more quickly than rich foods.

• Time of day
Guests tend to eat more at a cocktail reception in place of a dinner than at an after-dinner dessert reception or morning brunch. Not everyone has the time or the disposition to eat a European three-hour, five-course meal. On the other hand, crudités and a fruit tray are not going to satisfy a hungry dinner crowd. As a rule, people tend to eat lighter, smaller portioned meals at lunchtime than at dinnertime. Try to schedule the meal so that the main course will be served at a reasonable time.

## MEAT, POULTRY, AND SEAFOOD QUANTITIES

| meat and poultry | quantity per person (uncooked) |
|---|---|
| Beef, lamb, or pork (boneless) | 4 to 6 ounces |
| Steak or leg of lamb (bone-in) | 6 to 8 ounces |
| Pork chops (bone-in) | 1 large |
| Pork or beef ribs or shanks (bone-in) | 1 pound |
| Beef, pork, or lamb roasts (bone-in) | 8 to 11 ounces |
| Beef, pork, or lamb roasts (boneless) | 4 to 6 ounces |
| Chicken thighs, legs, or wings (bone-in) | 2 (3 to 4-ounce) pieces |
| Chicken breast (boneless and skinless) | 1 (6 to 8-ounce) breast |
| Chicken or turkey (whole) | 12 ounces to 1 pound |

| seafood | quantity per person (uncooked) |
|---|---|
| Crab meat, lobster meat, octopus, shrimp, scallops, squid | 4 to 5 ounces |
| Lobster (in shell) | 1½ to 2 pounds |
| Crab (in shell) | 1½ to 2 pounds |
| Mussels | 12 each |
| Oysters and clams | 4 to 6 each |
| Whole fish (not cleaned and guts intact) | 12 to 16 ounces |
| Whole fish (cleaned and guts removed) | 8 to 12 ounces |
| Fish fillets and steaks | 5 to 8 ounces |

## HORS D'OEUVRES AND SIDE DISHES SERVING QUANTITIES

| other foods | quantity per person (cooked or prepared) |
|---|---|
| Potatoes | 3 to 4 ounces |
| Salad | 3 to 4 ounces or 1 heaped cup |
| Vegetables | 3 to 4 ounces |
| Dessert | 4 ounces |
| Hors d'oeuvres | 4 to 5 ounces |
| Rice | 2 ounces |
| Pasta | 3 ounces |

## DO-IT-FOR-LESS WEDDING MENUS

The menus included here are examples of delicious, easy-to-make, do-it-for-less crowd-pleaser menus that can be adapted for any style of wedding. Use the whole menu or interchange with your own favorite recipes to make your reception a hit.

### Sunrise Brunch
Raspberry-Orange Champagne cocktail *(page 94)*

or Bellini *(page 94)*

Marinated Mushroom and Artichoke Salad *(page 136)*

Tomato and Sausage Frittata with Fresh Herbs *(page 137)*

Sage Biscuits with Honey Butter *(page 138)*

Sunrise Floral Cupcakes *(page 224)*

### In Full Bloom
Mimosa *(page 94)*

Garden Salad

Roasted Salmon with Lemon-Almond Pesto *(page 144)*

Haricots Vert with Wild Mushrooms and Pinenuts *(page 146)*

Rice Pilaf

Chocolate-Dipped Strawberries with Whipped Cream *(page 147)*

Pink Flower Cupcakes *(page 226)*

### Waterside Jewels
Limoncello Iced Tea *(page 94)*

Tropical Shrimp Ceviche with Parmesan Crostini *(page 152)*

Grilled Chicken Sandwiches with Sun-Dried Tomatoes and Arugula *(page 154)*

Lemon-Mint Pasta Bean Salad *(page 155)*

Cheesecake with Sea Star Cookies *(page 228)*

### Sunset Cocktails
Mango Tequila Sunset *(page 94)*

Caviar-Stuffed Eggs *(page 160)*

Goat Cheese with Tarragon and Edible Flowers *(page 163)*

Blue Cheese in Cherry Tomatoes *(page 162)*

Grilled Oysters on the Half Shell *(page 165)*

Proscuitto-Wrapped Scallops *(page 164)*

Grilled Chicken Satay with Peanut Sauce

Sunset Polka Dot Cake *(page 230)*

### French Countryside
Calvados Martini *(page 95)*

Niçoise Salad with Garlic Herb Dressing *(page 170)*

Classic Cassoulet with Crusty Bread *(page 172)*

Cheese Board with Fruit and Nuts *(page 174)*

Lemon Cake with Vanilla Frosting and Fresh Flowers *(page 234)*

### Amber Nights
Prosecco Cocktail *(page 95)*

Antipasti Platters of Salami, Olives, Artichoke Hearts, and Breadsticks *(page 180)*

Wild Mushroom Torta *(page 182)*

Roasted Pork Loin Roast with Sun-Dried Tomatoes and Olives *(page 184)*

Herbed Orzo *(page 181)*

Butter Cake with Sugared Fruit and Mocha Amaretto Frosting *(page 236)*

### Winter Wonderland
Hot Coffee Cocktail *(page 95)*

Demitasse of Creamy Carrot Ginger Soup *(page 190)*

Endive Salad with Apples, Pecans and Roquefort Cheese *(page 191)*

His and Hers Beef Wellingtons *(page 192)*

Lemon-Butter Broccolini *(page 197)*

Truffled Mashed Potatoes *(page 196)*

White Rose Cake *(page 240)*

### Island Spice
Caribbean Champagne Cocktail *(page 95)*

Mango, Pineapple, and Kiwi Salad *(page 202)*

Lobster Spring Rolls with Sweet Curry Dipping Sauce *(page 206)*

Chicken Trinidad with Rum Sauce *(page 204)*

Jasmine Rice with Golden Raisins *(page 209)*

Spice Cake with Gilded Pineapple Flowers *(page 244)*

## MIX-AND-MATCH MENUS

By mixing and matching the recipes in this book and by adding other simple ingredients, you can create a variety of other wonderful do-it-for-less menus. See our ideas for a starting point.

### Early Afternoon Wedding Picnic

Mimosa *(page 94)*

Grilled Chicken Sandwiches with Sun-Dried Tomatoes and Arugula *(page 154)*

Cheese Board with Fruit and Nuts *(page 174)*

In Full Bloom Pink Flower Cupcakes *(page 226)*

### Late Afternoon Elegant Sit-Down

Prosecco Cocktail *(page 95)*

Demitasse of Creamy Carrot Ginger Soup *(page 190)*

Wild Mushroom Torta *(page 182)*

Garden Salad

Lemon Cake with Vanilla Frosting and Fresh Flowers *(page 234)*

### Make-Ahead Formal Dinner

Bellini *(page 94)*

Goat Cheese with Tarragon and Edible Flowers *(page 163)*

His and Hers Beef Wellingtons *(page 192)*

Haricots Vert with Wild Mushrooms and Pinenuts *(page 146)*

Rice Pilaf

White Rose Cake *(page 240)*

### Make-Ahead Casual Buffet

Limoncello Iced Tea *(page 94)*

Blue Cheese in Cherry Tomatoes *(page 162)*

Proscuitto-Wrapped Scallops *(page 164)*

Tomato and Sausage Frittata with Fresh Herbs *(page 137)*

Sage Biscuits with Honey Butter *(page 138)*

Cheesecake with Sea Star Cookies *(page 228)*

### Family-Style Casual Wedding Dinner

Hot Coffee Cocktail *(page 95)*

Endive Salad with Apples, Pecans and Roquefort Cheese *(page 191)*

Classic Cassoulet with Crusty Bread *(page 172)*

Butter Cake with Sugared Fruit and Mocha Amaretto Frosting *(page 236)*

### Elegant Dinner Buffet

Calvados Martini *(page 95)*

Caviar Stuffed Eggs *(page 160)*

Roasted Pork Loin Roast with Sun-Dried Tomatoes and Olives *(page 184)*

Lemon-Butter Broccolini *(page 197)*

Truffled Mashed Potatoes *(page 196)*

Spice Cake with Gilded Pineapple Flowers *(page 244)*

### Seaside Cocktails and Appetizers

Mango Tequila Sunset *(page 94)*

Limoncello Iced Tea *(page 94)*

Tropical Shrimp Ceviche with Parmesan Crostini *(page 152)*

Lobster Spring Rolls with Sweet Curry Dipping Sauce *(page 206)*

Grilled Oysters on the Half Shell *(page 165)*

Grilled Chicken Satay with Peanut Sauce *(purchased)*

Sunrise Floral Cupcakes *(page 224)*

### Easy Wedding Lunch

Caribbean Champagne Cocktail *(page 95)*

Niçoise Salad with Garlic Herb Dressing *(page 170)*

Antipasti Platters of Salami, Olives, Artichoke Hearts, and Breadsticks *(page 180)*

Cheese Board with Fruit and Nuts *(page 174)*

Chocolate-Dipped Strawberries with Whipped Cream *(page 147)*

### Serve It Hot or Cold

Prosecco Cocktail *(page 95)*

Marinated Mushroom and Artichoke Salad *(page 136)*

Roasted Salmon with Lemon-Almond Pesto *(page 144)*

Herbed Orzo *(page 181)*

Lemon Broccolini *(page 197)*

Polka Dot Cake *(page 230)*

# DEVELOPING YOUR OWN MENU

Don't see what you want? If you want a menu that is completely different from the ones suggested on previous pages, go forth, and make
your own. When you create your own menu, you'll end up with a wedding that is entirely individual. While it's ambitious to want to try a new
recipe, keep in mind your cooking abilities, the amount of time you have
to prepare the food, and the quality of the recipe itself. The recipes in
*Do-It-for-Less! Weddings* evolved from years of catering, and we tested
each recipe twice while compiling the book. But not all recipes out there
receive the same level of attention, so you should always try to do a trial
run of any recipes you'll be serving to guests. You'll work out all the kinks
and reduce the potential for mistakes well before the wedding.

## Perfect balance

Once you have decided on your menu, write it down. How does it
sound? Do the courses flow naturally? Does reading the menu make
you hungry? It should! Menus should offer an interesting balance of
temperature, appearance, and texture. Consider the following points,
and plan accordingly.

• **Temperature**
Everything doesn't have to be served hot. Many flavors, in fact, are
overwhelmed by high heat and benefit from some cooling time at
room temperature. Likewise, a light salad or cooling sauce can offer a
much-needed relief from a spicy dish.

• **Flavor**
Flavors should complement each other and flow from appetizer to
entrée to dessert. If your first course is a balsamic-dressed green salad
and the wedding cake is an Italian torte, save the lamb tagine with jasmine rice for another day. Instead, pair the salad with Chicken Parmesan. Establishing a theme really helps with menu planning.

• **Color**
Think of how the finished plates will look. Is all the food one color? If
so, what can you add to make the plate more colorful? That plate of
slow-roasted pork with mushrooms and sautéed onions is going to
look rather bland with all that brown on brown. Serve the pork on a
bed of roasted red peppers and caramelized Brussels sprouts on the
side instead. Now your meal has color as well as flavor.

• **Texture**
Many happy couples forget to consider the various textures of the
foods they're serving. As with flavor and appearance, try not to repeat
foods with similar textures throughout your menu. If you are serving a
creamy comfort food like pasta alla vodka as your entrée, don't serve

buttery mashed potatoes alongside. A crunchy green vegetable would be a better choice.

• Mix It Up

Avoid repeating a single food item, food color, flavor, or cooking procedure (e.g., grilled everything) throughout the whole menu. Consider, for example, a menu of Pan-fried Goat Cheese with Side of Green Salad, Grilled Chicken with Parmesan Cream Sauce and Roasted Mixed Vegetables, Cheese Soufflés, Bananas Foster Cheesecake, Assorted Breads and Parmesan Grissini. As you can see, this menu is a little heavy on the cheese and, for most of us, would taste too rich. Now, there is nothing wrong with having a reception planned around desserts and cheese. It sounds delicious and your guests would love tasting all the varieties, but be aware that less is often more when it comes to food, especially with strong and spicy flavors. When serving fatty foods, serve something tart or acidic as an accompaniment. With your cheese plates, serve sliced fennel or pears to cleanse the palate. This will help cut through the richness. Mint sauce with lamb and orange sauce with duck are classic examples.

## Creating Visual Appeal

Making your food look as good as it tastes is not at all difficult. Here are a few simple rules:

• Color

Contrasts in color and texture add interest to plates. Your poached halibut may be delicious, but serving it with potatoes au gratin and pureed cauliflower soup might not do it justice. Instead, serve it with sautéed kale or steamed snow peas and roasted red potatoes. Add minced jalapeño and black beans to a corn salad. Swirl crème fraîche into colorful, smooth soups or sprinkle with chopped fresh chives.

• Shape

Cut peppers into strips or triangles. Slice green onions and asparagus on the diagonal. Julienne vegetables like carrots. Thinly slice pork loin and fan out on the plate.

• Texture

Garnish smooth soups with crisp croutons. Sprinkle toasted sesame seeds or slivered, toasted almonds over vegetables. Top meat with sautéed mushrooms or thinly sliced and fried onions.

• Height

Build the plate high: Place your vegetable and starch either right next to each other in the center of the plate or one on top of the other, and then place your meat on top or leaning up against the starch and vegetable. For example, if you are serving wild rice, asparagus spears, and a poached chicken breast, place a small mound of rice in the center of the plate. Lay the asparagus over the rice. Balance the chicken on top of the raft of asparagus so that one end is at the center of the rice and the other end rests on the plate.

• Plate size

Use a correctly sized plate. Tiny portions on huge plates are fine if you like the look of early '90s food-as-art, but to most of us, it looks as if the host is being cheap and the guests will leave hungry. Likewise, too much food piled on a small plate gives the overcrowded look of a "you can only visit the buffet once" food mountain.

## Whetting the Appetite

Posting a well-written menu or placing it on a table by the doorway to the reception venue adds anticipation for your guests on an already exciting day.

Instead of,

> Chicken and vegetables with cream

Impress your guests with,

> Pan-Seared Breast of Organic Poultry
> with a Parsley and Cream Reduction
> and a Selection of Farm-Fresh Seasonal Vegetables

## Garnishing

Accentuating your food with an appropriate garnish will make a big difference in presentation, and will make your hard work look like restaurant-quality. You don't have to spend hours carving elaborate vegetable creations to make your plates pop. Here are a few garnishing guidelines:

• Edible

All garnishes must be safe to eat — organic, if possible.

• Simple

Don't gild the lily. The garnish is there to enhance the food, not to compete with it.

- **Relevant**

Use a garnish that is relevant to the dish. Take an ingredient from the recipe and use that as your garnish. If your dish has chopped chives in it, then decorate the plate with two whole chives arranged in an X shape. Enhance your bar service with lemon twirls, or garnish your fish with a plump wedge of lemon. Using a citrus zester, make long curls of lemon zest and arrange it in a bundle on top of the fish. Or, quickly deep-fry the zest for a crunchy garnish.

- **Blossoms**

To decorate the plate, you can use edible flowers such as pansies, roses, lavender, nasturtium, and chive blossoms. Buy them from the produce section of the grocery store if they are available, or, if not, use organically grown flowers. Ask your florist if you need suggestions for a source. Do not use regular flowers from a florist without checking, as they are usually sprayed with pesticides.

- **Classic**

Parsley is a great garnish. It gives life to mashed potatoes, soups, stews, and any bland-looking food that needs a splash of color. Finely chop, and then dry in paper towels to stop the green color from transferring to other food. Use whole sprigs of flat-leaf parsley on the rim of a plate for an easy garnish.

- **Food as art**

For more elaborate garnishes, visit some Asian restaurants in your area, particularly Japanese and Thai restaurants. They frequently make intricate vegetable and fruit carvings and will sell you anything you ask for. To purchase garnishes to use for place cards, to decorate the buffet, or to adorn dinner plates speak to the manager. Or contact your local culinary school and ask for a student referral.

## Tableware

Choose dishes and utensils that fit the style of reception and reflect the months you spent planning every detail of your wedding, from choosing the perfect tablecloths to packaging the party favors. Disposable goods are appropriate for a casual or outdoor event. While plastic or paper plates are easier to dispose of or recycle and are much easier to store and transport, they may not lend the elegance you want. More formal events usually call for more formal china, flatware, and glassware. Plain white dishes look great with almost any theme or table setting, and are the most readily available from party rental stores. If you're planning on a more intimate guest list, you can buy them in bulk from stores like Pier One and Ikea or restaurant supply warehouses. A hostess can never own too many white plates, and you'll use them for years to come. If inviting an extremely large crowd, renting may be a better option.

If the budget simply does not allow for real china, don't despair. You'll find a wide selection of good-looking, sturdy, stylish products on the market to set the right tone for your event. You can even mix-and-match, using real flatware with a good quality disposable plate for the buffet. Disposable plates that look just like glass are now available, and make good compromises.

## Rent, Buy, or Borrow: There's a Cost to Freedom

All in all, there's no one perfect way to furnish the tableware, glassware, flatware, and other items you'll need to serve your guests. Purchasing plain white china can rival the cost of renting, but will it be an investment you'll appreciate, or a hassle to store after the wedding? If you think you'll do a lot of entertaining, white plates might last through many parties. If not, renting might be better. It's usually reasonably priced, and the convenience of having everything dropped off clean and picked up dirty (no one will have to wash up afterwards!) is not to be underestimated.

If you have a neighbor whose store of linens, dishes, and flatware could rival Martha Stewart's, and the offer of a loan has been made, consider carefully the responsibility you'll take on. You (or a family member or friend) will need to pick up the items — perhaps making several trips — return the items, and pony up for a replacement should anything be damaged. And a sincere thank-you will absolutely be in order, perhaps also a nice gift, whether the contribution is great or small.

# KEEPING THE FOOD SAFE

Have you ever felt queasy a few hours after eating at a party? The cause may not have been overeating; some unseen bacteria may have snuck into your miniature crab cakes or your chocolate mousse. Food contamination and food poisoning can be a serious problem. Follow this list of considerations to keep your food and guests safe.

### • Clean hands

Wash hands before, during, and after handling food, using soap, a nailbrush, and hot water. Wash hands after using the restroom, smoking, coughing, sneezing, or scratching, and don't cook with lotion on your hands.

### • Avoid jewelry

Jewelry can get caught in appliances and end up in the soup. Use common sense and discretion when cooking while wearing any jewelry, or better still, remove your jewelry altogether.

### • Secure hair

The rule for jewelry applies also to hair. If you don't want hair in the food, either tie your hair back or wear a hat.

### • Cover wounds

Cover any cuts or open wounds with proper dressing. Wear disposable plastic gloves over the dressing to prevent any infection from spreading. Remember to change your gloves when switching from raw meats and unwashed produce to cooked foods.

### • Avoid eating while cooking

If you are hungry, stop and take a break. Chewing food, gum, or toothpicks while cooking can lead to unwanted surprises in the food.

### • Tasting protocol

Fingers are for pointing, spoons are for tasting. Use a spoon and not your finger to taste the sauce for seasoning. After tasting, wash the spoon before using again. No double dipping. Alternatively, use plastic disposable spoons and discard after each use.

## Cleanliness is Perfection

Keeping your work area clean will reduce the risk of contamination.

### • Disinfect surfaces

Always wash cutting boards thoroughly with hot, soapy water when preparing different types of food. You don't want to contaminate your fruit and vegetables with chicken juices. Nor do you want your dessert to taste of garlic. Surprisingly, wooden cutting boards are safer to use than plastic for meats and poultry. Wash counters and work surfaces with hot, soapy water and an anti-bacterial cleanser or diluted bleach.

**HELPFUL HINT:**

Bacteria can thrive on kitchen sponges, rags, and dishtowels, so they should be washed frequently, preferably in a bleach solution. To quickly disinfect a sponge or rag, dampen and then microwave on high for 2 minutes.

• **Wash as you work**

Get into the habit of washing pots, pans, and dishes as you go to keep things running smoothly and prevent a huge pile of dishes at the end of the day that nobody wants to clean. If you have a dishwasher, always empty it before you start cooking. Stopping to put clean dishes away while you work will only slow you down.

## Food Inspection

There are strict health and safety guidelines enforced by government agencies for anyone selling food of any kind. Always buy from a reputable grocery store or supplier.

The first step to sanitation starts in the grocery store. When buying packaged meats or other high-protein foods such as milk and deli products, cream, cheese, or tofu, check the "use by" or "best before" dates to ensure optimum freshness. Sometimes if you look further back into the refrigerator case you will find fresher products. Beef, veal, and lamb should be red and fresh looking. Ground beef, turkey, or chicken that has a gray tone is usually a few days old.

As tempting as it seems, avoid buying fish or shellfish from vendors parked in a truck stop or on the side of the street with a cooler and one of those "100 shrimp for $10" signs. There is a reason why that shrimp is so unbelievably cheap. An exception to this loose rule is for those who live in areas with a large fishing industry. In certain parts of the country, you can find shrimp in stands by the side of the road that was caught only that morning, and it's often a great deal.

When buying whole fish, look for a fresh, mild ocean smell. The eyes should be clear and shiny, not cloudy or sunken. Look for a red or pink color around the gills and shiny, bright scales that are tight on the skin. Pass on any fish that is soft to the touch. When pressed, the flesh should be firm and elastic; it should not dent easily.

As most recipes call for fillets or steaks, and that is most likely how you will be buying your fish, you must rely on your sense of smell to judge freshness. If in doubt, don't buy it; choose frozen fish instead. It is often the freshest fish on the market because it is frequently frozen on the boat immediately after being caught.

## Safe Handling

Once you have selected your meat, place it in the lowest rack of the shopping cart where the juices will not drip onto ready-to-eat or raw foods. Meat "sealed" in plastic packaging can still drip everywhere and may contain bacteria that, if not thoroughly cooked or washed off of fruits and vegetables, could cause a guest to become sick. This transfer of bacteria is called cross-contamination and is responsible for many outbreaks of food poisoning. Be aware of cross-contamination when preparing food. If you use a cutting board to prepare raw chicken, do not use the same board for cutting lettuce unless the board has been thoroughly washed with hot, soapy water. A safer and more hygienic solution is to have cutting boards designated for specific duties, e.g., one for raw meats, one for cooked meats, and one for fruits and vegetables. Look for plastic cutting boards in a variety of colors, and allot one color for each duty. If you have only one cutting board, choose wood. Another alternative is to use disposable cutting boards available in grocery stores.

## Safe Storage

There are two reasons to store food properly: sanitation and expense. Holding foods at the proper temperatures in the proper containers will keep them from dehydration and spoilage. Spoiled food is money wasted; you want your food to last as long as possible in its ideal condition.

Proper refrigeration at all times preserves freshness and keeps bacteria at bay. Perishables must be kept at 40 degrees or less and frozen food at 32 degrees or less. Bacteria thrive between 40 degrees and 140 degrees. We call this the "danger zone." Foods should not be kept in this range for more than 4 hours. Keep this in mind when serving a buffet, storing leftovers, and grocery shopping.

Temperatures vary widely for properly cooked, safe-to-eat chicken, pork, and beef. See the guides on page 123 for proper cooking temperatures. For packaged goods, read the label. Many product labels display the correct cooking temperatures on them.

Leftover food should be cooled, placed in airtight containers, and refrigerated as soon as possible. Eat refrigerated leftovers within three days. Be sure to reheat them to a temperature of 170 degrees to destroy any bacteria.

Plan your grocery-shopping trip so that perishables are unrefrigerated for the shortest time possible. You may want to consider having a cooler packed with ice or reusable cooling packs in your car if you have delicate items such as seafood that need to be refrigerated. A cooler will also come in handy if you are shopping in the middle of summer or the ride home is a long one. Once home, store all food in proper, well-sealed storage containers. Below are guidelines for you to follow when storing food:

• **Breads**
Bread dries out faster in the refrigerator than at room temperature, but is less likely to get moldy. Store in paper or plastic. Alternatively, wrap tightly in plastic wrap, cover with aluminum foil, and freeze.

• **Canned goods**
Opened cans of food may be safely stored if covered tightly with plastic wrap. The exceptions are acidic fruits and vegetables like tomatoes, pineapple, and sauerkraut. These need to be stored in glass or plastic containers.

• **Cheese**
Most cheeses are best kept refrigerated, wrapped first in plastic wrap and then in a resealable plastic storage bag to keep odors out and moisture in. Firm and hard cheeses can be kept for several weeks. Fresh cheeses will spoil in seven to ten days because of their high-moisture content. Some cheeses that have become hard or dry may still be grated for

cooking or baking. Freezing is possible but not recommended because it changes the cheese's texture, making it mealy or tough.

• Chocolate

Wrap tightly in parchment paper, and then in foil. Store in a cool place, but not in the refrigerator; 60 degrees is ideal. Chocolate chips are low in cocoa solids, so they are less sensitive to temperature. Store chocolate chips in an airtight container at room temperature.

• Cooked food

Refrigerate cooked food immediately. Pour warm foods into pans so that the food is no more than 2 inches deep. Stir large pans occasionally while they cool to hasten the cooling process. Set a hot pan in an ice bath to cool the food faster and safer. Contrary to popular opinion, letting the pan cool at room temperature merely allows it to spend longer in the bacteria-breeding range of 40 to 140 degrees.

• Dairy

Milk should be stored below 40 degrees to prevent bacterial growth. Moving a gallon container of milk in and out of the refrigerator many times will shorten its life and increase the chance of bacterial growth. Don't pour milk that has been left out back into the container, as it can contaminate the whole container. Hard cheese can be stored at room temperature if room temperature is below 80 degrees. Wrap cheese in plastic to prevent mold. Eggs will usually keep for a few weeks if refrigerated. Store eggs on the interior refrigerator shelves and not in the door. The constant opening and closing can make the door the warmest part of the refrigerator. Butter picks up flavors from other foods, so always store it in a container or wrap it well.

• Dry goods

The ideal storage temperature for dry goods is 50 degrees.

• Fruits and vegetables

Rinse in cold water and pat dry. Remove any dead leaves. Use a salad spinner to dry greens as much as possible. Store the cleaned greens in a resealable plastic storage bag, and layer with paper towels. Most fruits keep well if refrigerated. To store soft berries, put them in one layer onto a cookie sheet lined with paper towels. Throw away any moldy ones. Cover lightly with additional paper towels, then refrigerate. Thick-skinned fruits can be kept at room temperature. All fruits should be checked daily. Remove and use over-ripe or bruised fruit right away. Do not refrigerate tomatoes. Potatoes and onions are best stored in a dark place at room temperature. Do not store potatoes and onions together; doing so makes each spoil faster. Potatoes that are refrigerated need a week or more at room temperature to restore their normal starch-sugar balance. Fresh mushrooms should be stored in a paper bag in the bottom of the refrigerator.

• Herbs

Stand fresh herbs upright in small glasses or plastic cups with an inch of water in the bottom, and then place a plastic bag loosely over the herbs. Alternatively, rinse fresh herbs and pat dry, then wrap in damp paper towels and put in resealable plastic storage bags. Dried herbs should be kept in as dark a place as possible and discarded after six months.

• Meats, poultry, and fish

Store meat, poultry, and fish in containers with sides to prevent dripping. Always store raw protein in the lowest section of the refrigerator, away from cooked food to prevent contamination from stray drips. Use disposable aluminum trays and pans to store wrapped meats. Store fish, liver, and ground meats loosely wrapped in the coldest part of the refrigerator, and do not store for more than one day. Remove the giblets and rinse fresh chicken before storing. Rewrap chicken well and use within two days.

• Spices

Buy spices in small amounts and store in cool, dark places. Bright lights and warm temperatures will shorten an already short shelf life. Most spices need to be replaced every six months.

## COOKED MEAT TEMPERATURE GUIDE

| chicken | temperature (°F) when done |
|---|---|
| Thigh | 175° to 180° |
| Breast | 175° to 180° |
| **beef** | **temperature (°F) when done** |
| Rare | 130° |
| Medium-rare | 140° |
| Medium | 150° |
| Medium-well | 165° |
| **lamb** | **temperature (°F) when done** |
| Rare | 130° |
| Medium-rare | 140° |
| Medium | 150° |
| Ground lamb | 165° |
| **pork** | **temperature (°F) when done** |
| All cuts | 165° to 170° |
| **veal** | **temperature (°F) when done** |
| Medium | 150° |
| Medium-well | 165° |

### Freezer Storage

Remove excess air from freezer bags to prevent freezer burn. Different foods benefit from different freezing methods. Follow these guidelines below for best results:

- **Berries.** You can freeze cranberries in their original packaging. For blackberries, blueberries, cherries, raspberries, and hulled strawberries, wash, dry, and then spread in a single layer on a baking sheet and freeze. When frozen, pour into resealable plastic storage bags.

- **Cakes.** Freeze frosted cakes uncovered until frozen solid before wrapping well to preserve the frosting.

- **Meat.** Separate pieces of meat with waxed paper before freezing to prevent them from sticking together.

### Defrosting Food

- **Refrigerate whenever possible.** For safety, thaw frozen foods in the refrigerator. Avoid the temptation to thaw food on the kitchen counter at room temperature or to run hot water over the food. This method gives bacteria an invitation to the party.

- **Other thawing options.** You can also run cold water over food that is tightly wrapped in plastic or use the microwave defrost setting. These methods of thawing must be followed with immediate cooking.

## IDEAL TEMPERATURES

| location | temperature (°F) | |
|---|---|---|
| Freezer | 0° | |
| Refrigerator | 8° to 40° | |
| Cool room temperature | 65° | |
| Warm room temperature | 70° to 75° | |
| Lukewarm or tepid liquid | 95° | |
| Warm liquid | 105° to 115° | |
| Hot liquid | 120° | |
| Boiling water | 212° | |
| Rising bread | 80° | |
| Low/slow oven | 180° to 225° | |
| Warm oven | 300° to 325° | |
| Moderate oven | 350° to 375° | |
| Hot oven | 400° to 450° | |
| Very hot oven | 475° to 500° | |

# FEEDING THE GUESTS

### How many *pounds* of salad?

Cooking for a crowd can be overwhelming if you are used to cooking for only a handful of people. The main obstacles for do-it-for-less wedding caterers include refrigeration, cooking space, and manpower. As the average household doesn't have a walk-in refrigerator and an arsenal of stoves, how can you pull off the wedding of your dreams? It would be nice to rent a restaurant kitchen for a day or so, but most liability insurance contracts prevent the restaurant from allowing anyone other than trained employees into the work area. Some larger places of worship in your community may have kitchen facilities available for rent; your ceremony venue may be one of them. If so, do all the main cooking there, taking advantage of any available refrigeration, and save the simple tasks for home.

If you are going to use a non-commercial kitchen, here are some ways to fully utilize what you have to work with:

• **Menu planning.**
Plan your menu carefully. Choose dishes that do not require refrigeration or that you can keep frozen until you are ready to put in the oven.

• **Prep ahead.**
Do as much cooking and preparation ahead of time as possible.

• **Freeze ahead.**
Freeze as much of the prepared food as you can.

• **Clear space.**
Clear as much refrigeration space as possible. If you live in a small apartment and have apartment-sized appliances, rent a refrigerator from a party rental supply company and put it on your porch or balcony.

• **Test sizes.**
Make sure the storage containers you are using will fit in the refrigerator, or keep your party food in resealable plastic storage bags in the refrigerator. These use much less space than plates, bowls, or other containers.

• **Adjust refrigerator.**
Set the temperature control to a cooler setting to compensate for the additional food if necessary.

• **Ask for help.**
Ask family, friends, or neighbors if they have a spare refrigerator or freezer in their garage that you can use if you are still short on space. Just label all of your food beforehand.

**GOOD DEALS IN COOKWARE**

If you're doing the cooking, you may need to acquire some extra or specialized cookware. Other than registering for such items on your wedding registry, try the following places for good deals:

• Antique malls

• Auctions and estate sales

• Department stores (*look for promotional sales and discounts*)

• Discount stores

• Garage sales

• Online auction sales (*www.Ebay.com*)

• Online cooking stores (*www.cooking.com or www.chefs.com*)

• Party supply stores

• Restaurant supply stores

• Swap meets (*great for copper cookware*)

• Storage companies (*selling unclaimed items*)

• Alternate cooling options.
Fill a plastic or galvanized tub with ice for your beverages so they don't take up valuable refrigerator space. If you don't have a plastic tub, use your washing machine or bathtub. Make sure it's sparkling clean, and line your tub with plastic if you have any worries. Keep extra ice in a small cooler for guests, and transfer the chilled drinks to the reception area to serve.

• Refrigerate protein.
Keep all protein refrigerated at all times.

• Storing produce.
Store produce in a cooler lined with ice or ice packs. Find a place to store room-temperature produce and dry goods as well.

• Measure ahead.
If you plan to use roasting or baking pans, check the dimensions of the oven and the refrigerator to make sure they fit.

• Adjust cooking times.
The more you fill the oven, the longer the food will take to cook, so allow for extra cooking time if necessary.

• Proper temperature.
Use meat thermometers whenever possible for accurate doneness.

• Creating baking space.
Invest in an extra cooking rack for your oven to create more space.

• Know your limits.
If you need help, enlist friends, family, or neighbors. Check the yellow pages for cooking schools in your area. Many culinary students will welcome the experience. Post a notice for a chef's assistant on the school's bulletin board for help a few weeks before the event.

## Get Organized

Before starting any recipe, read it thoroughly to fully understand each procedure. Next, prepare your "mise en place." This French term translates into having everything in place and ready to go, from ingredients and equipment to a preheated oven. Professional kitchens use this procedure to ensure a smooth operation. Keep the recipe close at hand and refer to it often; don't be caught off-guard midway through with a technique or ingredient you've never used before. Set out standard plastic or metal measuring cups for measuring dry ingredients, and glass or Pyrex measuring cups for fluid ingredients.

## All Things Equal

The knife cuts shown below give the professional standard for sizing. It is good to know the difference between "small dice" or "julienne." Not only does the finished dish look better if your cuts are uniform, it will also turn out better. Any recipe you make will have been written with these sizes in mind, and uniform shapes also allow for even cooking.

## STANDARD KNIFE CUTS

brunoise: ⅛ x ⅛ x ⅛-inch

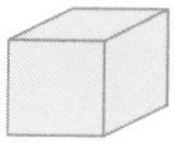

small dice: ¼ x ¼ ¼-inch

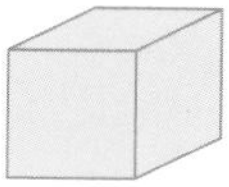

medium dice: ⅓ x ⅓ x ⅓-inch

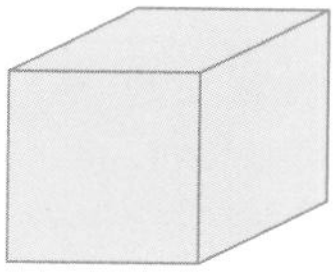

large dice: ½ x ½ x ½-inch

julienne: ⅛ x ⅛ x 1-inch

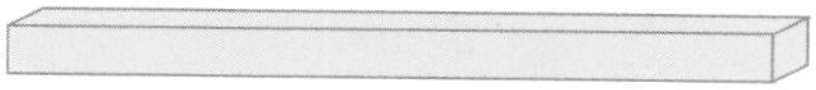

allumette: ⅛ x ⅛ x 2-inches

batonnet: ¼ x ¼ x 2½-inches

# SERVING THE MULTITUDES

If you look behind the scenes at a large catering event during service time, you'll see a carefully orchestrated dance as coordinated and precise as a military operation. You may not be inviting several hundred, but you can apply the same serving techniques that professional caterers use for your extravaganza.

How can you plate the food, serve all your guests simultaneously, and still keep the soup hot? For plated service, prepare a designated plating area. An extra table set up close to the dining area is perfect. If the kitchen is the only option, clear all counter-tops first, and then place a cutting board on a cool stovetop for additional space. You can also use the top of a washer and dryer if they aren't in a damp basement. If the food can be easily transported, consider using a garage or patio if weather and cleanliness permit. Cover the table with a towel or tablecloth to prevent the plates from slipping.

The food will stay hot longer if the plates are warm. Stack and warm them in a low oven (150 to 200 degrees), and do not be tempted to speed up the process by kicking up the heat. Hot plates not only burn fingers and take a long time to become cool enough to be handled, but they may also crack if too hot. Cool dessert and salad plates in the refrigerator or in a cooler.

Salads can be tossed just before serving, and plated and pre-set on the dining table. The easiest way to serve a mixed green salad is to wear disposable plastic gloves and place a handful of leaves within the inner rim of each plate. Clean any stray splatters of dressing from the rim before serving. If you are tight on space, consider plating half the salads just before serving, then plate the rest as the first half are being served.

Retaining two or more people to orchestrate the food service behind the scenes will be invaluable. Draw a plate presentation on a chart like the one on page 130 for the servers to follow, or make an actual sample plate of food before the serving begins. Designate one of the servers to be in charge, and make sure they are all thoroughly informed well before the event so that they can handle all of the service without your help. (See page 129 on hiring help.)

The most efficient system of plating is to have a team working in sequence. Each team member is responsible for one food item. With all the warm plates laid out, one team member starts by portioning out the food that will stay hot the longest — a bed of fettuccini — and serving it on every plate. Then a second follows, serving the garlic spinach on the side. A third adds the sliced chicken breast to the fettuccini, and a fourth follows with the alfredo sauce. If there are only two in a team, one person serves the fettuccini and the second person serves the spinach. While the spinach is being served, number one follows with the chicken breast and number two finishes with the sauce. With this style of plating, the food can be served to the guests quickly and in a steady stream. Food can be unpredictable, so be prepared for some inconsistencies with the plate presentation. Don't allow the servers to concern themselves if the dollop of cream on one dessert plate isn't as perfect as the dollop on another; the wedding will go on. The more you fuss with the food, the colder it gets.

If serving ice cream or sorbet in addition to the wedding cake, remove it from the freezer at least a half hour before serving. The larger the container, the longer it will take to soften. Have more than one ice cream scoop sitting in hot water, and alternate them to make scooping easier. If you have plenty of freezer space, pre-scoop the ice cream up to a day in advance and place on cookie sheets. Store covered in the freezer.

## HIRING CULINARY HELPERS

Even if you spend most of your parties either slaving away in the kitchen or making drinks to serve your guests, do not consider continuing in these habits on your wedding day! You might want to consider hiring a waiter or chef for the evening. An extra pair of hands can make all the difference at even the smallest gathering.

A staffing agency should be able to provide both waiters and chefs. Look under Bartending Services or Party Staffing in the yellow pages, or contact cooking schools or colleges with hospitality programs. Students may be able to apply the time worked to their externships. Some restaurant waiters and chefs may be available for private parties as well. And don't forget to enlist the help of teenagers, family, friends, and volunteers. If your family and friends are helping, remember that they are not there to be your servants — you get what you pay for.

The main difference between hiring from an agency and hiring on your own is that the agency will provide all the necessary insurance and legal documentation. If you hire someone privately, you may be responsible if that person becomes injured while in your employ. Check with your local employment office for legal requirements.

If you feel uncomfortable hiring a stranger sight-unseen, arrange a short meeting with him or her well in advance of the wedding. Is his appearance suitable? How many events has he worked? Does he have references? Discuss the structure of the wedding, go over the food, and describe the ingredients briefly: "The guests will arrive from the ceremony around 7:00 p.m.; we will have cocktails for an hour and then move into the dining room. The first course will be at 8:15, followed by the main course at 8:30. We'll then serve coffee and cut the cake."

Arrange an area for the wait staff or kitchen help to change their clothes and park their cars. Be specific with your instructions for dress code, appearance, and conduct.

A server will alleviate some of the pressure, especially if you are one of those entertaining whirlwinds that does absolutely everything for the party except harvesting grain to make the bread. Use a waiter to take over completely for the entire day of the wedding, including the preparation before and the clean-up after. Give the waiter a to-do list

## HOW MANY GUESTS PER SERVER?

The following is a guideline as to how many servers to hire:

• Butler-style reception: one server for 20 to 25 guests

• Buffet, assisted: one server for 40 guests

• Buffet, self-service: one server for 60 guests

• Sit-down dinner, formal: one server for 10 guests

• Sit-down dinner, informal: one server for 20 to 25 guests

• Open bar: one bartender and one wine server for 50 to 60 guests

of last-minute jobs while you get ready (and get married!), and make sure he can accomplish them without any assistance. The list could include heating up appetizers, lighting candles, filling up the ice bucket, or opening the red wine. Give him phone numbers, and make introductions with friends and family who are helping with the wedding in case something goes awry, and make sure everyone knows exactly how to pull off your vision. It might be helpful to keep notes for the staff over the months that you're planning. Discuss the locations of extra food and utensils, proper clean-up, what sort of time frame to expect, and who will pay him for the job — you'll be busy making your big getaway!

An experienced chef or kitchen helper can be a great investment to any event. You and your culinary friends and family can make as much food as you want before the event, then let the chef cook the last-minute items, allowing you all to enjoy the festivities. Or, arrange for the chef to come earlier in the day or even the day before to help you prepare the food. If you and only you can make your famous wild mushroom lasagna, then make it and freeze it ahead of time, but have him slice the bread, reheat the pans, clean the vegetables, wash the salad, make the dressing, and clean up the kitchen.

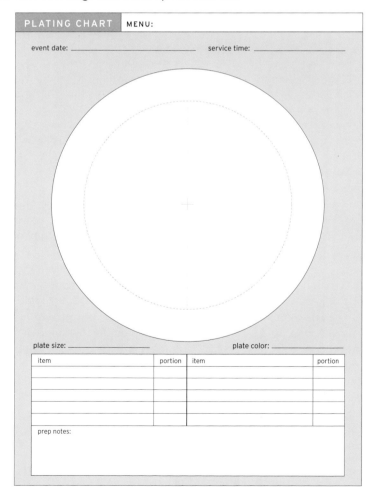

PLATING CHART    MENU:

event date: _____    service time: _____

plate size: _____    plate color: _____

| item | portion | item | portion |
|------|---------|------|---------|
|  |  |  |  |
|  |  |  |  |
|  |  |  |  |
|  |  |  |  |

prep notes:

# chapter 7
# do-it-for-less!
# wedding menus

This chapter offers eight complete wedding menus for those do-it-yourself couples wishing to take on the task of catering their own wedding (as discussed in detail in chapter 6). Each themed wedding contains a menu, a complete shopping list, plan-ahead tips, and decoration ideas including color themes and specific do-it-yourself and do-it-for-less decorating projects and ideas. Each menu includes detailed recipes and has a recommended drink (look for the individual drink recipes on page 94 of chapter 5), and a do-it-for-less wedding cake recipes and designs (found in chapter 8).

# sunrise brunch

While this menu is wonderful for brunch or lunch, you could also serve it for an early supper. The biscuits are divine.

**spring menu:**

marinated mushroom and artichoke salad

tomato and sausage frittata with fresh herbs

sage biscuits with honey butter

raspberry-orange champagne cocktail *(recipe page 94)*

bellini *(recipe page 94)*

sunrise floral cupcakes *(recipe page 224)*

## menu countdown

**1-2 weeks before:**
- Shop for nonperishables
- Buy beverages

**3 days before:**
- Shop for perishables
- Brown sausage and onion for frittata
- Mix together whipped butter and honey for biscuits

**2 days before:**
- Slice mushrooms, cucumbers, and bell pepper for salad; store separately in plastic bags
- Assemble and cook frittata; cover and chill
- Make biscuit dough; cover and chill

**1 day before:**
- Make salad dressing and marinate salad vegetables

**The morning of the wedding:**
- Chop dill and mix into marinating salad vegetables
- Bake biscuits

**1-2 hours ahead:**
- Reheat frittata and biscuits in a 275-degree oven until warm
- Assemble salad

**COLORS:** Pale and deep pink, daffodil yellow, and cabbage green will impart the gentle glow and feel of the sunrise and morning time. Incorporate a couple of intense colors such as cerise and red to add interest and drama. A softer palette would work, too: lavender, smoky slate, and palest yellow.

**INVITATIONS:** Send a simple invitation in mustard yellow or robin's-egg blue with a lace overlay or border. Or, layer several pieces of printed vellum in the hues of the wedding colors with the wedding details listed on each page. Mount on textured cardstock with a tie of antique ribbon or lace.

**SAVE-THE-DATE CARDS:** Send small boxes of biscotti or crumpets and wrap colorful ribbon around the box with a tag that reads the announcement. These can be homemade or purchased at a specialty store or café.

**FLOWERS:** Unopened, pale-colored ranunculus makes for a perfect morning bouquet while yellow calla lilies will be appropriate for bridesmaids. Branches of flowering cherry blossoms evoke springtime. For greenery, try rosemary. Bundles of white geraniums can decorate the ends of pews or the backs of chairs beautifully. Mixing younger flowers and buds with mature flowers mirrors the newness of life in early spring.

**CENTERPIECES:** Fill tall rectangular glass vases with water and add varieties of oranges, grapefruits, and other citrus fruits, both cut and whole. Float pastel-colored gerbera daisies on top.

**PLACE CARDS AND FAVORS:** Fill square Lucite boxes with wheatgrass and nestle the place card in the grass or attach to a wire and clip. These can double as favors. In addition, send guests home with assortments of morning teas, like Earl Grey or green, and tie the bundles with ribbon.

**DRESS SUGGESTIONS:** Choose a cap sleeve or another more conservative dress for the morning. A vintage lace dress would be perfect here. Go with a softer shade of white, as the morning light can make bright white look too severe.

**LOCATION:** An outdoor location will allow guests to enjoy the weather and time of day, maybe in a grove of dogwood trees or in a public garden. However, a small country chapel with stained glass windows also imparts the magical glow of morning.

**MUSIC:** Keep it light and fanciful with Spanish flamenco guitar music. Chamber music by Mozart with a string quartet or over speakers would also add to the mood.

# sunrise brunch shopping list: 1 to 2 weeks before

sunrise brunch

| ingredients | 12 people | 25 people | 50 people | 75 people |
|---|---|---|---|---|
| ✔ **dried herbs, spices, and extracts** | | | | |
| Black peppercorns | as needed | as needed | as needed | as needed |
| Cayenne pepper (optional) | ¼ ounce | ¼ ounce | ¼ ounce | ½ ounce |
| Sea salt | as needed | as needed | as needed | as needed |
| Table salt | as needed | as needed | as needed | as needed |
| **pantry items and dry goods** | | | | |
| All-purpose flour | 24 ounces | 3 pounds | 6 pounds | 9 pounds |
| Baking powder | 1 ounce | 2 ounces | 4 ounces | 6 ounces |
| Dijon mustard | ½ ounce | 1 ounce | 2 ounces | 3 ounces |
| Extra-virgin olive oil | 4 ounces | 8 ounces | 16 ounces | 25 ounces |
| Honey | 6 ounces | 8 ounces | 14 ounces | 22 ounces |
| Olive oil | 1 ounce | 1 ounce | 2 ounces | 4 ounces |
| Pine nuts | 2 ounces | 4 ounces | 8 ounces | 12 ounces |
| Quartered artichoke hearts | 2 (13.75-ounce) cans | 4 (13.75-ounce) cans | 8 (13.75-ounce) cans | 12 (13.75-ounce) cans |
| Vegetable cooking spray | as needed | as needed | as needed | as needed |
| White wine vinegar | 2 ounces | 4 ounces | 16 ounces | 24 ounces |

# sunrise brunch shopping list: up to 3 days before

| ingredients | 12 people | 25 people | 50 people | 75 people |
|---|---|---|---|---|
| ✔ **dairy, cheese, and deli** | | | | |
| Feta cheese | 6 ounces | 12 ounces | 24 ounces | 36 ounces |
| Heavy cream | 1 pint | 1 quart | 2 quarts | 3 quarts |
| Large eggs | 3 dozen | 5 dozen | 9 dozen | 13 dozen |
| Unsalted butter | 1 pound 2 ounces (4½ sticks) | 2¼ pounds (9 sticks) | 4½ pounds (18 sticks) | 6¾ pounds (27 sticks) |
| Whole milk | 1 pint | 1 quart | ½ gallon | 1 gallon |
| **meat and seafood** | | | | |
| Sweet Italian sausage | 1¼ pounds | 2½ pounds | 5 pounds | 7½ pounds |
| **fresh produce** | | | | |
| English or hot house cucumber | 1 | 2 | 4 | 6 |
| Dill | 1 large bunch | 1 large bunch | 1 large bunch | 1 large bunch |
| Sage leaves | ½ cup, plus 12 whole leaves | 1 cup, plus 24 whole leaves | 2 cups, plus 48 whole leaves | 3 cups, plus 72 whole leaves |
| Limestone lettuce | 2 heads | 4 heads | 8 heads | 12 heads |
| Plum or roma tomatoes | 3 | 6 | 12 | 18 |
| Red bell pepper | 1 | 2 | 4 | 6 |
| Red onion, medium-size | 1 | 1 | 2 | 3 |
| Small white button mushrooms | 1½ pounds | 3 pounds | 6 pounds | 9 pounds |

# marinated mushroom and artichoke salad

| ingredients | 12 people | 25 people | 50 people | 75 people |
|---|---|---|---|---|
| White wine vinegar | ¼ cup | ½ cup | 1 cup | 1½ cups |
| Honey | 1 tablespoon | 2 tablespoons | ¼ cup | ⅓ cup |
| Extra-virgin olive oil | ½ cup | 1 cup | 2 cups | 3 cups |
| Dijon mustard | 1 tablespoon | 2 tablespoons | ¼ cup | ⅓ cup plus 1 tablespoon |
| Sea salt | ¼ teaspoon | ½ teaspoon | 1 teaspoon | 1½ teaspoons |
| Freshly ground black pepper | ⅛ teaspoon | ¼ teaspoon | ½ teaspoon | ¾ teaspoon |
| Small white button mushrooms, halved | 1½ pounds | 3 pounds | 6 pounds | 9 pounds |
| Quartered artichoke hearts, drained | 2 (13.75-ounce) cans | 4 (13.75-ounce) cans | 8 (13.75-ounce) cans | 12 (13.75-ounce) cans |
| English or hothouse cucumber, thinly sliced in rounds | 1 | 2 | 4 | 6 |
| Red bell pepper, thinly sliced | 1 | 2 | 4 | 6 |
| Chopped fresh dill | 2 tablespoons | ¼ cup | ½ cup | ¾ cup |
| Limestone lettuce, washed and cut into bite-sized pieces | 2 heads | 4 heads | 8 heads | 12 heads |
| Pine nuts, toasted, for garnish (optional) | ¼ cup | ½ cup | 1 cup | 1½ cups |

 **do it ahead:**
Vegetables can be combined to marinate the night before and placed in a tightly sealed container.

 **helpful hint:**
Limestone lettuce is also sold as butter, Bibb, or Boston lettuce. Romaine lettuce is a perfectly fine substitute.

See page 184 for information on toasting pine nuts.

 **do it for less time:**
This is an easy recipe, but it does require quite a bit of chopping. If you have a food processor with a slicer attachment, you can make quick work of it.

 presentation:
For a very pretty effect, keep the leaves of one head of lettuce whole and arrange them on the bottom of your serving plate or bowl.

## directions:

1. Place the vinegar, honey, olive oil, mustard, salt, and pepper in the work bowl of a food processor or blender and blend until creamy.

2. Place the mushrooms, artichokes, cucumbers, and bell peppers in large resealable plastic bags. Divide the dressing among the bags.

3. Seal the bags and shake to coat with dressing. Let marinate for 20 minutes or up to 12 hours.

4. Just before serving, stir the dill into the vegetables.

5. To serve, place the lettuce in a deep serving platter or shallow serving bowl. Place the marinated vegetable mixture on top and toss lightly to combine. Garnish with the toasted pine nuts if using.

**serving size:** 1 heaping cup (1½ ounces) lettuce, ¼ cup marinated vegetables

## equipment:

- Food processor or blender
- Large resealable plastic bags

# tomato and sausage frittata with fresh herbs

| ingredients | 12 people | 25 people | 50 people | 75 people |
|---|---|---|---|---|
| Olive oil | 1 tablespoon | 2 tablespoons | ¼ cup | ⅓ cup plus 1 tablespoon |
| Sweet Italian sausage | 1¼ pounds | 2½ pounds | 5 pounds | 7½ pounds |
| Red onion, finely chopped | ½ medium-size | 1 medium-size | 2 medium-size | 3 medium-size |
| Feta cheese, crumbled | 6 ounces | 12 ounces | 24 ounces | 36 ounces |
| Fresh sage leaves | ¼ cup, chopped, plus 12 whole sage leaves for garnish | ½ cup, chopped, plus 24 whole sage leaves for garnish | 1 cup, plus 48 whole sage leaves for garnish | 1½ cups, plus 72 whole sage leaves for garnish |
| Eggs, large | 24 | 48 | 96 | 144 |
| Whole milk | 1½ cups | 3 cups | 6 cups | 9 cups |
| Sea salt | 1 teaspoon | 2 teaspoons | 4 teaspoons | 6 teaspoons |
| Freshly ground black pepper | ½ teaspoon | 1 teaspoon | 2 teaspoons | 3 teaspoons |
| Plum or roma tomatoes, sliced | 3 | 6 | 12 | 18 |

## equipment:

- 13 x 9 x 2-inch baking dishes
- Wooden spoon
- Large skillet
- Food processor or blender

## directions:

1. Preheat the oven to 325 degrees.

2. Evenly grease with olive oil one 13 x 9 x 2-inch baking dish for every 12 servings and set aside.

3. Working in batches, brown the sausage in a large skillet set over medium-high heat, breaking the sausage apart into small pieces as it cooks. Divide the cooked sausage evenly among the prepared baking dishes.

4. Sauté the onions in the same skillet until soft, about 5 minutes. Add the cooked onions to the baking dishes, and scatter the feta cheese and chopped sage over the onions.

5. Working in batches, place the eggs, milk, salt, and pepper into the work bowl of a food processor or blender and pulse until thoroughly combined, about 5 to 10 seconds. Pour over the sausage mixture, dividing evenly among the baking dishes.

6. Arrange the tomato slices and whole sage leaves on top of the frittata and bake for 55 to 60 minutes, or until the top is golden brown and the eggs are set (the frittata will puff slightly in the center). If the top of the frittata browns too quickly, cover the dish loosely with foil and continue baking until done.

7. Cut into squares and place on a serving platter. The frittata can be served hot, warm, or at room temperature.

serving size: 2½ x 3-inch piece

## do it ahead:

The frittata can be made entirely ahead of time. Let the finished frittata cool to room temperature, cover tightly in plastic wrap, then refrigerate for up to 2 days. To freeze, wrap also with foil, then freeze for up to 1 week. Serve hot, warm, or at room temperature.

## helpful hint:

Turkey sausage is a fine substitute for pork sausage. For a bit of heat, use half hot Italian sausage and half sweet Italian sausage. If sage is unavailable, you can substitute marjoram or oregano.

# sage biscuits with honey butter

| ingredients | 12 people | 25 people | 50 people | 75 people |
|---|---|---|---|---|
| **For the biscuits:** | | | | |
| Vegetable cooking spray | as needed | as needed | as needed | as needed |
| All-purpose flour | 4 cups | 8 cups | 16 cups | 24 cups |
| Baking powder | 2 tablespoons | ¼ cup | ½ cup | ¾ cup |
| Salt | 2 teaspoons | 1 tablespoon plus 1 teaspoon | 2 tablespoons, plus 2 teaspoons | ¼ cup |
| Cayenne pepper (optional) | ½ teaspoon | 1 teaspoon | 2 teaspoons | 1 tablespoon |
| Unsalted butter, chilled and cut into small pieces | 12 ounces (3 sticks) | 1½ pounds (6 sticks) | 3 pounds (12 sticks) | 4 ½ pounds (18 sticks) |
| Fresh sage leaves, chopped | ¼ cup | ½ cup | 1 cup | 1½ cups |
| Heavy cream | 1½ cups | 3 cups | 6 cups | 9 cups |
| Egg yolk, large | 1 | 2 | 4 | 6 |
| Milk | 1 tablespoon | 2 tablespoons | ¼ cup | 6 tablespoons |
| **For the honey butter:** | | | | |
| Unsalted butter, at room temperature | 6 ounces (1½ sticks) | 12 ounces (3 sticks) | 1½ pounds (6 sticks) | 36 ounces (9 sticks) |
| Honey | ⅓ cup plus, 1 tablespoon | ¾ cup | 1½ cups | 2¼ cups |

### do it ahead:
The biscuit dough can be made up to 1 month ahead if well wrapped in plastic wrap, then in foil, and frozen. Cut biscuits into desired shapes before freezing, and add an extra 1 to 2 minutes to the baking time.

### presentation:
Use a heart-shaped cutter for extra romance.

## directions:

1. Preheat the oven to 425 degrees. Lightly spray baking sheets with cooking spray.

2. Sift the flour, baking powder, salt, and cayenne together in a large bowl, in batches if necessary.

3. Using a pastry cutter or your fingertips, cut or rub the pieces of butter into the flour mixture until the mixture resembles very coarse meal. Be careful not to overwork the butter.

4. Gently incorporate the chopped sage.

5. Stir in the cream with a fork until the mixture is just moistened.

6. Transfer the mixture to a lightly floured work surface and briefly knead just until it comes together to form a dough.

serving size: 2 biscuits and 1½ tablespoons honey butter

# sage biscuits with honey butter (continued)

## equipment:

- Baking sheets
- Sifter
- Large mixing bowl
- Rolling pin
- 2-inch square or round cutter
- Pastry brush
- Electric hand mixer

## directions: (continued)

7. Roll the dough out to about ¾ inch thick.

8. Cut into 2-inch squares or, using a 2-inch round cutter, cut out the biscuits and place 1 inch apart on prepared baking sheets.

9. Reroll the scraps and cut out remaining biscuits, taking care not to let the dough get too warm from your hands.

10. The biscuits can be tightly covered and refrigerated at this point for up to 2 days or frozen up to several weeks.

11. If freezing, store on the baking sheets until frozen, then, if space is an issue, you can transfer to an airtight container or a resealable plastic bag. To bake, place the frozen biscuits on baking sheets, cover with plastic wrap, and thaw in the refrigerator a day before the event. Keep refrigerated until ready to bake.

12. Combine the egg yolks and milk in a small bowl and beat with a fork to mix. Brush the yolk mixture on the tops of the biscuits. Bake until lightly golden and cooked through, about 16 to19 minutes.

13. When ready to serve, whip the room-temperature butter with an electric mixer until light and fluffy, about 3 minutes. Drizzle the honey over the whipped butter and beat to combine. Serve with the warm biscuits.

# in full bloom

To make this menu as easy as possible, all the dishes can be served (and taste delicious!) at room temperature.

**spring menu:**

roasted salmon with lemon-almond pesto

haricots verts with wild mushrooms and pine nuts

garden salad *(purchased)*

rice pilaf *(purchased)*

artisan breads with butter *(purchased)*

chocolate-dipped strawberries with whipped cream

mimosa *(recipe page 94)*

in full bloom pink flower cupcakes *(recipe page 226)*

## menu countdown

**1-2 weeks before:**
- Shop for nonperishables
- Buy beverages

**2 days before:**
- Shop for perishables
- Make Lemon-Almond Pesto

**1 day before:**
- Cut lemon wedges for Roasted Salmon garnish
- Blanch haricots verts
- Make Chocolate-Dipped Strawberries

**1-2 hours ahead:**
- If serving at room temperature, prepare salmon on roasting pans, roast, and cover
- Assemble garden salad
- Slice and arrange artisan breads
- Whip cream

**Just before serving:**
- If serving hot, roast salmon and keep warm

**COLORS:** Pastel and watercolor-like shades including meringue yellow, pale pink, sage green, and sky blue. Punches of brighter colors like spring green and tomato red will keep the palette from looking overly diluted.

**INVITATIONS:** Find wallpaper or fabric samples with a floral or springlike prints and adhere to the backs of invitations. Cut with scalloped scissors or with pinking shears. Mix and match by pairing with strips of seersucker or plaid ribbon.

**SAVE-THE-DATE CARDS:** Send a packet of seeds with the announcement printed on the outside of the envelope. As the plant grows, it will remind the invitee of the upcoming event.

**FLOWERS:** Mix different textures, shapes, and sizes in abundant bouquets to impart the newness and hope of spring — the best value would be to concentrate on daisies, pastel-colored roses, and lilies but incorporate blue hydrangeas, pale daffodils, and calla lilies for variety and artistry.

**CENTERPIECES:** Find antique terrariums and fill with green, blossoming plants (real or faux) on the inside. Attach silk and wire butterflies inside and out. Finish by surrounding the perimeter with small twigs and white or silver spray-painted leaves. Begin growing wheatgrass or miniature rose bushes in antique tubs and containers well in advance of the wedding, and add wired silk butterflies or cut flowers in colored glass bottles.

**PLACE CARDS AND FAVORS:** Using origami paper, make paper flowers with directions found on the Internet, or purchase at an Asian specialty store. Put name cards on top. Place little nests with imitation sparrow or robin's eggs in teacups and saucers from the flea market. Nestle the place cards in the nest. Guests can use this for coffee and take home a one-of-a-kind favor.

**DRESS SUGGESTIONS:** Keep the mood of levity with chiffon and organza over heavier silks and embroidery. You might even incorporate a colored layer or overlay with your otherwise white dress, or wear a beautiful spring color. Have bridesmaids loosely pull their hair back and weave in colorful grosgrain ribbon. Construct a daisy tiara or wand for the flower girl.

**LOCATION SUGGESTIONS:** Arboretums and private gardens are always a great option, but an infrequently visited public garden or park is also a quaint place for a gathering.

**MUSIC:** Light and romantic tunes by Tony Bennett or Frank Sinatra will fit the bill. For a more contemporary play list, Norah Jones, Kings of Convenience, and Air will complement the carefree mood and spring season.

# in full bloom shopping list: **1 to 2 weeks before**

| ingredients | **12** people | **25** people | **50** people | **75** people |
|---|---|---|---|---|
| ✔ **dried herbs, spices, and extracts** | | | | |
| Almond extract | ½ ounce | ½ ounce | ½ ounce | ½ ounce |
| Black peppercorns | as needed | as needed | as needed | as needed |
| Sea salt | as needed | as needed | as needed | as needed |
| Table salt | as needed | as needed | as needed | as needed |
| **pantry items and dry goods** | | | | |
| Extra-virgin olive oil | 12 ounces | 20 ounces | 40 ounces | 60 ounces |
| Good-quality dark chocolate | 12 ounces | 24 ounces | 48 ounces | 72 ounces |
| Granulated sugar | 1 ounce | 3 ounces | 6 ounces | 8 ounces |
| Pine nuts | 3 ounces | 6 ounces | 12 ounces | 18 ounces |
| Unsalted roasted whole almonds | 12 ounces | 24 ounces | 72 ounces | 108 ounces |
| Vegetable shortening | 1 ounce | 1 ounce | 2 ounces | 3 ounces |

| ingredients | 12 people | 25 people | 50 people | 75 people |
|---|---|---|---|---|
| ✔ dairy, cheese, and deli | | | | |
| Unsalted butter | 2 ounces (½ stick) | 4 ounces (1 stick) | 8 ounces (2 sticks) | 12 ounces (3 sticks) |
| Heavy whipping cream | 1 half-pint | 1 pint | 1 quart | 1 quart plus 1 half-pint |
| meat and seafood | | | | |
| Salmon, whole sides with skin on | 4 pounds | 8½ to 9 pounds | 17 to 18 pounds | 25 to 26 pounds |
| fresh produce | | | | |
| Flat-leaf parsley | 1 small bunch | 2 small bunches | 4 small bunches | 6 small bunches |
| Garlic | 1 head | 2 heads | 4 heads | 6 heads |
| Haricots verts | 2½ pounds | 5 pounds | 10 pounds | 15 pounds |
| Large strawberries | 24 | 50 | 100 | 150 |
| Lemons | 9 | 19 | 38 | 57 |
| Mushrooms (any combination) | 8 ounces | 1 pound | 2 pounds | 3 pounds |

# roasted salmon

| ingredients | 12 people | 25 people | 50 people | 75 people |
|---|---|---|---|---|
| Extra-virgin olive oil | ½ cup, divided | ¾ cup, divided | 1½ cups, divided | 2¼ cups, divided |
| Salmon, whole sides with skin on | 4 pounds | 8½ to 9 pounds | 17 to 18 pounds | 25 to 26 pounds |
| Sea salt | to taste | to taste | to taste | to taste |
| Freshly ground black pepper | to taste | to taste | to taste | to taste |
| Lemons, cut into wedges for garnish | 4 | 8 | 16 | 24 |
| Lemon-Almond Pesto | (recipe follows) | (recipe follows) | (recipe follows) | (recipe follows) |

### do it ahead:
This dish can be served hot, or made the day before and served at room temperature or chilled.

### helpful hint:
You can make this with salmon fillets instead of whole sides of salmon for a sit-down plated meal. Buy fillets that are about 5 ounces each in weight. Leaving the skin on the salmon makes it easier to transfer to serving plates. However, if you can't find salmon with the skin on, the taste will not suffer.

### do it for less money:
Chicken breasts make an inexpensive substitute for the salmon, and are just as agreeable to the Lemon-Almond Pesto.

## directions:

1. Preheat the oven to 450 degrees.

2. Line large baking dishes (or baking sheets with shallow sides) with heavy-duty aluminum foil and liberally coat with half of the olive oil.

3. Place the salmon, skin-side down, on the baking dishes and drizzle with the remaining olive oil. Generously season the salmon with salt and pepper.

4. Place in the oven and roast until salmon has just cooked through, 12 to 15 minutes, depending upon thickness. To test doneness, insert a fork in the thickest part and twist; if the flesh flakes easily with just a little resistance, it is done.

5. Serve the salmon hot, at room temperature, or chilled, with pesto on the side or spooned on top. Garnish with lemon wedges.

serving size: 5 ounces

## equipment:
- Large baking dishes or rimmed baking sheets
- Aluminum foil

# lemon-almond pesto

| ingredients | 12 people | 25 people | 50 people | 75 people |
|---|---|---|---|---|
| Extra-virgin olive oil | 1 tablespoon, plus ¾ cup, divided | 2 tablespoons, plus 1½ cups, divided | ¼ cup, plus 3 cups, divided | ⅓ cup, plus 4½ cups, divided |
| Garlic, peeled and coarsely chopped | 1 head | 2 heads | 4 heads | 6 heads |
| Flat-leaf parsley, coarsely chopped | ¾ cup | 1½ cups | 3 cups | 4 cups |
| Unsalted roasted whole almonds | 12 ounces | 24 ounces | 48 ounces | 72 ounces |
| Freshly squeezed lemon juice | ½ cup (2 to 3 medium lemons), plus more to taste | 1 cup (4 to 6 medium lemons), plus more to taste | 2 cups (8 to 12 medium lemons), plus more to taste | 3 cups (12 to 18 medium lemons), plus more to taste |
| Sea salt | to taste | to taste | to taste | to taste |
| Freshly ground black pepper | to taste | to taste | to taste | to taste |
| Lemon zest | from 1 lemon | from 3 lemons | from 6 lemons | from 9 lemons |

## equipment:
- Citrus juicer
- Citrus zester
- Medium sauté pan
- Food processor

## directions:

1. Heat the smaller amount of olive oil in a sauté pan over medium-low heat.

2. Add the garlic and cook, stirring occasionally, until the garlic is lightly golden but not browned, about 5 minutes. Place the garlic in the work bowl of a food processor.

3. Working in batches if necessary, add the parsley, almonds, lemon juice, and remaining olive oil to the work bowl of the food processor. Pulse until the mixture is finely chopped, scraping down the sides of work bowl from time to time, until the mixture resembles a chunky paste. Add more olive oil if necessary.

4. Taste the pesto and adjust the seasoning by adding salt and pepper. Stir in the lemon zest.

5. Place in an airtight container and refrigerate for up to 2 days.

6. Bring to room temperature and stir before serving.

## helpful hint:
For extra nuttiness, toast the almonds before processing. Bake in a 350-degree oven for 10 to 15 minutes, stirring occasionally, or in a dry pan on the stove. The generous amount of garlic in this recipe will be warmly welcomed by your wedding guests, as its flavor will mellow and sweeten with cooking. Freshly squeezed lemon juice gives this pesto its sparkle, so don't substitute bottled juice.

## presentation:

For a very fancy — and drip-free — presentation, put the pesto in a piping bag fitted with a large tip and pipe a curling wave or swirl of pesto down the center of each side of salmon.

## do it ahead:
This pesto can be made up to 2 days in advance. Store in an airtight container and refrigerate. Bring to room temperature before serving.

serving size: 1 to 2 tablespoons

# haricots verts with wild mushrooms and pine nuts

| ingredients | 12 people | 25 people | 50 people | 75 people |
|---|---|---|---|---|
| Haricots verts, trimmed | 2½ pounds | 5 pounds | 10 pounds | 15 pounds |
| Mushrooms, sliced (use any combination of button, cremini, shiitake, chanterelle, porcini, or oyster) | 8 ounces | 1 pound | 2 pounds | 3 pounds |
| Unsalted butter | 2 ounces (½ stick) | 4 ounces (1 stick) | 1 cup (2 sticks) | 12 ounces (3 sticks) |
| Salt | to taste | to taste | to taste | to taste |
| Freshly ground black pepper | to taste | to taste | to taste | to taste |
| Pine nuts, toasted | 3 ounces | 6 ounces | 12 ounces | 18 ounces |

### helpful hint:

Haricots verts are thin, snappy French green beans. They cook much faster than the more common blue lake variety, which is two to three times the size of haricots verts. You can certainly use blue lake green beans; just cut them in half before cooking. You will also need to blanch them in boiling water for 4 to 5 minutes before sautéing. You can also substitute asparagus for the green beans if they are in season. See page 184 for toasting pine nuts.

### do it ahead:

Blanch the haricots verts the day before, then run cold water over them to stop the cooking. Sauté them in melted butter just before serving.

## directions:

1. Fill a large pot with salted water and bring to a boil over high heat.

2. Working in batches if necessary, add the haricots verts to the pot and let the water come back up to a boil; cook for 1 minute.

3. Drain, then run cold water over the beans to stop the cooking, and then drain again. The haricot verts can be prepared up to this point a day in advance.

4. Melt a tablespoon of butter in a large sauté pan.

5. Working in batches if necessary, add the mushrooms and sauté over medium-high heat until they have released their liquid and are starting to brown, about 5 minutes. Remove the mushrooms from the pan and reserve.

6. Working in batches, melt the remaining butter in the sauté pan. Add the haricots verts and sauté until heated through, about 4 minutes. Stir in the reserved mushrooms.

7. Season with salt and pepper, and sprinkle with the toasted pine nuts.

## equipment:

- Large pot
- Colander
- Large sauté pan

serving size: about 3 ounces

# chocolate-dipped strawberries with whipped cream

| ingredients | 12 people | 25 people | 50 people | 75 people |
|---|---|---|---|---|
| Fresh strawberries, preferably with stems, rinsed and dried completely | 24 large | 50 large | 100 large | 150 large |
| Good-quality dark chocolate | 12 ounces | 24 ounces | 48 ounces | 72 ounces |
| Vegetable shortening | 2 teaspoons | 1 tablespoon, plus 1 teaspoon | 2 tablespoons, plus 2 teaspoons | 4 tablespoons |
| Heavy whipping cream | ¾ cup | 1½ cups | 3 cups | 4½ cups |
| Granulated sugar | 3 tablespoons | ⅓ cup | ⅔ cup | 1 cup |
| Almond extract | ½ teaspoon | 1 teaspoon | 2 teaspoons | 1 tablespoon |

## equipment:

- Baking sheets
- Waxed paper
- Medium sauté pan
- Heavy saucepan or double boiler
- Silicone spatula or wooden spoon
- Electric hand or stand mixer

## directions:

1. Line baking sheets with waxed paper. Place the chocolate and shortening in a heavy saucepan over very low heat or in a double boiler. Stir frequently until the chocolate has melted and the mixture is smooth. Remove from the heat.

2. Holding each strawberry by the stem end, dip into the melted chocolate. Place on the prepared baking sheets and allow to cool at room temperature for 25 minutes. Keep cool or chilled until ready to serve.

3. Less than an hour before serving, place the whipping cream, sugar, and almond extract in a large bowl and beat with an electric mixer until soft but firm peaks form. The cream will double in volume, so work in batches if necessary. Cover with plastic wrap, and keep chilled until ready to use. Serve strawberries with a dollop of whipped cream on the side for dipping.

## do it ahead:

Add to this dessert a scoop of vanilla ice cream. Place the scoops of ice cream on a baking sheet lined with waxed paper, and freeze. Once frozen, you can consolidate the scoops and wrap tightly in plastic wrap.

The strawberries can be dipped the day before if kept in a cool place.

The whipped cream can be made up to 8 hours in advance if stored in a sieve set over a bowl and refrigerated.

## helpful hint:

If large strawberries with stems are unavailable, buy 3 to 4 medium strawberries per person. Substitute any flavor extract you like for the almond. Try vanilla, rum, brandy, orange, or coconut. Do not even try to substitute baking chocolate, but feel free to use a quality white or milk chocolate bar instead of the dark. Roll strawberries in sweetened shredded coconut while the chocolate is still wet.

serving size: 2 strawberries and 2 tablespoons whipped cream

# waterside jewels

This is a picnic-style party. The ceviche is served to guests as they arrive. The sandwiches and pasta salad can be put into individual lunch boxes or baskets for guests to pick up.

## summer menu:

tropical shrimp ceviche

**parmesan crostini**

grilled chicken sandwiches with sun-dried tomatoes and arugula

**lemon-mint pasta bean salad**

cookies *(purchased)*

**limoncello iced tea** *(recipe page 94)*

cheesecake with star cookies and fresh flowers
*(recipe page 228)*

## menu countdown

**1-2 weeks before:**
• Shop for nonperishables
• Buy beverages

**3 days before:**
• Shop for perishables
• Squeeze citrus for ceviche
• Slice baguettes for Parmesan Crostini

**2 days before:**
• Make Parmesan Crostini
• Grill chicken for sandwiches
• Make Lemon-Mint Pasta Bean Salad

**1 day before:**
• Marinate shrimp ceviche
• Cut up mango, pineapple, and onions for ceviche

**The morning of the wedding:**
• Assemble sandwiches
• Individually wrap sandwiches and pasta salad and put into lunch boxes or baskets
• Complete ceviche assembly

**COLORS:** Tropical colors of punch pink, ocean blue, sea green, aqua, and sunny marigold. Temper the vibrancy with sandy neutrals or go for the elegance of all-white with colored accents.

**INVITATIONS:** Stain correspondence-size paper with tea or burn the edges with a match, and print on the invitations using a cursive or calligraphy font. Buy green and brown bottles in bulk at a flea market; roll up the invitations and stuff down the bottlenecks. Mail using cardboard tubes.

**SAVE-THE-DATE CARDS:** Make a mix CD of artists like the Beach Boys and Bob Marley, and slip it into a cardstock envelope printed with the details of the event. Ebay or used record stores are good places to look. Or, write the details in the sand, photograph it, and mount the photo on a woven mat with raffia accents or on tropical printed papers.

**FLOWERS:** Easy, draping flowers fit the mood of easy casual elegance. Use cascading flowers like bougainvillea and wisteria to embellish chairs, stands, even the candelabras. For other arrangements, lilies are an excellent place to start (tiger lilies, stargazer lilies) because of their moderate cost, large size, and visual impact. Save the pricier orchids and hibiscus as accents for your bridal bouquet, or use potted, individual orchids as elegant centerpieces that do double-duty as gifts for special guests. Cover the tops of bamboo poles with palmetto foliage and secure with raffia to mark off the center aisle.

**CENTERPIECES:** Fill large vases halfway with water and one-quarter of the way with sand, starfish, and seashells. Place on crinkled burlap. Cut the stems off hot-pink flowers and string into a miniature lei to encircle the vases. Use small pebbles or large tropical leaves to embellish. Make arrangements of driftwood, pillar candles, and white flowers for a more muted presentation.

**PLACE CARDS AND FAVORS:** Small cakes on saucers, decorated with brown sugar, will look like little sandcastles. You can mount the place cards on toothpicks and mark each castle with a guest's name. Personalized flip-flops in foam or hemp can double as footwear at the reception. Handwrite names in icing onto fish-shaped sugar cookies to use as place cards. Loop ribbon through a small hole in a sand dollar and write the name, date, and location of the wedding as a memento and Christmas tree ornament.

**DRESS SUGGESTIONS:** For bridesmaids, skip the solid colors and try a hombre or a graphic floral print. Have the groomsmen go sans tie and opt for a bright linen button-down. Guests will love the casual attire — just don't forget to inform them on the invitation.

**LOCATION SUGGESTIONS:** Find a shoreline bed-and-breakfast or a restaurant with a full ocean view. Small thatched-roof beach huts and over-the-water bungalows are perfect for intimate ceremonies. Seaside restaurants with large porches or outdoor seating would be good options.

**MUSIC:** Acoustic guitar with seaside-rock sensibilities like Jack Johnson, Jimmy Buffett, or indie band Mission to the Sea. For a more sophisticated mood, put on Brazilian jazz from artists like Astrud Gilberto and Stan Getz.

**ALTERNATE BEACH THEME:** Create a Pacific Northwest or Atlantic seaboard feel with cooler, softer tones such as chambray blue and burlap brown. String white lights along a picket fence on the beach and shift to peonies and calla lilies. Bundle pale-colored tulips or wheatgrass in small wooden boxes for clean and elegant centerpieces. Mark the entrance to the chapel with a old banana-seat bicycle decked out in flowers and ribbon. Use clean crab traps and driftwood as decoration. Dress your bridesmaids in modest silk shantung sheath dresses for a mid-century look, and bring out the big band music, Duke Ellington-style, to invite a swinging, festive mood.

# waterside jewels shopping list: **1 to 2 weeks before**

| ingredients | **12** people | **25** people | **50** people | **75** people |
|---|---|---|---|---|
| ✓ **dried herbs, spices, and extracts** | | | | |
| Black peppercorns | as needed | as needed | as needed | as needed |
| Sea salt | as needed | as needed | as needed | as needed |
| Table salt | as needed | as needed | as needed | as needed |
| **pantry items and dry goods** | | | | |
| Extra-virgin olive oil | 7 ounces | 14 ounces | 28 ounces | 42 ounces |
| Garbanzo beans | 1 (14.5-ounce) can | 2 (14.5-ounce) cans | 4 (14.5-ounce) cans | 6 (14.5-ounce) cans |
| Olive oil | 4 ounces | 8 ounces | 16 ounces | 24 ounces |
| Olive oil cooking spray | as needed | as needed | as needed | as needed |
| Red kidney beans | 1 (14.5-ounce) can | 2 (14.5-ounce) cans | 4 (14.5-ounce) cans | 6 (14.5-ounce) cans |
| Small shell pasta | 2 pounds | 4 pounds | 8 pounds | 12 pounds |

# waterside jewels shopping list: up to 3 days before

| ingredients | 12 people | 25 people | 50 people | 75 people |
|---|---|---|---|---|
| ✔ **dairy, cheese, and deli** | | | | |
| Fresh mozzarella | 2½ pounds | 5 pounds | 10 pounds | 15 pounds |
| Parmesan cheese, grated | 6 ounces | 12 ounces | 24 ounces | 36 ounces |
| Sun-dried tomato tapenade or sun-dried tomato pesto | 10 ounces | 20 ounces | 40 ounces | 60 ounces |
| **meat and seafood** | | | | |
| Boneless, skinless chicken breasts | 6 (6-ounce) | 13 (6-ounce) | 25 (6-ounce) | 38 (6-ounce) |
| Raw shrimp | 2½ pounds medium-to-large (16-20 count) | 5 pounds medium-to-large (16-20 count) | 10 pounds medium-to-large (16-20 count) | 15 pounds medium-to-large (16-20 count) |
| **miscellaneous** | | | | |
| Baguettes | 2 | 3 | 6 | 9 |
| Sandwich-sized rolls | 12 | 25 | 50 | 75 |
| **fresh produce** | | | | |
| Arugula | 3 ounces | 6 ounces | 12 ounces | 18 ounces |
| Cilantro | 2 small bunches | 4 small bunches | 8 small bunches | 12 small bunches |
| Flat-leaf parsley | 1 small bunch | 2 small bunches | 4 small bunches | 6 small bunches |
| Grapefruit | 1 | 2 | 3 | 5 |
| Green onions | 4 | 1 bunch | 2 bunches | 3 bunches |
| Lemons | 6 | 12 | 24 | 36 |
| Limes | 19 | 39 | 77 | 121 |
| Medium mangoes | 2 | 3 | 6 | 9 |
| Mint | 1 small bunch | 2 small bunches | 4 small bunches | 6 small bunches |
| Pineapple | 1 | 1 | 2 | 3 |
| Red onion | 1 | 1 | 2 | 3 |

waterside jewels

# tropical shrimp ceviche

| ingredients | 12 people | 25 people | 50 people | 75 people |
|---|---|---|---|---|
| Freshly squeezed lime juice | 1 cup (about 1¼ pounds limes) | 2 cups (about 2¾ pounds limes) | 4 cups (about 5⅓ pounds limes) | 6 cups (about 8 pounds limes) |
| Freshly squeezed lemon juice | ½ cup (2 to 3 medium lemons) | 1 cup (4 to 6 medium lemons) | 2 cups (8 to 12 medium lemons) | 3 cups (12 to 18 medium lemons) |
| Freshly squeezed grapefruit juice | ½ cup (about ½ large grapefruit) | 1 cup (about 1 pound grapefruit) | 2 cups (about 2 pounds grapefruit) | 3 cups (about 3 pounds grapefruit) |
| Raw shrimp, peeled and deveined | 2½ pounds medium-to-large (16-20 count) | 5 pounds medium-to-large (16-20 count) | 10 pounds medium-to-large (16-20 count) | 15 pounds medium-to-large (16-20 count) |
| Sea salt | 1 teaspoon | 2 teaspoons | 1 tablespoon plus 1 teaspoon | 2 tablespoons plus 2 teaspoons |
| Red onion, minced | ⅓ cup | 1 medium | 2 medium | 3 medium |
| Mangoes, peeled, pitted, and diced | 2 medium | 3 medium | 6 medium | 9 medium |
| Pineapple, peeled, cored, and diced | ½ pineapple | 1 pineapple | 2 pineapples | 3 pineapples |
| Cilantro, chopped | ½ cup, plus 12 small sprigs for garnish | 1 cup, plus 25 small sprigs for garnish | 2 cups, plus 50 small sprigs for garnish | 3 cups, plus 75 small sprigs for garnish |
| Limes, cut into wedges for garnish | 3 limes | 7 limes | 13 limes | 25 limes |
| Parmesan Crostini | (recipe follows) | (recipe follows) | (recipe follows) | (recipe follows) |

## do it for less time:
You can squeeze the citrus fruits, strain the liquid, and store in the refrigerator up to 5 days in advance or freeze up to a month. Seal tightly in an airtight container. If freezing, thaw 1 to 2 days before the event in the refrigerator. For faster work of the shrimp, buy good-quality frozen, EZ-Peel, or peeled and deveined raw shrimp. Buy mango already sliced in the produce section of your grocery store. If you can't find fresh mango, it's perfectly acceptable to use frozen.

## helpful hint:
U15 shrimp are an ideal size for this recipe, but 16-20 count might be more economical. (These numbers refer to the number of shrimp per pound. So, U15s have about 15 shrimp per pound; 16-20s have 16 to 20 shrimp per pound.) You can certainly use smaller shrimp; just buy the same total weight.

## directions:

1. Combine the lime, lemon, and grapefruit juices.

2. Place the shrimp in resealable plastic bags (only fill the bags half-full, and double the bags for security). Divide the citrus juice evenly among the bags.

3. Seal the bags, squeezing out the excess air, and refrigerate for at least 12 hours or up to 24 hours. The shrimp will "cook" in the acid.

4. After marinating, add the salt, onion, mango, pineapple, and chopped cilantro to shrimp and toss to coat.

5. Spoon the ceviche into small glasses or martini glasses and garnish with a sprig of cilantro and a wedge of lime. Serve with the Parmesan Crostini.

• Fresh citrus juice makes all the difference in the taste of this recipe. It'll take some time to squeeze the juice, but you can do it a few days ahead of time.

serving size: about 4 shrimp

## equipment:
• Large resealable plastic bags

# parmesan crostini

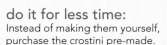

| ingredients | 12 people | 25 people | 50 people | 75 people |
|---|---|---|---|---|
| Baguettes, long, thin, sliced ¼-inch thick on the diagonal | 2 | 3 | 6 | 9 |
| Olive oil cooking spray | as needed | as needed | as needed | as needed |
| Parmesan cheese, grated | 6 ounces | 12 ounces | 24 ounces | 36 ounces |
| Sea salt | to taste | to taste | to taste | to taste |

## equipment:

• Baking sheets

## directions:

1. Preheat the oven to 375 degrees.

2. Spray the baguette slices with olive oil cooking spray to lightly coat. Turn the slices over and spray the other side. Place the baguette slices close together on baking sheets.

3. Sprinkle with a pinch of Parmesan cheese and a light dusting of sea salt.

4. Bake until the cheese is golden brown, watching the crostini carefully to be sure they don't burn. Remove the baking sheets from the oven.

5. Let the crostini cool to room temperature, and then store in airtight containers for up to 2 days.

serving size: 2 crostini

## do it ahead:

Make these up to 2 days in advance and store at room temperature in airtight containers.

## do it for less time:

Instead of making them yourself, purchase the crostini pre-made.

## presentation:

Place servings of ceviche in small glasses or cups, and nestle the glasses in trays of crushed ice to keep them cold.

# grilled chicken sandwiches with sun-dried tomatoes and arugula

| ingredients | 12 people | 25 people | 50 people | 75 people |
|---|---|---|---|---|
| Boneless, skinless chicken breasts | 6 large | 13 large | 25 large | 38 large |
| Olive oil | ½ cup | 1 cup | 2 cups | 3 cups |
| Salt | to taste | to taste | to taste | to taste |
| Freshly ground black pepper | to taste | to taste | to taste | to taste |
| Sandwich-sized rolls, sliced in half | 12 | 25 | 50 | 75 |
| Sun-dried tomato tapenade or sun-dried tomato pesto | 1¼ cups | 2½ cups | 5 cups | 7½ cups |
| Fresh mozzarella, sliced ¼ inch thick | 2½ pounds | 5 pounds | 10 pounds | 15 pounds |
| Arugula | 2½ ounces | 5 ounces | 10 ounces | 15 ounces |

**helpful hint:**
Arugula (also known as rocket) isn't always available. You can use baby spinach or watercress as a substitute. Olive tapenade also makes a delicious spread for these sandwiches. You can find it in the gourmet foods aisle, or you can make it yourself. If you don't have an outdoor grill, you can use a stovetop grill pan to cook the chicken.

**do it for less time:**
Some large club stores sell high-quality, frozen grilled chicken breasts. Buy some before and have a taste test. These are a great time-saving alternative.

## directions:

1. Preheat the grill to high (or place a grill pan over high heat).

2. Make 2 thin fillets from each chicken breast by cutting them all the way through horizontally. If necessary, flatten the chicken to an even thickness with the flat end of a meat mallet or pounder.

3. Brush both sides of the chicken with olive oil and sprinkle generously with salt and pepper.

4. Grill the chicken for 2 to 3 minutes on each side, or until cooked through. (The chicken can be grilled the day before. If grilling ahead of time, set the chicken aside to cool, then cover and refrigerate until ready to assemble the sandwiches.)

5. Spread the insides of the rolls with the sun-dried tomato tapenade. Place a piece of chicken and 2 slices of mozzarella on the bottom of each roll. Top with the arugula and finish with the tops of the rolls. Wrap the sandwiches in parchment or waxed paper if serving in individual lunch boxes.

serving size: 1 sandwich with 3½ ounces chicken

## equipment:

- Grill or grill pan
- Meat mallet
- Pastry brush

# lemon-mint pasta bean salad

waterside jewels

| ingredients | 12 people | 25 people | 50 people | 75 people |
|---|---|---|---|---|
| Small shell pasta | 2 pounds | 4 pounds | 8 pounds | 12 pounds |
| Extra-virgin olive oil | ¾ cup plus 2 tablespoons, divided | 1½ cups plus ¼ cup, divided | 3 cups plus ½ cup, divided | 4½ cups plus ¾ cup, divided |
| Green onions, thinly sliced | 4 | 1 bunch | 2 bunches | 3 bunches |
| Garbanzo beans, rinsed and drained | 1 (14.5-ounce) can | 2 (14.5-ounce) cans | 4 (14.5-ounce) cans | 6 (14.5-ounce) cans |
| Red kidney beans, rinsed and drained | 1 (14.5-ounce) can | 2 (14.5-ounce) cans | 4 (14.5-ounce) cans | 6 (14.5-ounce) cans |
| Mint, chopped | ½ cup | 1 cup | 2 cups | 3 cups |
| Flat-leaf parsley, chopped | ½ cup | 1 cup | 2 cups | 3 cups |
| Freshly squeezed lemon juice | ¼ cup (1 to 2 medium lemons) | ½ cup (2 to 3 medium lemons) | 1 cup (4 to 6 medium lemons) | 1½ cups (6 to 9 medium lemons) |
| Salt | to taste | to taste | to taste | to taste |
| Freshly ground black pepper | to taste | to taste | to taste | to taste |

## equipment:
- Large pot
- Colander
- Small mixing bowl
- Whisk

## directions:
1. Cook the pasta in boiling salted water according to package directions until just ever so slightly underdone. Rinse under cool running water, shake well to drain, and toss with the smaller amount of olive oil.

2. Add the green onions, garbanzo and kidney beans, mint, and parsley, and toss to combine.

3. Whisk together the remaining olive oil and lemon juice. Add to the pasta, tossing to coat. Season with salt and pepper to taste.

4. Keep chilled for up to 2 days before serving.

## do it ahead:
This salad can be made 2 days ahead.

## presentation:
If serving this menu in individual lunch boxes, small Chinese take-out containers work very well for holding the salad. Or use plastic cups covered with waxed paper and tied with a ribbon.

155

# sunset cocktail party

These wedding appetizers can be done entirely outside with just a grill to heat up two of them.

**summer menu:**

caviar-stuffed eggs

**blue cheese in cherry tomatoes**

goat cheese with tarragon and edible flowers

**prosciutto-wrapped scallops**

grilled oysters on the half shell

**grilled chicken satay with peanut sauce**
*(purchased from local restaurant)*

mango tequila sunset *(recipe page 94)*

**sunset polka dot cake** *(recipe page 230)*

## menu countdown

**1-2 weeks before:**
- Shop for nonperishables
- Buy beverages
- Place orders for chicken satay

**3 days before:**
- Shop for perishables
- Make flavored butter for oysters

**2 days before:**
- Make filling for cherry tomatoes
- Make filling for eggs
- Confirm order for chicken satay

**1 day before:**
- Assemble goat cheese logs
- Pick up the chicken satay
- Purchase whole oysters
- Fill eggs with stuffing
- Prepare scallops

**The morning of the wedding:**
- Clean and shuck the oysters; keep on ice in the refrigerator. Hold for no more than 1 hour
- Garnish eggs
- Fill and garnish tomatoes

**COLORS:** Bold colors against the backdrop of night are best; try tangerine orange, cobalt blue, and twilight yellow.

**INVITATIONS:** Choose a glossy finish and opt for a modern sans serif font over calligraphy.

**SAVE-THE-DATE CARDS:** Adhere a photo of the couple to a card with bold graphic flowers and a dark background; or, use something as simple as stationery with a martini glass embossed at the top.

**FLOWERS:** Any bold and exotic flowers will make for spectacular décor. Try birds of paradise, plumeria, hibiscus, amaryllis, and tiger lilies. Use candles whenever possible; they will make the floral arrangements glow at twilight.

**CENTERPIECES:** Fill rectangular hurricanes with water and fill with river rocks and koi-colored goldfish. Hang oversized, colorful paper lanterns across the room, polka-dotting the reception area with bright hues.

**PLACE CARDS AND FAVORS:** Place martini glasses at each setting and set a toothpick with olives inside. Hang the place card from the toothpick with a thin red ribbon. Let guests take home the martini glass as well as a wedding mix CD that you compiled.

**DRESS SUGGESTIONS:** Pick a festive color like fuchsia and have bridesmaids find their own dresses, which can be a little more on-trend and hip. If the wedding is near the ocean, have the wedding party layer their attire with leis instead of traditional bouquets and boutonnieres.

**LOCATION SUGGESTIONS:** A large sailboat or small yacht would fit the bill, but any deck or waterside patio will work just as well. Restaurants, lounges, and small art galleries are perfect inside alternatives and often provide a great view of the sunset. You'll need one large table or several small tables for the food, or have 2 or 3 servers pass trays of food. Guests can stand, or you can offer some scattered chairs and tables. Tall cocktail tables where guests stand are nice for conversation and are available at most rental companies.

**MUSIC:** Saturate the air with sultry jazz by John Coltrane or Chet Baker. Sprinkle in easy and familiar dance tunes by the Village People and the KC and the Sunshine Band as the night goes on.

# sunset cocktail party shopping list: **1 to 2 weeks before**

| ingredients | **12** people | **25** people | **50** people | **75** people |
|---|---|---|---|---|
| ✔ **dried herbs, spices and extracts** | | | | |
| Black peppercorns | as needed | as needed | as needed | as needed |
| Sea salt | as needed | as needed | as needed | as needed |
| White pepper | as needed | as needed | as needed | as needed |
| **miscellaneous** | | | | |
| Short bamboo skewers | 24 | 50 | 100 | 150 |
| **pantry items and dry goods** | | | | |
| Dijon mustard | 1 ounce | 2 ounces | 4 ounces | 6 ounces |
| Extra-virgin olive oil | 2 ounces | 4 ounces | 8 ounces | 12 ounces |
| Mayonnaise | 4 ounces | 8 ounces | 16 ounces | 24 ounces |
| Red wine vinegar | ½ ounce | 1 ounce | 2 ounces | 3 ounces |
| Water crackers | 48 | 100 | 200 | 300 |

# sunset cocktail party shopping list: up to 3 days before

| ingredients | 12 people | 25 people | 50 people | 75 people |
|---|---|---|---|---|
| ✔ **dairy, cheese, and deli** | | | | |
| Blue cheese | 3 ounces | 6 ounces | 12 ounces | 18 ounces |
| Cream cheese | 6 ounces | 12 ounces | 24 ounces | 36 ounces |
| Goat cheese | 12 ounces | 25 ounces | 50 ounces | 75 ounces |
| Large eggs | 1 dozen | 3 dozen | 5 dozen | 7 dozen |
| Salted butter | 6 ounces (1½ sticks) | 10 ounces (2½ sticks) | 20 ounces (5 sticks) | 30 ounces (7½ sticks) |
| Sour cream | 4 ounces | 8 ounces | 16 ounces | 24 ounces |
| **meat and seafood** | | | | |
| Black lumpfish caviar | ½ ounce | 1 ounce | 2 ounces | 3 ounces |
| Oysters | 24 | 50 | 100 | 150 |
| Prosciutto | 8 ounces | 16 ounces | 32 ounces | 48 ounces |
| Scallops, each 1½ inches across | 24 | 50 | 100 | 150 |
| **fresh produce** | | | | |
| Cherry or grape tomatoes | 1 dry pint | 2 dry pints | 4 dry pints | 6 dry pints |
| Chives for garnish | as needed | as needed | as needed | as needed |
| Tarragon | 2 small bunches | 4 small bunches | 8 small bunches | 10 small bunches |
| Dill sprigs for garnish | 24 | 50 | 100 | 150 |
| Edible flowers or petals | 1 ounce | 2 ounces | 4 ounces | 6 ounces |
| Flat-leaf parsley | 1 small bunch | 1 small bunch | 1 small bunch | 1 small bunch |
| Lemons | 6 | 13 | 25 | 38 |
| Limes | 6 | 13 | 25 | 38 |
| Red onion | 1 | 1 | 1 | 2 |
| Red radishes | 3 | 6 | 12 | 18 |

sunset cocktail party

# caviar-stuffed eggs

sunset cocktail party

| ingredients | 12 people | 25 people | 50 people | 75 people |
|---|---|---|---|---|
| Large eggs | 12 | 25 | 50 | 75 |
| Mayonnaise | ½ cup | 1 cup | 2 cups | 3 cups |
| Sour cream | ¼ cup | ½ cup | 1 cup | 1½ cups |
| Dijon mustard | 2 tablespoons | ¼ cup | ½ cup | ¾ cup |
| Sea salt | ¼ teaspoon | ½ teaspoon | 1 teaspoon | 1½ teaspoons |
| White pepper | ⅛ teaspoon | ¼ teaspoon | ½ teaspoon | ¾ teaspoon |
| Black lumpfish caviar | 1 tablespoon (½ ounce) | 2 tablespoons (1 ounce) | 4 tablespoons (2 ounces) | 6 tablespoons (3 ounces) |
| Red radishes, cut in half and thinly sliced | 3 | 6 | 12 | 18 |
| Small dill springs for garnish | 24 | 50 | 100 | 150 |

### do it ahead:
Let fresh eggs sit in your refrigerator for a week before hard-boiling them; they will peel more easily. You can hard-boil them up to 5 days in advance. Before peeling, place the hard-boiled eggs in warm water for a few minutes; the shells will slip off much easier. A day or two before the reception, peel and halve the eggs and make the egg filling. Fill the eggs with stuffing the night before and keep refrigerated. Garnish the morning of your event.

### do it for less money:
You can use any type of caviar for this recipe that you prefer. Lumpfish caviar is an excellent-tasting, inexpensive choice. Some less expensive caviar may "bleed" a little, but it tastes just fine.

## equipment:

- Large pot
- Piping bag
- Large star or round pastry tip

## directions:

1. Hard-boil the eggs, in batches if needed: Place the eggs in a large pan and cover with cold water. Bring the pan to a boil over high heat, then cover the pan and turn off the heat. Let sit for 14 minutes, then rinse the eggs under cool running water to avoid a green ring around the yolk.

2. Peel the eggs and cut in half lengthwise and remove the yolks, reserving the hard-boiled white halves. Place the yolks in a bowl and mash with a fork (or use a food processor) until nearly smooth. Add the mayonnaise, sour cream, mustard, salt, and pepper. Continue stirring until the mixture is smooth. Taste and adjust the seasoning.

3. Place the filling in a piping bag or resealable plastic bag fitted with a large star or round tip. Fill the egg white halves with the yolk mixture. Refrigerate to keep chilled.

4. Shortly before serving, top each egg half with a scant ⅛ teaspoon of caviar, two slices of radish, and a dill sprig.

serving size: 2 pieces

# blue cheese in cherry tomatoes

| ingredients | 12 people | 25 people | 50 people | 75 people |
|---|---|---|---|---|
| Cherry or grape tomatoes | 36 | 75 | 150 | 225 |
| Cream cheese, room temperature | 6 ounces | 12 ounces | 24 ounces | 36 ounces |
| Blue cheese, coarsely crumbled | 3 ounces | 6 ounces | 12 ounces | 18 ounces |
| Sour cream | ¼ cup | ½ cup | 1 cup | 1½ cups |
| Sea salt | to taste | to taste | to taste | to taste |
| Freshly ground black pepper | to taste | to taste | to taste | to taste |
| Snipped chives for garnish | as needed | as needed | as needed | as needed |

## do it ahead:
Make the filling for the tomatoes up to 2 days ahead, and refrigerate in an air-tight container until ready to use.

## helpful hint:
A tomato spoon, which looks like a small melon baller with teeth, easily removes the seeds of the tomato.

## presentation:
Buy the multicolored cherry or grape tomatoes if they are available. Serve on a bed of mâche (a watercress-like green with small, pretty leaves) frisée, or curly endive for a really beautiful presentation. If you set the tomatoes on a bed of greens for a cushion, you won't have to bother slicing off the bottoms for balance.

## directions:

1. Using a very sharp knife, slice just a sliver off the bottom of each tomato so that they sit flat and to ensure that they won't roll around on the serving tray. Slice ¼ inch off the top of each tomato and, using a tomato spoon or small melon baller, scoop out some of the seeds to create a cup.

2. Place the cream cheese, blue cheese, and sour cream in the work bowl of a food processor and blend until smooth. Taste and adjust the seasoning with salt and pepper.

3. Place the cheese in a piping bag or resealable plastic bag fitted with a medium-size star tip. Fill the tomatoes with the cheese mixture.

4. Garnish with chives before serving.

## equipment:
- Tomato spoon
- Food processor
- Piping bag
- Small star-shaped pastry tip

serving size: 3 tomatoes

# goat cheese with tarragon and edible flowers

| ingredients | 12 people | 25 people | 50 people | 75 people |
| --- | --- | --- | --- | --- |
| Goat cheese | 12 ounces | 25 ounces | 50 ounces | 75 ounces |
| Small edible flowers or petals | ½ cup | 1 cup | 2 cups | 3 cups |
| Tarragon leaves, chopped | ½ cup | 1 cup | 2 cups | 3 cups |
| Water crackers | 48 | 100 | 200 | 300 |

## equipment:
• Waxed paper

## directions:

1. Lay a piece of waxed paper, about 12 inches long, on a clean work surface. Place about 1 cup of the goat cheese on the waxed paper and roll into logs about 1½ inches across. Repeat until all of the cheese is formed into logs. (You don't have to do this if you buy goat cheese already formed into logs.)

2. Freeze for 15 minutes to harden.

3. Unroll the cheese and place on a clean piece of waxed paper. Press flowers, petals, and tarragon leaves into the surface of the cheese. Roll up in the clean waxed paper and chill until ready to use.

4. Serve on a platter with crackers.

## do it for less time:
Buy French goat cheese known as chèvre. If you buy it already formed into logs, half the work is done!

## presentation:
Green grapes (or the tiny champagne grapes if they are available) look beautiful on the serving platter with this appetizer.

## helpful hint:
To make individual servings for passing appetizers on a tray, freeze the cheese logs until very firm and slice into ½-inch slices.

• Any type of cracker or crostini will work with this recipe.

serving size: 4 crackers and 1 tablespoon cheese

# prosciutto-wrapped scallops

| ingredients | 12 people | 25 people | 50 people | 75 people |
|---|---|---|---|---|
| Scallops, about 1½ inches across | 24 | 50 | 100 | 150 |
| Prosciutto, cut into half-inch strips | 8 ounces | 16 ounces | 32 ounces | 48 ounces |
| Short bamboo skewers, soaked in water for 15 minutes | 24 | 50 | 100 | 150 |
| Extra-virgin olive oil | ¼ cup | ½ cup | 1 cup | 1½ cups |
| Sea salt | to taste | to taste | to taste | to taste |
| Freshly ground black pepper | to taste | to taste | to taste | to taste |
| Lemons, cut into wedges for garnish | 6 | 13 | 25 | 38 |

**do it for less money:**
If your scallops are smaller than about an inch across, plan on buying 3 per guest. Soak bamboo or wood skewers in water for at least 15 minutes before using to prevent burning when on the grill.

**do it ahead:**
These hors d'oeuvres can be assembled the day before and cooked on the grill at the wedding.

## directions:

1. Rinse the scallops well under cold water. Pat them dry with paper towels, and then wrap each scallop with a strip of prosciutto. Secure the prosciutto by skewering each scallop with a short bamboo skewer. Brush with the olive oil and sprinkle with salt and pepper. Place the skewers on baking sheets or serving trays and cover tightly with plastic wrap. Chill until ready to grill.

2. Preheat the grill to high. Grill the scallops for 1 to 2 minutes per side, or until just cooked through and opaque. Be careful not to overcook. Place the finished scallops on a plate covered with paper towels for a minute before removing to a serving platter. Serve the skewers hot with lemon wedges.

## equipment:
- Bamboo skewers
- Pastry brush
- Baking sheets

serving size: 2 scallops

# grilled oysters on the half shell

| ingredients | 12 people | 25 people | 50 people | 75 people |
|---|---|---|---|---|
| Salted butter, room temperature | 6 ounces (1½ sticks) | 10 ounces (2½ sticks) | 20 ounces (5 sticks) | 30 ounces (7½ sticks) |
| Flat-leaf parsley, chopped | 2 tablespoons | ¼ cup | ½ cup | ¾ cup |
| Red onion, minced | ¾ cup | ¼ cup | ½ cup | ¾ cup |
| Freshly ground black pepper | ¼ teaspoon | ½ teaspoon | 1 teaspoon | 1½ teaspoons |
| Red wine vinegar | 1 tablespoon | 2 tablespoons | ¼ cup | ⅓ cup |
| Oysters, shucked, left in the half shell | 24 | 50 | 100 | 150 |
| Limes, cut into wedges for garnish | 6 | 13 | 25 | 32 |

## equipment:
- Oyster glove
- Oyster knife
- Electric hand or stand mixer
- Grill

## directions:

1. Place the butter, parsley, onion, pepper, and red wine vinegar in a bowl and beat with an electric mixer until well combined. Cover tightly with plastic wrap and chill for at least 12 hours.

2. Preheat the grill to high or turn on the broiler.

3. Place a teaspoon of the butter mixture on each oyster in its half shell. Place the shells on the grill, oyster-side up, and cook until the butter has melted and begins to bubble, 1 to 2 minutes. Remove with tongs to a serving tray and serve hot with wedges of lime.

## do it ahead:
The butter can be made 3 days in advance. Cover tightly and refrigerate until ready to use.

## helpful hint:
If you haven't shucked oysters before, it's good to have a practice run before the wedding, or find someone to help you. You'll need an oyster glove (or a thick towel) and an oyster knife for each person helping to shuck. Be careful not to lose the delicious "liquor" or juice from the oyster.

You can broil the oysters if you don't have a grill.

## do it for less money:
Check on the size of the oysters available. You might want to adjust the number you buy, as some varieties are quite large and you can get by with 1 per person. On the other hand, smaller varieties might require 3 per person. This recipe is for large-size oysters, about 2 x 3½ inches each. If you use smaller ones, but don't increase the quantity, you can make less of the butter mixture.

serving size: 2 oysters

# french countryside dinner

This menu is great for dinner or lunch. It's served family-style; each table of guests receives its own beautifully plated serving platter of food, which makes for a wonderful (and edible!) centerpiece.

niçoise salad with garlic-herb dressing

classic cassoulet with crusty bread

cheese board with fruit and nuts

calvados martini *(recipe page 95)*

lemon cake with vanilla frosting and fresh flowers
*(recipe page 234)*

## menu countdown

**1-2 weeks before:**
- Shop for nonperishables
- Buy beverages

**3 days before:**
- Shop for perishables
- Make the cassoulet except for the last 15 minutes of cooking, leaving off the breadcrumbs

**2 days before:**
- Cook potatoes and haricots verts for Niçoise Salad; chill

**1 day before:**
- Assemble Niçoise Salad and cover with damp paper towels and plastic wrap; chill
- Clean fruits for cheese board

**The morning of the wedding:**
- Make Garlic-Herb Dressing
- Cut fruits for cheese board

**1-2 hours ahead:**
- Finish cassoulet
- Assemble cheese board

## french countryside dinner decorating ideas:

**COLORS:** Bright colors reminiscent of Provence, such as poppy red, royal purple, lavender, navy blue, and canary yellow. Mix mossy greens and ecru whites to hint at mountains and sky and to put the bright color in context. Use rustic flowered prints for linens.

**INVITATIONS:** Print on parchment paper using calligraphy and layer with speckled cotton vellum. Spritz the invitation lightly with lavender water or perfume to transport your guests through the scent of Provence.

**SAVE-THE-DATE CARDS:** Print an ancient Occitan poem on very thick, colored, cotton bond paper and insert into vellum sleeves with the announcement printed on the back.

**FLOWERS:** Pick bold flowers to match the beauty of the landscape such as peonies, irises, and sunflowers. An array of wildflowers like Indian paintbrush, evening primrose, and varieties of sage are also appropriate. Use old shutters, wheelbarrows, buckets, and window boxes as containers. Be sure to accompany flowers with a lot of greenery to impart an untamed feeling.

**CENTERPIECES:** Find antique bird cages and place mason jars filled with twigs, lavender, and votive candles inside. Decorate the perimeter with other hints of the French countryside such as grape leaves and basil. Encircle cylindrical hurricane lamps with wildflowers and ivy. Place a pillar candle inside and light before the reception begins.

**PLACE CARDS AND FAVORS:** Find antique miniature figurines of roosters, horses, and antiquated people and adhere the place cards. Or prop the cards against antique bud vases or trinket boxes. If the reception is outside, provide wide-brimmed straw hats or fans for your guests. Send guests home with fragrant French-milled soap or herbes de Provence tied in twine.

**DRESS SUGGESTIONS:** Have bridesmaids wear linen tie-waist dresses and silk scarves around their necks. For the bride, choose something European country-casual but sophisticated like a silk, knee-length embroidered dress with a sheer neckline and keyhole back.

**LOCATION SUGGESTIONS:** If you can't find your way to Provence, a barn, vineyard, or countryside inn is a great place to simulate the feel. Find somewhere with fresh air and plenty of landscape for the eyes to take in.

**MUSIC:** Try French jazz from artists like Quintette du Hot Club de France, Karrin Allyson, and Jean-Luc Ponty. Or try popular French artists like Carla Bruni and Coralie Clément.

french countryside

| ingredients | **12** people | **25** people | **50** people | **75** people |
|---|---|---|---|---|
| ✔ **alcohol** | | | | |
| Dry white wine | 1 bottle | 1 bottle | 2 bottles | 3 bottles |
| **dried herbs, spices, and extracts** | | | | |
| Black peppercorns | as needed | as needed | as needed | as needed |
| Large bay leaves | 2 | 4 | 8 | 12 |
| Sea salt | as needed | as needed | as needed | as needed |
| **pantry items and dry goods** | | | | |
| Assorted fruits, nuts, or olives | 1½ pounds | 3 pounds | 6 pounds | 9 pounds |
| Champagne vinegar | 4 ounces | 8 ounces | 16 ounces | 24 ounces |
| Crackers or sliced baguette | 1½ pounds | 3 pounds | 6 pounds | 9 pounds |
| Dijon mustard | ½ ounce | 1 ounce | 2 ounces | 3 ounces |
| Dried white beans | 2 pounds | 4½ pounds | 8 pounds | 12 pounds |
| Extra-virgin olive oil | 10 ounces | 20 ounces | 40 ounces | 60 ounces |
| Low-sodium chicken broth | 1 gallon | 2½ gallons | 5 gallons | 7 gallons |
| Oil-cured olives | 2 (10-ounce) jars | 4 (10-ounce) jars | 8 (10-ounce) jars | 12 (10-ounce) jars |
| Panko breadcrumbs | 3 cups | 6 cups | 10 cups | 14 cups |
| Vegetable cooking spray | 1 can | 1 can | 1 can | 1 can |

# french countryside shopping list: up to 3 days before

| ingredients | 12 people | 25 people | 50 people | 75 people |
|---|---|---|---|---|
| ✓ **dairy, cheese, and deli** | | | | |
| Cheese (assorted) | 1⅔ pounds | 3½ pounds | 7 pounds | 10½ pounds |
| Large eggs | 1 dozen | 3 dozen | 5 dozen | 7 dozen |
| Unsalted butter | 12 ounces (3 sticks) | 24 ounces (6 sticks) | 3 pounds (12 sticks) | 4½ pounds (18 sticks) |
| **meat and seafood** | | | | |
| Kielbasa sausage | 2½ pounds | 5 pounds | 10 pounds | 15 pounds |
| Skin-on chicken thighs | 24 | 50 | 100 | 150 |
| Thick-cut bacon | 8 ounces | 1 pound | 2 pounds | 3 pounds |
| **fresh produce** | | | | |
| Cherry, pear, or grape tomatoes | 1 pound | 2 pounds | 4 pounds | 6 pounds |
| Fennel bulb | 1 | 2 | 4 | 6 |
| Parsley | 1 small bunch | 2 small bunches | 4 small bunches | 6 small bunches |
| Thyme | 1 small bunch | 2 small bunches | 4 small bunches | 6 small bunches |
| Garlic | 1 head | 2 heads | 4 heads | 6 heads |
| Haricots verts or small green beans | 1 pound | 2 pounds | 4 pounds | 6 pounds |
| Hothouse or English cucumber | 1 | 2 | 4 | 6 |
| Yellow onions, large | 1 | 3 | 6 | 9 |
| Limestone lettuce | 3 heads | 5 heads | 10 heads | 15 heads |
| Small red potatoes | 1½ pounds | 3 pounds | 6 pounds | 9 pounds |
| Yellow or orange bell peppers | 2 | 4 | 8 | 12 |

# niçoise salad

| ingredients | 12 people | 25 people | 50 people | 75 people |
|---|---|---|---|---|
| Small red potatoes, cut into wedges | 1½ pounds | 3 pounds | 6 pounds | 9 pounds |
| Haricots verts or small green beans | 1 pound | 2 pounds | 4 pounds | 6 pounds |
| Limestone lettuce, leaves rinsed and patted dry | 3 heads | 5 heads | 10 heads | 15 heads |
| Yellow or orange bell peppers, cored and thinly sliced | 2 | 4 | 8 | 12 |
| Cherry, pear, or grape tomatoes, halved | 1 pound | 2 pounds | 4 pounds | 6 pounds |
| Hothouse or English cucumber, cut in half lengthwise and thinly sliced | 1 | 2 | 4 | 6 |
| Fennel bulb, thinly sliced | 1 | 2 | 4 | 6 |
| Large eggs, hard-boiled and peeled | 12 | 25 | 50 | 75 |
| Oil-cured olives | 1½ cups | 3 cups | 6 cups | 9 cups |
| Garlic-Herb Dressing | (recipe follows) | (recipe follows) | (recipe follows) | (recipe follows) |

### helpful hint:
Traditionally, a Niçoise salad contains tuna. We've left it out of our recipe because the main dish is so hearty. It also serves as a great vegetarian dish in this form. Limestone lettuce is also known as butter, Boston, or Bibb lettuce. You can substitute any attractive head lettuce you prefer.

See page 161 for instructions on hard-boiling a perfect egg.

### do it ahead:
Chop and prep everything 2 days ahead, then assemble the salad the night before. Cover with damp paper towels and plastic wrap, and chill until ready to serve.

### presentation:
If any specialty ingredients are available, like purple fingerling potatoes or heirloom tomatoes, by all means, use those! They will, in almost all cases, make fine substitutes and also work nicely to add color to the dish. Pass breadsticks or an assortment of fancy crackers in a basket lined with fragrant rosemary.

## directions:

1. Bring a large pot of salted water to a boil over high heat. Add the potatoes and simmer until tender but still firm enough to hold their shape. Drain and allow to cool.

2. Bring another pot of water to a boil and blanch the haricots verts for 2 minutes. Drain and let sit under cold running water for a minute to stop the cooking.

3. Divide the lettuce leaves among the serving platters, using at least 1 platter for each table. Arrange the leaves to make a bed for the remaining ingredients.

4. Divide the potatoes, haricots verts, peppers, tomatoes, cucumbers, fennel, eggs, and olives evenly among the platters. Attractively arrange them in little bundles or piles atop the lettuce. Serve with dressing on the side.

serving size: 1½ cups of salad

## equipment:
- 2 large pots
- Colander

# garlic-herb dressing

| ingredients | 12 people | 25 people | 50 people | 75 people |
|---|---|---|---|---|
| Garlic cloves, crushed | 4 | 8 | 16 | 24 |
| Champagne vinegar | ½ cup | 1 cup | 2 cups | 3 cups |
| Dijon mustard | 1 tablespoon | 2 tablespoons | ¼ cup | ⅓ cup |
| Extra-virgin olive oil | 1¼ cups | 2½ cups | 5 cups | 7½ cups |
| Sea salt | to taste | to taste | to taste | to taste |
| Freshly ground black pepper | to taste | to taste | to taste | to taste |
| Fresh thyme leaves | 1 tablespoon | 2 tablespoons | ¼ cup | ⅓ cup |

## equipment:
• Food processor or blender

## directions:
1. Place the garlic, vinegar, and mustard in the work bowl of a food processor or blender and pulse to combine. Add the oil and process until creamy and emulsified. Add the salt and pepper to taste. Add the thyme and pulse to incorporate. Chill until ready to serve.

## do it ahead:
You can make this dressing 1 to 2 days in advance, except for the thyme. Just before serving, stir in the thyme, blending well to emulsify.

## helpful hint:
If you can't find champagne vinegar, you can use sherry vinegar, apple cider vinegar, or a good-quality white wine vinegar.

serving size: 1 to 2 tablespoons

# classic cassoulet

| ingredients | 12 people | 25 people | 50 people | 75 people |
|---|---|---|---|---|
| Dried white beans, picked over and rinsed | 2 pounds | 4½ pounds | 8 pounds | 12 pounds |
| Low-sodium chicken broth | 1 gallon | 2½ gallons | 5 gallons | 7 gallons |
| Fresh parsley | 3 sprigs, plus ¾ cup chopped | 6 sprigs, plus 1½ cups chopped | 12 sprigs, plus 3 cups chopped | 18 sprigs, plus 4½ cups chopped |
| Large bay leaves | 2 | 4 | 8 | 12 |
| Fresh thyme | 8 sprigs | 16 sprigs | 32 sprigs | 48 sprigs |
| Unsalted butter, melted | 12 ounces (3 sticks) | 24 ounces (6 sticks) | 3 pounds (12 sticks) | 4½ pounds (18 sticks) |
| Garlic, minced | 6 cloves | 1 head | 2 heads | 3 heads |
| Chicken thighs, skin-on | 24 | 50 | 100 | 150 |
| Sea salt | to taste | to taste | to taste | to taste |
| Freshly ground black pepper | to taste | to taste | to taste | to taste |
| Vegetable cooking spray | as needed | as needed | as needed | as needed |
| Thick-cut bacon | 8 ounces | 1 pound | 2 pounds | 3 pounds |
| Yellow onion, chopped | 1 large | 3 medium-size | 6 medium-size | 9 medium-size |
| Dry white wine | 1 cup | 2 cups | 4 cups | 6 cups |
| Kielbasa sausage, sliced diagonally into 1-inch pieces | 2½ pounds | 5 pounds | 10 pounds | 15 pounds |
| Panko breadcrumbs | 3 cups | 6 cups | 10 cups | 14 cups |

**do it ahead:**
You can make this 3 days ahead with great results — cassoulet only gets better the longer it sits.

## directions:

1. Cover the beans with cold water by 2 inches in a large pot and soak at room temperature for 8 to 24 hours. Drain and rinse. Place the beans in 1 or more stock-pots. Add chicken broth, making sure beans are covered by 2 inches of broth. If needed, add water so that beans are covered. Divide the parsley sprigs, bay leaves, and half the thyme among the total number of pots. Tie each bundle together with kitchen twine to make a bouquet garni, and add to the pots. Bring to a boil over high heat. Reduce the heat, cover, and simmer for 1½ to 2 hours, until the beans are just tender,

## equipment:

- Large pots
- Kitchen twine
- Large mixing bowl
- Baking sheets
- Large skillet
- Roasting pans

## directions: (continued)

adding more chicken broth as needed to keep the beans submerged. Drain the beans, reserving the cooking liquid and discarding the herbs.

2. While the beans are cooking, preheat the oven to 375 degrees. Place half of the melted butter and all of the garlic in a large bowl. Working in batches, toss the chicken in the butter mixture to coat. Place the chicken on baking sheets, skin-side up. Season generously with salt and pepper and bake for 35 minutes, or until the skin is nicely browned.

3. Generously spray baking or roasting pans with vegetable cooking spray and set them aside. Cook the bacon until crisp in a large skillet over medium-high heat. Remove the bacon from the skillet and coarsely chop. Drain all but 2 tablespoons of the bacon fat from the skillet and sauté the onions for 7 minutes, or until lightly golden and translucent. Add the wine to the onions, increase the heat to high, and cook for another 5 minutes.

4. Divide the beans among the prepared roasting pans and add the thyme sprigs and sausage slices. Sprinkle with the chopped bacon. Pour the onion mixture over the beans and bacon. Add the chicken thighs, skin-side up. Add just enough reserved cooking liquid to the roasting pans to cover the beans and sausage but leave the top of the chicken dry. Set the cassoulet pans on foil-covered baking sheets and bake uncovered for 25 minutes.

5. While the cassoulet is cooking, mix the panko and remaining butter together. Stir in half of the chopped parsley, and add salt and pepper to taste. Sprinkle the breadcrumbs generously over the tops of the pans of cassoulet, and continue cooking until the crumbs are golden brown, about 15 minutes longer. Garnish with the reserved chopped parsley. Serve hot, accompanied by warm crusty rolls or baguettes.

serving size: 2 chicken thighs

## do it ahead:

If making the cassoulet ahead of time, you will need to set the dish in an ice bath to bring down the temperature quickly before refrigerating. Place a thick layer of ice cubes in the bottoms of several large pans (use pans that are larger than the cassoulet pans). Put the cassoulet pans on top of ice and pour enough cold water into the pans to come within an inch of the top of the cassoulet. Let sit for 20 minutes. Alternatively, cover the bottom of a clean sink with ice cubes, set the pan on top, and carefully run cold water in the sink to come within 1 inch of the top of the pan. Once the cassoulet is room-temperature, remove from ice bath, cover tightly in plastic wrap, and refrigerate. Do not stack the pans on top of one another, as this will keep them from cooling down.

## helpful hint:

Go all-out and use confit duck legs, 1 per person, in place of the chicken. Duck confit is made by cooking the duck in duck fat. Decadent and delicious! And expensive. You'll have to order the duck confit from a gourmet butcher shop.

Buy the best crusty rolls or baguettes you can find and warm them before serving.

You can use any type of pre-cooked sausage that you like. A chicken sausage will work, as would a spicy sausage.

## do it or less time:

You can buy garlic pre-peeled. It comes in plastic tubs, vacuum-sealed bags, or Styrofoam packages in the produce department, and the quality is comparable to fresh, whole bulbs.

# cheese board with fruit and nuts

| ingredients | 12 people | 25 people | 50 people | 75 people |
|---|---|---|---|---|
| Total of cheese, chosen from the following list | 1⅔ pounds | 3½ pounds | 7 pounds | 10½ pounds |
| Crackers or sliced baguette | 1½ pounds | 3 pounds | 6 pounds | 9 pounds |
| Total of fruit, nuts, or olives, chosen from the following list | 1½ pounds | 3 pounds | 6 pounds | 9 pounds |

**helpful hint:**
A selection of 3 to 5 cheeses is plenty, especially as a "tasting flight," and when it is part of a larger menu.

Choose cheeses based on contrasting tastes and textures; balance the sweet with the pungent, the firm with the creamy. Select cheeses made from different types of milk, starting with a goat's milk and then move on to cow's or sheep's milk.

## directions:

1. Slice the fruit as needed, and store fruits like apples and pears in water with plenty of lemon to keep them from oxidizing. Arrange the items on several serving trays and or platters. Provide plenty of cheese knives and toothpicks for the guests to serve themselves easily.

### cheese selection:

• Mimolette: A semi-hard cheese with an easy, mild flavor similar to Edam. Can be a bit difficult to find, but is available in specialty cheese shops. Pairs wonderfully with fruit.

• Montchèvre Goat Milk Brie: A very nice, clean Brie with a smooth texture.

• Petit Basque: An excellent cheese with lots of flavor and a consistent crowd-pleaser. Can be somewhat challenging to find, but can be ordered. Heavenly served next to fruits and nuts.

• Petit Pont l'Eveque: A soft cow's milk cheese that is creamy, pale in color, and mild in flavor, but very aromatic. Some might say stinky. But one man's stinky is another man's divine, and it will set off the platter nicely.

• Saint Agur: A mild, French double-cream blue cheese that will appeal to most people. Its buttery texture helps tame the pungent "blueness." Absolutely wonderful with a sweet fruit.

• Belletoile Triple-Cream Brie: When you think of the perfect French Brie, this is it. It's a mild-tasting Brie and very creamy with 70 percent cream.

• Chèvre (any kind): Chèvre has a completely different texture and mouth feel than other cheeses. It tangy flavor pairs beautifully with fruit jellies and condiments.

### cheese board additions:

• Fresh fruit such as pears, grapes, apples, and figs

• Roasted or candied nuts

• Olives, roasted red peppers, quince paste, fig preserves, cornichons or gherkins, or capers

serving size: 2 ounces cheese; 2 ounces crackers; 2 ounces fruit, nuts, or other condiments

# amber nights

This menu is easily set up for a buffet or sit-down service, and can be dressed up for a more sophisticated wedding or down for a casual wedding with a rustic feel.

## fall menu:

antipasti platters of salami, olives, artichoke hearts, and breadsticks

herbed orzo

wild mushroom torta

roasted pork loin roast with sun-dried tomatoes and olives

prosecco cocktail *(recipe page 95)*

butter cake with sugared fruit and mocha amaretto frosting *(recipe page 236)*

## menu countdown

**1-2 weeks before:**
- Shop for nonperishables
- Buy beverages

**3 days before:**
- Shop for perishables
- Prepare mushroom tortas

**2 days before:**
- Prepare orzo, except for the herbs
- Prepare stuffing for pork

**1 day before:**
- Stuff pork, but do not cook
- Prepare antipasti platters, but do not open breadstick packages

**The morning of the wedding:**
- Cook pork loin; let sit for 20 to 30 minutes before slicing
- Arrange antipasti platters and breadsticks

**1-2 hours ahead:**
- Reheat mushroom tortas and garnish with fresh thyme
- Arrange on platters of arugula or watercress
- Mix basil and parsley into the orzo

**COLORS:** Old-world terracotta, Bordeaux, ginkgo green, and harvest yellow are earthy and sensual yet sophisticated.

**INVITATIONS:** Instead of using regular paper, find one with a texture to impart a more robust, earthy feel. Embellishments around the corners such as a grapevine in gold are also a perfect accent.

**SAVE-THE-DATE CARDS:** Print a small square announcement on papyrus or parchment and adhere to the back of hammered or embellished copper coasters.

**FLOWERS:** Dramatic arrangements of sunflowers, hydrangeas, and dahlias are majestic like the landscape of Italy. Gerbera daisies, geraniums, and miniature carnations are good substitutes that are easier to fund. In addition, use fruits like grapes, plums, and apricots to deepen the European country feel, and use a lot of greenery including climbing vines and herbs like thyme and rosemary.

**CENTERPIECES:** Fill a wine decanter a quarter of the way up with water; color the water a deep purple (using equal drops of red and blue); and insert a few long stemmed white flowers, such as French white tulips and Queen Anne's Lace. Be sure not to do this too far in advance, as the flowers will take in the coloring.

**PLACE CARDS AND FAVORS:** Bundle corks together with bright metallic ribbon and nestle the name card between the corks. Send guests home with chocolate biscotti wrapped in cheesecloth and secured with twine.

**DRESS SUGGESTIONS:** Have bridesmaids wear rich, decadent tones like burgundy or marigold and drape strands of necklaces in rich citrine and smoky quartz. Skip the bow tie and have the groom and groomsmen wear white button-downs with dark navy suits.

**LOCATION SUGGESTIONS:** Try an old church, where interesting architectural elements are still intact; a quaint farmhouse; or a vineyard if you are in the Pacific Northwest.

**MUSIC:** Play operas by Puccini or hire a string quartet. If that feels pretentious or too sophisticated, opt for big band jazz by Duke Ellington and Count Basie.

| ingredients | 12 people | 25 people | 50 people | 75 people |
|---|---|---|---|---|
| ✔ **alcohol** | | | | |
| White wine, like Pinot Grigio | 1 (750-ml) bottle | 1 (750-ml) bottle | 2 (750-ml) bottles | 3 (750-ml) bottles |
| **dried herbs, spices, and extracts** | | | | |
| Black peppercorns | as needed | as needed | as needed | as needed |
| Sea salt | as needed | as needed | as needed | as needed |
| Table salt | as needed | as needed | as needed | as needed |
| **frozen items** | | | | |
| Prepared pie crusts | 2 (15-ounce) packages | 3 (15-ounce) packages | 6 (15-ounce) packages | 9 (15-ounce) packages |
| **pantry items and dry goods** | | | | |
| Extra-virgin olive oil | 4 ounces | 8 ounces | 16 ounces | 24 ounces |
| Fire-roasted red bell peppers | 1 (15.5-ounce) jar | 2 (15.5-ounce) jars | 4 (15.5-ounce) jars | 6 (15.5-ounce) jars |
| Marinated artichoke hearts | 1 (15.5-ounce) jar | 2 (15.5-ounce) jars | 4 (15.5-ounce) jars | 6 (15.5-ounce) jars |
| Marinated green and black olives | ½ pound | 1 pound | 2 pounds | 3 pounds |
| Olive oil | 1 ounce | 2 ounces | 4 ounces | 6 ounces |
| Orzo pasta | 2½ pounds | 5 pounds | 10 pounds | 15 pounds |
| Panko breadcrumbs | 1 cup | 2 cups | 4 cups | 6 cups |
| Pine nuts | 4 ounces | 8 ounces | 1 pound | 1½ pounds |
| Pitted kalamata olives | ½ pound | 1 pound | 2 pounds | 3 pounds |
| Pre-made Parmesan breadsticks | 36 | 75 | 150 | 225 |
| Sun-dried tomatoes | ½ pound | 1 pound | 2 pounds | 3 pounds |
| Vegetable cooking spray | as needed | as needed | as needed | as needed |

# amber nights shopping list: **up to 3 days before**

| ingredients | **12** people | **25** people | **50** people | **75** people |
|---|---|---|---|---|
| ✔ **dairy, cheese, and deli** | | | | |
| Heavy whipping cream | 1 pint | 1 quart | 1 quart, plus 1 pint | 2 quarts |
| Large eggs | ½ dozen | 1 dozen | 2 dozen | 3 dozen |
| Parmesan cheese | 3 ounces | 6 ounces | 12 ounces | 18 ounces |
| Unsalted butter | 4 ounces (1 stick) | 8 ounces (2 sticks) | 12 ounces (3 sticks) | 1 pound (4 sticks) |
| **meat and seafood** | | | | |
| Center-cut boneless pork loin roasts | 2 (about 5 pounds total) | 3 (9 to 10 pounds total) | 6 (about 18 pounds total) | 9 (about 27 pounds total) |
| Dry salami | ¾ pound | 1½ pounds | 3 pounds | 4½ pounds |
| Prosciutto | ¾ pound | 1½ pounds | 3 pounds | 4½ pounds |
| **fresh produce** | | | | |
| Basil | 1 small bunch | 1 small bunch | 2 small bunches | 3 small bunches |
| Dried porcini mushrooms | 1 ounce | 2 ounces | 4 ounces | 6 ounces |
| Flat-leaf parsley | 1 small bunch | 2 small bunches | 3 small bunches | 4 small bunches |
| Thyme | 1 small bunch | 1 small bunch | 1 small bunch | 2 small bunches |
| Oranges | 1 | 2 | 4 | 4 |
| Red onions | 1 | 1 | 1 | 2 |
| Shallots | 4 to 5 | 8 to 10 | 16 to 18 | 24 to 26 |
| Shitake mushrooms | ¼ pound | ½ pound | 1 pound | 1½ pounds |
| Small cremini mushrooms | 1 pound | 2 pounds | 4 pounds | 6 pounds |

# antipasti with parmesan breadsticks

| ingredients | 12 people | 25 people | 50 people | 75 people |
|---|---|---|---|---|
| Dry salami, thinly sliced | ¾ pound | 1½ pounds | 3 pounds | 4½ pounds |
| Prosciutto, thinly sliced | ¾ pound | 1½ pounds | 3 pounds | 4½ pounds |
| Marinated artichoke hearts, drained and sliced in half | 1 (15.5-ounce) jar | 2 (15.5-ounce) jars | 4 (15.5-ounce) jars | 6 (15.5-ounce) jars |
| Marinated green and black olives | ½ pound | 1 pound | 2 pounds | 3 pounds |
| Fire-roasted red bell peppers, drained and sliced | 1 (15.5-ounce) jar | 2 (15.5-ounce) jars | 4 (15.5-ounce) jars | 6 (15.5-ounce) jars |
| Pre-made Parmesan breadsticks | 36 | 75 | 150 | 225 |

**helpful hint:**
You can swap out any of the antipasti ingredients for others you prefer. Marinated mushrooms, celery sticks, pancetta, and pieces of Parmesan or Asiago cheese all make great additions.

Make sure to ask your butcher to separate thin slices of prosciutto with parchment or waxed paper to keep them from sticking together.

## directions:

1. Divide all the ingredients among several serving platters or trays and arrange attractively.

serving size: 5 to 6 ounces and 3 breadsticks

# herbed orzo

| ingredients | **12** people | **25** people | **50** people | **75** people |
|---|---|---|---|---|
| Orzo pasta | 2½ pounds | 5 pounds | 10 pounds | 15 pounds |
| Extra-virgin olive oil | ½ cup | 1 cup | 2 cups | 3 cups |
| Sea salt | to taste | to taste | to taste | to taste |
| Freshly ground black pepper | to taste | to taste | to taste | to taste |
| Red onion, finely chopped | ¼ cup | ½ cup | 1 cup | 1½ cups |
| Flat-leaf parsley, minced | 2 tablespoons | ¼ cup | ½ cup | ¾ cup |
| Basil, cut into chiffonade | ¼ cup | ½ cup | 1 cup | 1½ cups |
| Orange zest | 1 tablespoon | 2 tablespoons | ¼ cup | ⅓ cup |

amber nights

## equipment:

- Large pot
- Colander
- Citrus zester

## directions:

1. Set a large pot of salted water over high heat and bring to a boil. Cook the pasta until al dente. Drain and toss the pasta with olive oil to coat. Season with salt and pepper, and stir in the onion. Toss with the parsley, basil, and orange zest. Chill or serve at room temperature.

## do it ahead:

You can cook the orzo, drain it, toss it with a little olive oil, and store in resealable plastic bags up to 2 days ahead. Stir in the herbs on the day of the event.

## helpful hint:

If you cannot find orzo pasta, you can use riso, orecchiette, or any very small-size pasta.

To make a chiffonade of basil, stack 6 or 7 basil leaves and roll them up tightly. Slice the basil very thinly so that you have fine ribbons.

serving size: 3 to 4 ounces

# wild mushroom torta

| ingredients | **12** people | **25** people | **50** people | **75** people |
|---|---|---|---|---|
| Dried porcini mushrooms | 1 ounce | 2 ounces | 4 ounces | 6 ounces |
| Boiling water | 1½ cups | 3 cups | 5 cups | 7½ cups |
| Vegetable cooking spray | as needed | as needed | as needed | as needed |
| Unsalted butter, melted | 2 ounces (½ stick) | 4 ounces (1 stick) | 8 ounces (2 sticks) | 12 ounces (3 sticks) |
| Prepared pie crust | 2 (15-ounce) packages | 3 (15-ounce) packages | 6 (15-ounce) packages | 9 (15-ounce) packages |
| Shiitake mushrooms, sliced | ¼ pound | ½ pound | 1 pound | 1½ pounds |
| Small cremini mushrooms, quartered | 1 pound | 2 pounds | 4 pounds | 6 pounds |
| Eggs | 4 large | 8 large | 16 large | 24 large |
| Egg yolks | 2 large | 4 large | 8 large | 12 large |
| Freshly ground black pepper | ½ teaspoon | 1 teaspoon | 2 teaspoons | 1 tablespoon |
| Sea salt | 1 teaspoons | 2 teaspoons | 4 teaspoons | 2 tablespoons |
| Fresh thyme leaves | ½ tablespoon chopped, plus whole sprigs for garnish | 1 tablespoon chopped, plus whole sprigs for garnish | 2 tablespoons chopped, plus whole sprigs for garnish | 3 tablespoons chopped, plus whole sprigs for garnish |
| Heavy cream | 1 cup plus 2 tablespoons | 2¼ cups | 4½ cups | 6¾ cups |

**do it ahead:**
The tortas can be made 3 days ahead and gently reheated before serving. Leave them in the muffin tins after baking and let cool to room temperature. Cover and refrigerate until ready to reheat.

presentation:
Place each mushroom torta on a bed of arugula or watercress for a lovely presentation. Use whole or half sprigs of thyme for a simple but beautiful garnish.

## directions:

1. Preheat the oven to 350 degrees. Place the porcini mushrooms in a large bowl and cover with boiling water; let soak for 30 minutes. Drain the mushrooms through a fine sieve, reserving half of the mushroom liquid and discarding any sediment. Finely chop the softened porcini mushrooms.

2. Spray the muffin tins with vegetable cooking spray and set aside. Lay the pie crust on a flat work surface and cut into 5-inch circles, rerolling scraps to make enough for 1 crust per person. (You can use a flattened paper muffin tin liner as a cutting guide.) Press the pie crust into the bottoms and sides of the muffin tins. Bake for 10 to 12 minutes, or until lightly golden. Remove from the oven and let cool slightly.

amber nights

# wild mushroom torta (continued)

## equipment:

- Large bowl
- Fine sieve
- Muffin tins
- Rolling pin
- Large skillet
- Food processor

## directions: (continued)

3. Meanwhile, working in batches, heat the remaining butter over medium-high in a large skillet. Add the shiitake and cremini mushrooms and sauté until they've released their liquid and are starting to brown, about 5 minutes.

4. Place the reserved mushroom liquid, eggs, egg yolks, pepper, and salt in the work bowl of a food processor, in batches if necessary, and blend until smooth. Add the cream and pulse until combined. Add the chopped porcini mushrooms and the minced thyme, pulsing once or twice to blend. Divide the mixture among the muffin tins. Arrange the shiitake and cremini mushrooms on top. Bake until the filling has set, about 30 minutes. Serve hot, warm, or at room temperature.

serving size: 1 torta

# roasted pork loin roast with sun-dried tomatoes and olives

| ingredients | 12 people | 25 people | 50 people | 75 people |
|---|---|---|---|---|
| Shallots, finely chopped | ¾ cup (about ⅔ pound shallots) | 1½ cups (about ¾ pound shallots) | 3 cups (about 1½ pounds shallots) | 4½ cups (about 2¼ pounds shallots) |
| Unsalted butter | 2 ounces (½ stick) | 4 ounces (1 stick) | 8 ounces (2 sticks) | 12 ounces (3 sticks) |
| Sun-dried tomatoes, chopped | ½ pound | 1 pound | 2 pounds | 3 pounds |
| Pitted kalamata olives, chopped | ½ pound | 1 pound | 2 pounds | 3 pounds |
| Pine nuts, toasted | ¾ cup | 1½ cups | 3 cups | 4½ cups |
| Panko breadcrumbs | 1 cup | 2 cups | 4 cups | 6 cups |
| Parmesan cheese, shredded | 1 cup | 2 cups | 4 cups | 6 cups |
| Flat-leaf parsley, chopped | ¼ cup | ½ cup | 1 cup | 1½ cups |
| Salt | ¾ teaspoon, plus more to taste | 1½ teaspoons, plus more to taste | 1 tablespoon, plus more to taste | 1½ tablespoons, plus more to taste |
| Freshly ground black pepper | ½ teaspoon, plus more to taste | 1 teaspoon, plus more to taste | 2 teaspoons, plus more to taste | 1 tablespoon, plus more to taste |
| Center-cut boneless pork loin roasts | 2 (about 5 pounds total), not tied | 3 (9 to 10 pounds total), not tied | 6 (about 18 pounds total), not tied | 9 (about 27 pounds total), not tied |
| Olive oil | 2 tablespoons | ¼ cup | ½ cup | ¾ cup |
| White wine, like Pinot Grigio | ½ (750-ml) bottle | 1 (750-ml) bottle | 2 (750-ml) bottles | 3 (750-ml) bottles |

## helpful hints:

Pork might be the most adaptable and flavorful meat to serve your wedding crowd. If you are hosting any pork-haters, you can cut a pocket into a chicken breast and stuff it with the same stuffing.

To toast pine nuts, place on a baking sheet in a 325-degree oven for about 5 minutes. Watch carefully, as they can turn from toasted to burned in a flash. Remove from the baking sheet immediately, or they will continue to cook.

You can substitute any oil-cured or marinated olives for kalamata.

## directions:

1. Preheat the oven to 375 degrees. Heat the butter in a large skillet over medium heat. Add the shallots and sauté until golden, about 10 minutes. Add the sun-dried tomatoes, olives, and pine nuts and stir to combine. Remove from the heat and stir in the breadcrumbs, Parmesan cheese, parsley, salt, and pepper.

2. Insert a long, thin knife lengthwise through the center of the end of each pork loin. Turn the loin and insert knife into the other end to make a long cavity through the center of the loin. Enlarge the opening to 1 to 1½ inches across. Divide the stuffing among the pork loins. Rub the entire outside of the pork loins with olive oil and season generously with salt and pepper.

amber nights

Fyi helpful hints

184

## equipment:

- Large skillet
- Long, thin knife
- Shallow baking dishes or rimmed baking sheets
- Aluminum foil
- Medium saucepan
- Wooden spoon
- Sieve

## directions: (continued)

3. Place in shallow baking dishes and roast about 40 minutes, or until a meat thermometer inserted into the thickest part of the meat (being careful to avoid the stuffing) registers 160 degrees. Remove the loins from the baking dish and cover loosely with foil to keep warm.

4. Meanwhile, bring the wine to a boil in a medium saucepan. Pour the hot wine into the still-hot baking dishes used to roast the pork loins, stirring and scraping up all the browned bits stuck to the bottom. (Be careful — if a glass baking dish is chilled, it could break when filled with a hot liquid.) Pour the wine back into saucepan, along with all the browned bits. Bring to a boil over high heat, reduce the heat to medium and let boil for 10 minutes to reduce. Remove from the heat and strain.

5. Slice the pork into 5- to 6-ounce portions and serve with the wine sauce.

serving size: 5 to 6 ounces

# winter wonderland

This menu is easily set up as a buffet and can be dressed up or down for a casual wedding or for a more sophisticated wedding. It works well for lunch as well as for dinner.

## winter menu:

demitasse of creamy carrot ginger soup

endive salad with apples, pecans, and roquefort cheese

his and hers beef wellingtons

truffled mashed potatoes

lemon-butter broccolini

hot coffee cocktail *(recipe page 95)*

white rose cake *(recipe page 240)*

## menu countdown

**1-2 weeks before:**
- Shop for nonperishables
- Buy beverages
- Prepare soup and freeze

**4 days before:**
- Shop for duxelles and filets

**3 days before:**
- Make duxelles for Wellingtons

**2 days before:**
- Sear filets for Wellingtons
- Shop for remaining perishables

**1 day before:**
- Assemble Wellingtons
- Make vinaigrette for salad
- Combine lemon-butter for broccolini
- Blanch broccolini
- Thaw soup

**The morning of the wedding:**
- Slice apples and toss with lemon juice

**1-2 hours ahead:**
- Warm soup
- Assemble salad and keep chilled
- Assemble mashed potatoes and keep warm

**At the last minute:**
- Bake the Beef Wellingtons
- Sauté broccolini and toss with lemon-butter
- Pour soup into cups and garnish
- Plate Beef Wellington, broccolini, and mashed potatoes

**COLORS:** Mimic the winter landscape by using tonal whites such as cream, vanilla, and winter white. Whitewashed colors like sage, mushroom brown, and dove gray are also beautiful complements to true whites. Accent with silver, gold, bronze, or metallic frosty blue to spark the magic of the season. If the wedding is before Christmas, contrast with cheery crimson and forest green.

**INVITATIONS:** Print using a metallic ink and send in a Bordeaux-colored envelope lined in gold or a festive plaid. Stamp with a wax seal. Or try white paper with silver printing in a metallic pale blue envelope. Seal with a clear sticker printed with a white snowflake.

**SAVE-THE-DATE CARDS:** Find vintage or handmade ornaments online and send to invitees with the announcement printed either on the box or on a tag attached to the ornament. If vintage ornaments are not available, silver ball ornaments will also work beautifully.

**FLOWERS:** Keep the "blanket of white" idea in mind while choosing flowers. Dusty miller, silver-dollar eucalyptus, and baby-blue eucalyptus, mixed with white flowers such as roses, crocus, and lilies convey the right mood. Insert splashes of color with arrangements using brilliant Christmas poinsettias, holly, and ivy.

**CENTERPIECES:** Bundle branches together and stand up vertically, binding them together with twine or ribbon. Or purchase rosemary topiaries trimmed in the shape of miniature Christmas trees. Surround with pine cones, holly, pine needles, white candles, and even winter fruits such as pears and apples. Spray-paint with white and/or silver to give the effect of being dusted with snow. Use metallic runners on thick white tablecloths for a spark of festivity.

**PLACE CARDS AND FAVORS:** Adhere place cards onto tin stars or tin snowflakes. Serve guests small boxes of chocolate truffles with the couple's names and wedding date printed on the lid. Christmas sugar cookies make excellent favors when delicately frosted and bagged in silver or white gift bags topped with sparkly tissue paper. Tie silver bows to the outside of frosted-glass tea-light holders and then fill them with a white or silver candle. If you find a tea light with a winter or holiday smell, this makes the small gift even more charming.

**DRESS SUGGESTIONS:** Find vintage brooches from the flea market and have bridesmaids wear them in their hair. You can forego the bouquets for bridesmaids by providing muffs or candle lanterns instead. For the bride, accent the white with crimson lipstick and a poinsettia in the hair.

**LOCATION SUGGESTIONS:** Cozy inns or lodges with grand fireplaces set the mood perfectly. However, locations that showcase the winter wonderland outside are also fitting, such as art galleries and some banquet halls. The Christmas season is also a perfect time to have an intimate wedding at someone's home.

**MUSIC:** Billie Holiday and other old jazz greats such as Dizzy Gillespie and Charlie Bird have Christmas and winter-themed albums that will certainly warm the hearts of your guests. Also consider music from Handel's *Messiah* for a regal repertoire. Imagine a recessional of the Hallelujah chorus — what fun!

# winter wonderland shopping list: **1 to 2 weeks before**

| ingredients | 12 people | 25 people | 50 people | 75 people |
|---|---|---|---|---|
| ✔ **alcohol** | | | | |
| Brandy | 4 ounces | 8 ounces | 16 ounces | 24 ounces |
| **dried herbs, spices, and extracts** | | | | |
| Black peppercorns | as needed | as needed | as needed | as needed |
| Sea salt | as needed | as needed | as needed | as needed |
| **frozen items** | | | | |
| Frozen puff pastry | 4 sheets | 8 sheets | 16 sheets | 24 sheets |
| Prepared mashed potatoes | 3 pounds | 6 pounds | 12 pounds | 18 pounds |
| **pantry items and dry goods** | | | | |
| Dijon mustard | 1½ ounces | 3 ounces | 6 ounces | 8 ounces |
| Dried cherries or cranberries | 4 ounces | 8 ounces | 1 pound | 1½ pounds |
| Extra-virgin olive oil | 8 ounces | 16 ounces | 32 ounces | 48 ounces |
| Low-sodium chicken broth | 40 ounces | 80 ounces | 160 ounces | 240 ounces |
| Olive oil | 4 ounces | 8 ounces | 15 ounces | 22 ounces |
| Pecan halves | 3 ounces | 6 ounces | 12 ounces | 18 ounces |
| Truffle oil | 1 ounce | 2 ounces | 3 ounces | 4 ounces |

# winter wonderland shopping list: up to 4 days before

| ingredients | 12 people | 25 people | 50 people | 75 people |
|---|---|---|---|---|
| ✔ **dairy, cheese, and deli** | | | | |
| Heavy cream | 1 half-pint | 1 pint | 1 quart | 1 quart |
| Large eggs | 1 dozen | 1 dozen | 1 dozen | 1 dozen |
| Roquefort cheese | 2 ounces | 4 ounces | 8 ounces | 12 ounces |
| Unsalted butter | 4 ounces (1 stick) | 8 ounces (2 sticks) | 1 pound (4 sticks) | 24 ounces (6 sticks) |
| **meat and seafood** | | | | |
| Filet mignon steaks | 12 (4-ounce) | 25 (4-ounce) | 50 (4-ounce) | 75 (4-ounce) |
| Pâté de foie gras (optional) | 1¼ pounds | 2½ pounds | 5 pounds | 7½ pounds |
| **fresh produce** | | | | |
| Broccolini | 2 pounds | 4 pounds | 8 pounds | 12 pounds |
| Button or cremini mushroom caps and stems | 2¼ pounds | 4½ pounds | 9 pounds | 12 pounds |
| Carrots | 1½ pounds (about 7-8 medium carrots) | 3 pounds (about 15 medium carrots) | 6 pounds (about 30 medium carrots) | 9 pounds (about 30 medium carrots) |
| Celery | 2 stalks | 3 stalks | 6 stalks | 9 stalks |
| Chives | 1 small bunch | 1 small bunch | 2 small bunches | 3 small bunches |
| Endive | 3 heads (about 1 pound) | 6 to 7 heads (about 2 pounds) | 13 to 14 heads (about 4 pounds) | 18 to 20 heads (about 6 pounds) |
| Flat-leaf parsley | 1 small bunch | 1 small bunch | 1 small bunch | 2 small bunches |
| Ginger root | 1 2-inch piece | 1 4-inch piece | 1 6-inch piece | 1 8-inch piece |
| Rosemary | 1 small bunch | 2 small bunches | 3 small bunches | 4 small bunches |
| Thyme | 1 small bunch | 1 small bunch | 2 small bunches | 3 small bunches |
| Gala, Pink Lady, or Fuji apples | 1 | 2 | 4 | 6 |
| Granny Smith or Pippin apples | 1 | 2 | 4 | 6 |
| Large onions | 1 | 1 | 2 | 3 |
| Leeks | 1 | 1 | 2 | 3 |
| Lemons | 3 | 6 | 12 | 18 |
| Shallots | 8 | 16 | 32 | 48 |

# demitasse of creamy carrot ginger soup

| ingredients | 12 people | 25 people | 50 people | 75 people |
|---|---|---|---|---|
| Olive oil | 1½ tablespoons | 3 tablespoons | 1/3 cup | ½ cup |
| Leeks, white and pale green part only, sliced | ¾ cup (about ½ leek) | 1½ cups (about 1 leek) | 3 cups (about 2 leeks) | 4½ cups (about 3 leeks) |
| Large onion, chopped | ½ onion | 1 onion | 2 onions | 3 onions |
| Celery, chopped | 2 stalks | 3 stalks | 6 stalks | 9 stalks |
| Fresh ginger, peeled and grated | 2 tablespoons (about 2 ounces unpeeled) | ¼ cup (about 4 ounces unpeeled) | ½ cup (about 8 ounces unpeeled) | ¾ cup (about 12 ounces unpeeled) |
| Low-sodium chicken broth | 5 cups | 10 cups | 20 cups | 30 cups |
| Carrots, peeled and sliced | 1½ pounds (about 7 medium carrots) | 3 pounds (about 15 medium carrots) | 6 pounds (about 30 medium carrots) | 9 pounds (about 45 medium carrots) |
| Sea salt | to taste | to taste | to taste | to taste |
| Freshly ground black pepper | to taste | to taste | to taste | to taste |
| Chives, snipped in half | 6 | 13 | 25 | 38 |

### do it ahead:
This soup can be made 1 to 2 weeks in advance and frozen. Thaw in the refrigerator 2 days before serving. Reheat gently over medium heat and keep warm over low heat until ready to serve.

### presentation:
Serve this in demitasse or espresso cups or in tiny bowls or sake cups. To serve in sake cups, make half the amount specified below. Top with a chive trimmed in half. Balance a toasted baguette round or breadstick cracker on the edge of each bowl.

## directions:

1. Set a large pot over medium-high heat and add the oil. Add the leek, onion, celery, and ginger. Sauté until the onion is soft, about 5 minutes. Add the broth and carrots and bring to a boil. Reduce the heat, cover, and simmer until the carrots are soft, about 30 minutes.

2. Working in batches, purée the carrot mixture in the work bowl of a food processor or blender until smooth.

3. Before serving, season to taste with salt and pepper, and then garnish with chives.

## equipment:

- Large pot
- Food processor or blender
- Ladle

serving size: ½ cup

# endive salad with apples, pecans, and roquefort cheese

| ingredients | 12 people | 25 people | 50 people | 75 people |
|---|---|---|---|---|
| Dijon mustard | 3 tablespoons | ⅓ cup | ⅔ cup | 1 cup |
| Freshly squeezed lemon juice | ¼ cup (1 to 2 medium lemons) | ½ cup (2 to 3 medium lemons) | 1 cup (4 to 6 medium lemons) | 1½ cups (6 to 9 medium lemons) |
| Sea salt | to taste | to taste | to taste | to taste |
| Freshly ground black pepper | to taste | to taste | to taste | to taste |
| Extra-virgin olive oil | 1 cup | 2 cups | 4 cups | 6 cups |
| Shallots, minced | 3 tablespoons | ⅓ cup | ⅔ cup | 1 cup |
| Rosemary, minced | 1 tablespoon, plus small sprigs for garnish | 2 tablespoons, plus small sprigs for garnish | ¼ cup, plus small sprigs for garnish | 6 tablespoons, plus small sprigs for garnish |
| Flat leaf parsley, minced | 2 tablespoons | ¼ cup | ½ cup | ¾ cup |
| Dried cherries or cranberries | ¾ cup | 1½ cups | 3 cups | 4½ cups |
| Granny Smith or Pippin apple, cored and chopped into tiny cubes | 1 apple | 2 apples | 4 apples | 6 apples |
| Gala, Pink Lady, or Fuji apple, cored and chopped into tiny cubes | 1 apple | 2 apples | 4 apples | 6 apples |
| Pecan halves, toasted | ¾ cup | 1½ cups | 3 cups | 4½ cup |
| Endive, leaves separated | 3 heads (about 1 pound) | 6 to 7 heads (about 2 pounds) | 13 to 14 heads (about 4 pounds) | 18 to 20 heads (about 6 pounds) |
| Crumbled Roquefort cheese | ½ cup (2 ounces) | 1 cup (4 ounces) | 2 cups (8 ounces) | 3 cups (12 ounces) |

## equipment:

- Baking sheet for toasting nuts
- Blender or food processor

## directions:

1. To make the vinaigrette, place the mustard and lemon juice in a blender or in the work bowl of a food processor. Season with salt and pepper, and blend to combine and dissolve the salt. Add the olive oil and blend until creamy. Add the shallots, rosemary, and parsley, and pulse once or twice until combined. Taste and adjust seasonings. Store in an airtight container up to a day in advance.

2. Combine the dried cherries and chopped apples in a medium mixing bowl. Add the dressing and stir to coat well. If not serving immediately, store in an airtight container in the refrigerator for up to 5 hours.

3. Just before serving, stir the toasted pecans into the apple mixture. Divide the endive leaves among salad plates. If using 2 endive leaves per person, place the first one horizontally pointing right, and place the other beneath it horizontally pointing left. If using 3 leaves per person, add the third leaf below the others and point again to the right. Alternatively, arrange the leaves in a star shape with each "petal" pointing outward.

4. Place a comfortable amount of the apple mixture (½ to 1 tablespoon) in the pointed end of each endive. Sprinkle each plate with a bit of Roquefort cheese to garnish.

serving size: 2 or 3 endive leaves

## do it ahead:

You can make the vinaigrette and wash the endive leaves the day before the reception. Store the washed leaves in layers with paper towels in resealable plastic bags and refrigerate until ready to plate. You can chop the apples and prepare the filling for the endive leaves the morning of the party; the lemon in the vinaigrette will keep the apples from turning.

## helpful hint:

If endive is difficult to find, substitute arugula or other bitter green. Allow 1 ounce of greens (about 1 cup) per person. You can substitute hazelnuts or walnuts for the pecans, or candied or spiced nuts for an extra touch. Any blue cheese works well here, including Roquefort, Gorgonzola, Stilton.

fyi

# his and hers beef wellingtons

| ingredients | 12 people | 25 people | 50 people | 75 people |
|---|---|---|---|---|
| Button or cremini mushroom caps and stems, cleaned and halved | 2¼ pounds | 4½ pounds | 9 pounds | 12 pounds |
| Olive oil | ¼ cup, or as needed for sautéing | ½ cup, or as needed for sautéing | 1 cup, or as needed for sautéing | 1½ cups, or as needed for sautéing |
| Unsalted butter | 1 ounce (2 tablespoons) | 2 ounces (½ stick) | 4 ounces (1 stick) | 6 ounces (1 ½ sticks) |
| Shallots, minced | 6 | 12 | 24 | 36 |
| Sea salt | to taste | to taste | to taste | to taste |
| Freshly ground black pepper | to taste | to taste | to taste | to taste |
| Brandy | ½ cup | 1 cup | 2 cups | 3 cups |
| Heavy cream | ¼ cup | ½ cup | 1 cup | 1½ cups |
| Filet mignon steaks, about 1 inch thick | 12 (4-ounce) | 25 (4-ounce) | 50 (4-ounce) | 75 (4-ounce) |
| Frozen puff pastry, thawed | 4 sheets | 8 sheets | 16 sheets | 24 sheets |
| Pâté de foie gras, sliced into ¼-inch-thick pieces (optional) | 1¼ pounds | 2½ pounds | 5 pounds | 7½ pounds |
| Large eggs | 3 | 6 | 12 | 18 |
| Water | 2 tablespoons | ¼ cup | ½ cup | ½ cup |

**$ do it for less money:**
Typical Beef Wellington calls for a slice of foie gras atop the filet. This decadent addition takes an already delicious dish and makes it utterly sinful. If your local grocer doesn't carry it, substitute a smooth duck or chicken pâté or order a canned foie gras online. It's quite good and will keep for months. You can keep costs down by omitting the foie gras, and your guests will still love the dish.

**do it ahead:**
The duxelles (mushroom mixture) can be prepared up to 3 days before assembling the Beef Wellingtons. The filets can be seared 2 days before serving. The Wellingtons can be assembled the day before serving and then baked immediately before serving.

## directions:

1. To make the mushroom duxelles, pulse the mushrooms in batches in the bowl of a food processor until finely chopped, but not mushy. Set a large skillet over medium heat and add 2 tablespoons olive oil and the butter. Add the shallots and sauté until softened and lightly golden, about 5 minutes.

2. Add 2 more tablespoons of olive oil to the shallots, increase the heat to medium-high, and stir in the mushrooms. Season generously with salt and pepper to taste, and sauté until the mushrooms have released their juices. (You will likely need to cook the mushrooms in batches or have several sauté pans going at once. Use 2 tablespoons of olive oil to sauté each pan of mushrooms. Divide the brandy and heavy cream evenly among the batches or pans so that all the mushrooms can absorb their flavors.)

## equipment:

- Food processor
- Large skillets
- Wooden spoon
- Instant-read thermometer
- Medium mixing bowl
- Rolling pin
- Baking sheets
- Parchment paper
- Cookie cutters (heart-shaped or initials)
- Pastry brush

| Doneness | Seared Temperature | Finished Beef Wellington |
| --- | --- | --- |
| Rare | 110 degrees | 130 degrees |
| Medium-rare | 120 degrees | 140 degrees |
| Medium | 130 degrees | 150 degrees |
| Medium-well | 145 degrees | 165 degrees |
| Well done | 150 degrees | 170 degrees |

## directions: (continued)

3. Once the mushrooms have released their juices, stir in the brandy. When the brandy has completely evaporated, stir in the heavy cream and remove the pan from the heat. Spread the mixture in large, rimmed sheet pans to cool quickly in the refrigerator, and then transfer to an airtight container until ready to assemble the Wellingtons. The duxelles can be made up to 3 days in advance.

4. Pat the filet mignons dry with paper towels and generously season with salt and pepper on both sides. Set a large, heavy skillet over high heat. Add a tablespoon of olive oil and sear the filets just until browned on both sides and an instant-read thermometer registers 110 degrees for rare. (The filets will cook again in the oven, so it's important not to overcook them during the searing process.)

5. The filets can be seared 2 days in advance. Let cool, and then cover and refrigerate until ready to assemble the Wellingtons. If assembling immediately, let the filets cool at least 30 minutes before proceeding.

6. Prepare an assembly line for the Wellingtons: a floured workspace for rolling out the dough, the seared and cooled filets, the pâté (if using), and the duxelles. Combine the eggs and water in a mixing bowl, whisking until well combined. Line the baking sheets with parchment paper.

serving size: 1 Wellington

## presentation:

For a personalized entrée, monogram each Beef Wellington with the wedding couple's initials. Roll out extra puff pastry dough and cut out their initials with alphabet cookie cutters. Affix the letters to the assembled Wellingtons with egg wash, intertwining the letters if possible. Alternatively, use cookie cutters to top each pastry with a decoration related to the theme, such as holly leaves for Christmas. Be sure to buy plenty of extra dough for these additional touches.

## directions: (continued)

7. Working with only 1 sheet at a time, cut the puff pastry dough into four pieces. Roll out each square to 6 or 7 inches. Place a seared filet in the middle, spread with the pâté (if using), and top with ¼ cup of the duxelle mixture.

8. If topping the Wellingtons with initials or a decoration, fold one corner of the dough over the top of the duxelles. Brush the opposite corner of dough with egg wash and fold over the first piece of dough. Repeat with the remaining two corners, pressing out any excess air and crimping the seams to seal. Place the Wellington seam-side down on a baking sheet covered with parchment paper, and continue assembling the remaining Wellingtons. To decorate the Wellingtons, roll out additional dough and cut out initials or decorative elements with cookie cutters or a knife. Affix to the top of each Wellington with egg wash.

## directions: (continued)

9. For a simpler but still festive look, form the pastry into "purses" instead. As with the first method, roll out the dough, place the filet in the center, and top with the duxelles. Brush the visible dough with egg wash. Pull one of the corners up to the middle and work your way around the filet, pulling up the dough as you go and pinching it together in the center to form a "purse." Crimp the center to seal well; the dough on top will fluff out much like tissue paper from a gift bag. Place the finished Wellington upright on a baking sheet covered in parchment.

10. Cover the assembled pastries loosely with plastic wrap and refrigerate for at least 30 minutes until the dough is chilled or up to a day in advance until ready to bake. Cover and refrigerate the remaining egg wash to use before baking.

11. When ready to bake, preheat the oven to 425 degrees and gently brush the chilled Wellingtons with egg wash. Bake the pastries until golden brown, about 20 minutes, and turn the baking sheets midway if needed for even cooking. Serve immediately.

# truffled mashed potatoes

| ingredients | 12 people | 25 people | 50 people | 75 people |
|---|---|---|---|---|
| Prepared mashed potatoes, thawed in the refrigerator if frozen | 3 pounds | 6 pounds | 12 pounds | 18 pounds |
| Truffle oil | 1½ tablespoons | 3 tablespoons | ⅓ cup | ½ cup |
| Chives, finely chopped | ¼ cup | ½ cup | 1 cup | 1½ cups |
| Sea salt | to taste | to taste | to taste | to taste |
| Freshly ground black pepper | to taste | to taste | to taste | to taste |
| Unsalted butter, melted (optional) | 2 ounces (½ stick) | 4 ounces (1 stick) | 8 ounces (2 sticks) | 12 ounces (3 sticks) |
| Heavy cream, warmed (optional) | ⅓ cup | ¾ cup | 1½ cups | 2¼ cups |

### do it for less time:
We call for already-prepared mashed potatoes here. Look for fresh or frozen. You will be stunned at how good some of them taste, but you must try a variety before the big day as they're not all created equal. One thing's for sure: there's no comparison to dry spud flakes, and many guests will mistake these doctored potatoes for homemade. We've had good luck with Alexia Mashed Potatoes, which are distributed nationwide.

### do it for less money:
If you have plenty of time to spare and want to save a few dollars, make your own mashed potatoes. Peel and chop 5 pounds of potatoes per 12 guests. Bring to a boil in a large pot of water and cook until tender. Mash with a potato masher or ricer, and stir in butter and warmed whole milk until the desired consistency is reached. Complete the recipe as directed.

### do it ahead:
Prepare the recipe up to 2 hours in advance and keep warm and creamy in a Crock-Pot set on low to free up stove-top and oven space. Just before serving, stir in a splash of warm milk or cream if the potatoes become too stiff.

## directions:

1. Heat the mashed potatoes in the microwave or on the stovetop according to package directions. When the potatoes are hot, stir in half the truffle oil, the chives, and salt and pepper. Taste, adding more truffle oil, salt, and pepper to taste. (If making ahead, place the warmed potatoes in a Crock-Pot set on low. Stir in the chives just before serving.) For creamier potatoes, add the butter and cream, a little at a time, until the desired consistency is reached.

## equipment:
- Microwave
- Large Pot
- Crock-Pot (optional)

serving size: 3 to 4 ounces

# lemon-butter broccolini

| ingredients | 12 people | 25 people | 50 people | 75 people |
|---|---|---|---|---|
| Broccolini, stems trimmed | 2 pounds | 4 pounds | 8 pounds | 12 pounds |
| Olive oil | 2 tablespoons | ¼ cup | ½ cup | ¾ cup |
| Unsalted butter, room temperature | 1 ounces (2 tablespoons) | 2 ounces (½ stick) | 4 ounces (1 stick) | 6 ounces (1½ sticks) |
| Freshly squeezed lemon juice | 2 tablespoons (1 small lemon) | ¼ cup (1 to 2 medium lemons) | ½ cup (2 to 3 medium lemons) | ¾ cup (3 to 5 medium lemons) |
| Lemon zest | 2 tablespoons (2 to 3 medium lemons) | ¼ cup (4 to 6 medium lemons) | ½ cup (8 to 12 medium lemons) | ¾ cup (12 to 18 medium lemons) |
| Sea salt | to taste | to taste | to taste | to taste |
| Freshly ground black pepper | to taste | to taste | to taste | to taste |

## equipment:

- Citrus zester
- Citrus juicer
- Large pot
- Large sauté pan

## directions:

1. Place a large pot of salted water over high heat and bring to a boil. Working in batches if necessary, blanch the broccolini for 1 minute until bright green. Place under cold running water or plunge in a large bowl of ice water to stop the cooking; drain well. If making ahead, store the drained broccolini in resealable plastic bags in the refrigerator.

2. Bring the broccolini to room temperature before sautéing. Working in batches, heat a large sauté pan over medium-high heat. Add 1 tablespoon of oil and 1 tablespoon of butter for each batch, and add as much broccolini as will comfortably fit (don't crowd!). Sauté for 2 to 3 minutes, until warmed through but still bright green and crisp-tender. Toss with the lemon zest and lemon juice, and season with salt and pepper. Serve immediately.

## helpful hint:

Broccolini looks like small broccoli with very long, green stems. It is actually a cross between broccoli and Chinese kale. If you can't find broccolini at your local grocery, you can replace it with many green vegetables to great success. Broccoli, asparagus, sugar snap peas, spinach, green beans, or baby bok choy would all work fabulously well.

## do it for less time:

You can reduce the quantity of zest to match the number of lemons you're juicing. The taste won't have as bright a lemon flavor, but you'll still get the lemony overtones.

## do it ahead:

You can blanch the broccolini the day before and refrigerate. Bring to room temperature before sautéing. Zest and juice the lemons a day in advance and store in the refrigerator.

serving size: 2½ ounces (3 to 4 stalks)

# island spice

Everything in this menu can be made ahead of time and reheated the day of your wedding. The meal can also be stretched by adding orders of vegetable stir fry from a Chinese or Thai restaurant.

winter menu:

mango, pineapple, and kiwi salad

chicken trinidad with rum sauce

lobster spring rolls with sweet curry dipping sauce

jasmine rice with golden raisins

caribbean champagne cocktail *(recipe page 95)*

spice cake with gilded pineapple flowers and star anise *(recipe page 244)*

## menu countdown

**1-2 weeks before:**
- Shop for nonperishables
- Buy beverages

**5 days before:**
- Make flour mixture for chicken and store in a resealable plastic bag

**3 days before:**
- Shop for perishables
- Squeeze lime juice for vinaigrette and refrigerator
- Make curry dipping sauce — except for the peanuts or cilantro — and refrigerate

**2 days before:**
- Make vinaigrette for salad and refrigerate
- Fry chicken, cover, and refrigerate
- Cut vegetables for spring rolls and store separately in refrigerator
- If frozen, thaw lobster meat in refrigerator

**1 day before:**
- Cut fruit for salad and refrigerate
- Clean and cut romaine leaves, wrap in paper towels, and store in plastic bag in refrigerator
- Make rum sauce for chicken and refrigerate
- Make and fry spring rolls, cover, and refrigerate
- Soak raisins in rum

**The morning of the wedding:**
- Add vinaigrette to fruit salad and marinate
- Add peanuts and cilantro to Sweet Curry Dipping Sauce

**1-2 hours ahead:**
- Make rice, stir in soaked raisins, and keep warm. Reheat rice in microwave just before serving, if necessary
- Finish cooking chicken and keep warm in oven
- Reheat rum sauce
- Reheat spring rolls
- Reheat sweet curry dipping sauce or bring to room temperature

**COLORS:** Sultry crimson; metallics like aged gold and copper, pearl, jade green.

**INVITATIONS:** Use a darker tone of paper, like a turmeric or cinnamon brown, and add touches of gold around the perimeter. Also use gold script for font and use tissue paper or vellum with a swirly texture or pattern like paisley.

**SAVE-THE-DATE CARDS:** Find gold-foiled note cards and have the announcement printed in a very fancy, calligraphy font. Paste onto the backs of small square blocks of mosaic tiles found at the hardware store. Send it in a parchment paper box with a silk ribbon tied around.

**FLOWERS:** Try some exotic fragrant flowers like orchids, anise, or geranium but concentrate on striking fruits and herbs like pomegranates, mint, and figs. Tie poppy pods or chinaberries to the backs of the seats in the reception hall. Use small pots of bamboo as accent pieces.

**CENTERPIECES:** Use large, round, baked clay plates, which are easily found at flea markets, and fill to overflowing with aromatic leafy herbs such as cilantro, parsley, and mint. Set a few white pillar candles on top and sprinkle with gold paillettes and other beads. Add to the island feel by using coconut shells or tortoise-shell bowls filled with salt and pepper for a useful table decoration.

**PLACE CARDS AND FAVORS:** Find flat round discs made of steel or silver that has been hammered or antiqued. Have the names of guests engraved in them. These can double as favors, as they can be used as coasters. Another suggestion is to use miniature tasseled silk pillows and secure place cards on them with a push pin or silk ribbon.

**DRESS SUGGESTIONS:** Have bridesmaids wear simple column dresses in satin or silk shantung and drape a silk shawl around their shoulders. Adorn your hair with decorative pins or flowers. Color and drama is key, so even while you're wearing white, try a pop of color like wearing gold shoes or having your hands painted with henna.

**LOCATION SUGGESTIONS:** Having the reception at an old theater or reception hall will convey the drama and showcase the rich colors and textures you are using. Try to find a place that is a little bit darker, more mysterious, that you can light up with the soft glow of candles. If the wedding is outside, plenty of clear stringing lights will certainly set the mood without risk of being blown out by the wind.

**MUSIC:** Tunes from Imogen Heap or Olive have upbeat, worldly overtones. To create a more brooding, intense atmosphere, incorporate Mazzy Star or Massive Attack. However, more traditional, Hollywood glamour tunes from the Rat Pack or Shirley Horn certainly invite the right mood, too.

# island spice shopping list: **1 to 2 weeks before**

| ingredients | **12** people | **25** people | **50** people | **75** people |
|---|---|---|---|---|
| ✔ alcohol | | | | |
| Dark rum | 4 ounces | 8 ounces | 16 ounces | 24 ounces |
| Golden rum | 6 ounces | 12 ounces | 24 ounces | 36 ounces |
| **dried herbs, spices, and extracts** | | | | |
| Black peppercorns | as needed | as needed | as needed | as needed |
| Cayenne pepper | ½ ounce | ½ ounce | ½ ounce | ½ ounce |
| Ground cinnamon | ½ ounce | ½ ounce | ½ ounce | ½ ounce |
| Ground ginger | ½ ounce | ½ ounce | ½ ounce | ½ ounce |
| Sea salt | as needed | as needed | as needed | as needed |
| Table salt | as needed | as needed | as needed | as needed |
| **frozen foods** | | | | |
| Orange-passion fruit juice concentrate | 8 ounces | 16 ounces | 32 ounces | 48 ounces |
| **miscellaneous** | | | | |
| Egg roll wrappers | 12 | 25 | 50 | 75 |
| **pantry items and dry goods** | | | | |
| All-purpose flour | 6 ounces | 12 ounces | 1½ pounds | 2¼ pounds |
| Black sesame seeds | ½ ounce | 1 ounce | 2 ounces | 3 ounces |
| Canola oil | 4 ounces | 8 ounces | 16 ounces | 24 ounces |
| Coconut milk | 6 ounces | 10 ounces | 20 ounces | 30 ounces |
| Golden raisins | 6 ounces | 12 ounces | 24 ounces | 32 ounces |
| Honey | 5 ounces | 9 ounces | 18 ounces | 27 ounces |
| Jasmine rice | 3 cups | 6 cups | 12 cups | 18 cups |
| Olive oil | 1 ounce | 2 ounces | 4 ounces | 6 ounces |
| Peanut oil | 16 ounces | 1 quart | 2 quarts | 3 quarts |
| Roasted and salted peanuts | 2 ounces | 3 ounces | 6 ounces | 9 ounces |
| Roasted and salted pistachios | 2 ounces | 3 ounces | 6 ounces | 9 ounces |
| Seasoned rice vinegar | 1 ounce | 2 ounces | 4 ounces | 6 ounces |
| Sesame oil | ½ ounce | 1 ounce | 2 ounces | 3 ounces |
| Sliced almonds | 4 ounces | 8 ounces | 1 pound | 1½ pounds |
| Thai red curry paste | ½ ounce | 1 ounce | 2 ounces | 3 ounces |
| Unsweetened shredded coconut | 10 ounces | 20 ounces | 40 ounces | 60 ounces |

# island spice shopping list: up to 3 days before

| ingredients | 12 people | 25 people | 50 people | 75 people |
|---|---|---|---|---|
| ✔ **dairy, cheese, and deli** | | | | |
| Heavy cream | 1 half-pint | 1 half-pint | 1 pint | 1 quart |
| Unsalted butter | 8 ounces (2 sticks) | 1 pound (4 sticks) | 2 pounds (8 sticks) | 3 pounds (12 sticks) |
| **meat and seafood** | | | | |
| Pre-cooked lobster meat | ½ pound | 1¼ pounds | 2½ pounds | 3¾ pounds |
| Boneless, skinless chicken breasts | 12 (6-ounce) | 25 (6-ounce) | 50 (6-ounce) | 75 (6-ounce) |
| **fresh produce** | | | | |
| Celery | 1 stalk | 2 stalks | 4 stalks | 6 stalks |
| Chives | ½ small bunch | 1 small bunch | 1 small bunch | 2 small bunches |
| Cilantro | 1 small bunch | 2 small bunches | 3 small bunches | 5 small bunches |
| Mint | 2 small bunches | 4 small bunches | 8 small bunches | 12 small bunches |
| Green onions | 1 bunch | 2 bunches | 4 bunches | 6 bunches |
| Hearts of romaine | 4 | 8 | 16 | 24 |
| Kiwis | 6 | 12 | 24 | 36 |
| Large carrot | 1 | 2 | 4 | 6 |
| Large eggs | 1 dozen | 1 dozen | 2 dozen | 3 dozen |
| Lemons | 1 | 1 | 1 | 2 |
| Limes, medium-size | 3 | 5 | 10 | 15 |
| Mangoes | 4 | 9 | 18 | 27 |
| Medium zucchini | 1 | 2 | 4 | 6 |
| Pineapple | 1 | 2 | 4 | 6 |
| Red bell pepper | 1 | 2 | 4 | 6 |
| Seedless red grapes | 12 ounces | 1½ pounds | 3 pounds | 4½ pounds |

# mango, pineapple, and kiwi salad

island spice

| ingredients | 12 people | 25 people | 50 people | 75 people |
|---|---|---|---|---|
| Freshly squeezed lime juice | ¼ cup (about 2 or 3 medium limes) | ½ cup (about 5 medium limes) | 1 cup (about 10 medium limes) | 1½ cups (about 15 medium limes) |
| Canola oil | ½ cup | 1 cup | 2 cups | 3 cups |
| Honey | 1 tablespoon | 2 tablespoons | ¼ cup | ⅓ cup |
| Sea salt | to taste | to taste | to taste | to taste |
| Freshly ground black pepper | to taste | to taste | to taste | to taste |
| Mangoes, peeled, pitted, and diced | 4 | 9 | 18 | 25 |
| Pineapple, peeled, cored, quartered, and sliced | 1 | 2 | 4 | 6 |
| Kiwis, peeled, halved, and sliced | 6 | 12 | 24 | 36 |
| Seedless red grapes, halved | 1½ cups | 3 cups | 6 cups | 9 cups |
| Green onions, thinly sliced diagonally | ½ bunch | 1 bunch | 2 bunches | 3 bunches |
| Black sesame seeds | 1 tablespoon | 2 tablespoons | ¼ cup | ⅓ cup |
| Hearts of romaine (inner leaves 6 inches and smaller), leaves separated | 4 | 8 | 16 hearts | 24 |

### do it for less time:
Buy mango already sliced in the produce section of your grocery store. If you can't find fresh mango, it's perfectly acceptable to use frozen. You can use a good-quality bottled lime juice like Nellie and Joe's Key West Lime Juice in place of the fresh lime juice.

### do it ahead:
Make the vinaigrette 2 days before and cut up all the fruit the day before.

### do it for less money:
Canned mandarin orange sections are a good way to stretch this salad.

## equipment:

- Microwave
- Large pot
- Crock-Pot (optional)

## directions:

1. Place the lime juice, canola oil, and honey in the work bowl of a food processor. Blend until mixture is creamy and emulsified. Add salt and pepper to taste. You can make this 2 days ahead up to this point if placed in an airtight, nonreactive container and refrigerated. Shake well before using.

2. Place the mango, pineapple, kiwi, grapes, and green onions in a large bowl. Add sesame seeds and vinaigrette, tossing well to coat. Cover a serving platter with the romaine leaves. Spoon the salad over the leaves.

## helpful hint:

Zest the limes before juicing them and use the zest elsewhere: make lime sugar to use in a dessert recipe, stir 2 teaspoons into rice for citrus-scented rice, or just freeze it for other uses.

Warm citrus will produce more juice than cold citrus; microwave limes for 10 seconds before juicing and roll them on the counter to get the most juice from each lime. Use a citrus reamer for juicing and place a fine-mesh strainer over a measuring cup to catch seeds.

fyi

serving size: 3 to 4 ounces

# chicken trinidad with rum sauce

island spice

| ingredients | 12 people | 25 people | 50 people | 75 people |
|---|---|---|---|---|
| Peanut oil for frying | about 16 ounces | about 1 quart | about 2 quarts | about 3 quarts |
| All-purpose flour | 1 cup | 2 cups | 4 cups | 6 cups |
| Sea salt | ½ tablespoon | 1 tablespoon | 2 tablespoons | 3 tablespoons |
| Freshly ground black pepper | 1 teaspoon | 2 teaspoons | 1 tablespoon | 1½ tablespoon |
| Cayenne pepper | ½ teaspoon | 1 teaspoon | 2 teaspoons | 1 tablespoon |
| Ground ginger | ½ teaspoon | 1 teaspoon | 2 teaspoons | 1 tablespoon |
| Ground cinnamon | 1 teaspoon | 2 teaspoons | 1 tablespoon, plus 1 teaspoon | 2 tablespoons, plus 2 teaspoons |
| Large eggs, lightly beaten | 5 | 10 | 20 | 30 |
| Unsweetened shredded coconut | 3½ cups | 7 cups | 14 cups | 21 cups |
| Boneless, skinless chicken breasts | 12 (6-ounce) | 25 (6-ounce) | 50 (6-ounce) | 75 (6-ounce) |
| Orange–passion fruit juice concentrate, room temperature | 8 ounces | 16 ounces | 32 ounces | 48 ounces |
| Dark rum | 4 ounces | 8 ounces | 16 ounces | 24 ounces |
| Unsalted butter, cut into pieces, room temperature | 8 ounces (2 sticks) | 1 pound (4 sticks) | 2 pounds (8 sticks) | 3 pounds (12 sticks) |
| Heavy cream, at room temperature | ⅓ cup plus 1 tablespoon | ¾ cup | 1½ cups | 2¼ cups |
| Chives, finely chopped | 2 tablespoons | ¼ cup | ½ cup | ¾ cup |
| Salt | to taste | to taste | to taste | to taste |
| Freshly ground black pepper | to taste | to taste | to taste | to taste |
| Sliced almonds for garnish, toasted (optional) | ¾ cup | 1½ cups | 3 cups | 4½ cups |
| Fresh mint for garnish | 12 sprigs | 25 sprigs | 50 sprigs | 75 sprigs |

**helpful hint:**
Be sure to use unsweetened coconut, as sweetened coconut will burn. Use a deep saucepan to make the sauce to avoid splashing liquid, especially when incorporating the butter with an electric mixer.

# chicken trinidad with rum sauce (continued)

## equipment:

- Large, heavy-bottomed pot
- Whisk
- Large slotted spoon
- Baking sheets
- Paper towels
- Large saucepan
- Electric hand mixer

## directions:

1. Preheat the oven to 375 degrees. Heat 4 inches of oil in a heavy-bottomed pot at least 8 inches deep, until the surface of the oil just starts to ripple, about 350 degrees. You can test a pinch of coconut in the oil; if it starts to sizzle immediately, the oil's ready.

2. Whisk together the flour, salt, pepper, cayenne, ginger, and cinnamon. In an assembly line, line up dishes of the flour mixture, beaten eggs, and coconut. Dredge the chicken breasts in flour mixture, shaking to remove excess, then dip in beaten eggs. Roll the breasts in the shredded coconut to cover all sides.

3. Using a slotted spoon, carefully place the chicken breasts in the hot oil and fry until golden brown, 1-2 minutes. Remove the chicken breasts from the oil with a slotted spoon, and drain on paper towels. (The chicken can be made to this point up to 2 days ahead if covered and refrigerated.) Make sure the oil comes back up to 350 degrees before adding another batch of chicken, and replenish the oil as necessary.

4. After all breasts are done, place on baking sheets in the oven and bake for 25 to 30 minutes, or until the juices run clear. Remove from the oven and set aside.

5. Meanwhile, combine the juice concentrate and rum in a large saucepan, and bring to a boil over high heat. Reduce the heat to medium and let boil for 8 minutes, or until the liquid has reduced by one-quarter. Remove the sauce from the heat and, using an electric mixer on low, whisk in the butter ¼ cup at a time until all of the butter is incorporated and the sauce is smooth. Stir in the heavy cream. Stir in chives. Season with salt and pepper. Pour some of the sauce on serving platters and place the chicken on top. Place the rest of the sauce in bowls to be served alongside the chicken. Garnish with sliced almonds and mint sprigs.

## do it for less money:

If you can't find orange-passion fruit juice concentrate you can use orange juice concentrate instead.

## do it ahead:

If frying the chicken in advance, place the chicken directly on baking sheets after frying, let cool to room temperature, and wrap securely in plastic wrap before storing in the refrigerator. Store the chicken pieces in a single layer, as stacking damages their crisp crusts. Before serving, bring to room temperature, unwrap, and put in oven to finish cooking.

serving size: 1 (6-ounce) chicken breast, 2 tablespoons sauce

# lobster spring rolls

| ingredients | 12 people | 25 people | 50 people | 75 people |
|---|---|---|---|---|
| Pre-cooked lobster meat | ½ pound | 1¼ pounds | 2½ pounds | 3¾ pounds |
| Olive oil | 2 tablespoons | ¼ cup | ½ cup | ¾ cup |
| Large carrot, julienned | 1 | 2 | 4 | 6 |
| Celery, julienned | 1 stalk | 2 stalks | 4 stalks | 6 stalks |
| Red bell pepper, cored, seeded, and julienned | 1 | 2 | 4 | 6 |
| Medium zucchini, julienned | 1 | 2 | 4 | 6 |
| Green onions, very thinly sliced | 2 | 4 | 8 | 12 |
| Chopped cilantro | ½ cup, plus whole sprigs for garnish | 1 cup, plus whole sprigs for garnish | 2 cups, plus whole sprigs for garnish | 3 cups, plus whole sprigs for garnish |
| Salt | to taste | to taste | to taste | to taste |
| Freshly ground black pepper | to taste | to taste | to taste | to taste |
| Peanut oil for frying | as needed | as needed | as needed | as needed |
| Egg roll wrappers | 12 | 25 | 50 | 75 |
| Sweet Curry Dipping Sauce | (recipe follows) | (recipe follows) | (recipe follows) | (recipe follows) |

**do it ahead:**
Do not attempt to assemble the lobster rolls in advance and then fry them just before the event, as the wrappers will disintegrate from the filling's moisture. You can, however, prepare them completely ahead of time — prepare filling, assemble the rolls, fry, and store in the refrigerator — and then rewarm in the oven to crispen just before serving.

**do it for less money:**
Replace half of the lobster with bay or rock shrimp to make this dish more economical, or use all shrimp.

## directions:

1. Pick over the lobster meat to remove any shell pieces. Coarsely chop meat. If using raw shrimp in lieu of lobster, shell, devein, and coarsely chop the meat.

2. Heat the olive oil in a large skillet over medium-high heat. Working in batches if necessary, sauté the carrots for 5 minutes. Add the celery and bell pepper, and continue cooking for 5 more minutes. Add the lobster and zucchini; cook just until heated through, about 3 minutes. Remove from the heat, stir in the green onions and cilantro, and season with salt and pepper to taste.

3. Fill a large, deep saucepan with peanut oil to come one-third of the way up the sides of the pan. Heat over medium until the surface of the oil just starts to ripple, about 350 degrees.

## equipment:

- Large skillet
- Large, heavy-bottomed saucepan
- Wooden cutting board
- Tongs or slotted spoon
- Paper towels

## directions: (continued)

4. Place the egg roll wrappers on a clean work surface (a damp wooden cutting board works best to keep the wrappers from sticking). Place 2 tablespoons of the lobster and vegetable mixture down the center of each wrapper, leaving an inch of space at the top and bottom. Fold in the top and bottom of the wrapper first. Fold one side of the wrapper over filling and roll like a burrito until the wrapper completely encompasses the filling. Moisten the edge and press to seal. Make all the egg rolls, keeping them covered until ready to fry.

5. Using tongs or a slotted spoon, carefully place the rolls 6 to 9 at a time, depending upon the size of the saucepan (to ensure even cooking, rolls should not be crowded in the saucepan), in the hot oil. Cook, turning so they brown evenly, until they turn a light golden brown. Remove from the oil with tongs or a slotted spoon and drain on paper towels. (The lobster rolls can be made up to this point a day ahead if they are covered and refrigerated. Place on baking sheets and bake for 10 to 15 minutes in a 350-degree oven to reheat.)

6. To serve, slice the lobster rolls diagonally through the center and place on serving trays with bowls of Sweet Curry Dipping Sauce. Garnish with cilantro sprigs.

## do it for less time:

Frozen lobster meat is fine to use in this recipe. Thaw in the refrigerator for 2 days before using. For quicker work of the vegetable prep, use a julienne peeler tool (it looks like a vegetable peeler with a deeply serrated blade) to cut the carrots and zucchini. Or use a mandoline if you have one.

serving size: 1 spring roll

# sweet curry dipping sauce

island spice

| ingredients | 12 people | 25 people | 50 people | 75 people |
|---|---|---|---|---|
| Thai red curry paste | 1 tablespoon | 2 tablespoons | ¼ cup | ⅓ cup |
| Coconut milk | ¾ cup | 1¼ cups | 2½ cups | 3¾ cups |
| Sesame oil | 1 tablespoon | 2 tablespoons | ¼ cup | ⅓ cup |
| Honey | ½ cup | 1 cup | 2 cups | 3 cups |
| Seasoned rice vinegar | 2 tablespoons | ¼ cup | ½ cup | ¾ cup |
| Freshly squeezed lemon juice | 1½ teaspoons | 1 tablespoon | 2 tablespoons | 3 tablespoons |
| Roasted and salted peanuts, finely chopped | ¼ cup | ½ cup | 1 cup | 1½ cups |
| Cilantro for garnish, finely chopped | 1 tablespoon | 2 tablespoons | ¼ cup | ⅓ cup |

### do it ahead:
The sauce can be made a day in advance except for the peanuts and cilantro. Stir peanuts in just before serving to keep their crunch, and garnish with cilantro.

### helpful hint:
Seasoned rice vinegar, or mirin, is much sweeter than plain rice vinegar. You can use plain rice vinegar for a less sweet sauce.

Lightly spray a measuring cup with vegetable cooking spray before measuring honey for less mess and a more accurate measurement.

## directions:

1. Place curry paste and coconut milk in a large saucepan over medium heat, stirring frequently for 3 minutes to just bring to a simmer. Reduce the heat to low and whisk in the oil, honey, and rice vinegar, and whisk until smooth. (The sauce can be made to this point up to 1 day ahead. Cover tightly and refrigerate until the day of the event, and bring to room temperature or reheat.) Remove from the heat and stir in the peanuts. The sauce can be served warm or at room temperature. Garnish bowl with chopped cilantro.

## equipment:
- Large saucepan
- Whisk

serving size: about 1 tablespoon

# jasmine rice with golden raisins

| ingredients | 12 people | 25 people | 50 people | 75 people |
| --- | --- | --- | --- | --- |
| Golden raisins | 1 cup | 2 cups | 4 cups | 6 cups |
| Golden rum | ¾ cup (6 ounces) | 1½ cups (12 ounces) | 3 cups (24 ounces) | 4½ cups (36 ounces) |
| Water | 4½ cups | 9 cups | 18 cups | 27 cups |
| Sea salt | 1 teaspoon | 2 teaspoons | 4 teaspoons | 6 teaspoons |
| Jasmine rice, rinsed | 3 cups | 6 cups | 12 cups | 18 cups |
| Roasted and salted pistachios, chopped, for garnish (optional) | ¼ cup | ½ cup | 1 cup | 1½ cups |

## equipment:

- Glass or plastic mixing bowl
- Large pot
- Sieve or fine colander

## directions:

1. Place the raisins and golden rum in a nonreactive bowl and let soak for 12 to 24 hours to plump the raisins and infuse them with flavor.

2. Bring the water to a boil in a large pot over high heat. Add the salt and rice, and stir to combine. Cover the pot and reduce the heat to low. Cook the rice for 15 minutes, or until done. Drain the raisins and stir into the cooked rice, fluffing with a fork. Remove the rice to large serving bowls and garnish with pistachios. Serve hot.

## do it for less time:

To save time, purchase frozen jasmine rice and microwave just before serving.

## helpful hint:

Any long-grain white rice can be substituted for the jasmine. Use spiced rum for an extra punch of flavor to the dish.

serving size: ¾ cup

# chapter 8
# making your own
# wedding cake

You can save a substantial amount of money by making your own wedding cake. Bakeries typically price wedding cakes by the slice — from $1.50 to $6.00 per slice for relatively standard cakes. Any extras you add — liquors, nuts, fillings, marzipan — also add to the cost. Handmade specialties like sugar paste flowers can easily increase the price exponentially up to $10.00 to $15.00 per slice. Costs rise even more for couture cakes from top-tier bakers like Sylvia Weinstock, who create masterpieces from flour, sugar, and butter.

Follow our tricks of the trade in this chapter to create your own fabulous cake or to shave costs when hiring a professional baker. For less than $150, you can end up with a cake that serves 75 guests, tastes moist and delicious, and looks beautiful as well.

The cakes in this book are made with packaged cake mixes. We used Betty Crocker and Duncan Hines in testing our receipes, but you'll find many reputable brands on the market. Martha Stewart and the Barefoot Contessa both produce delicious cakes, although the price runs more than $10 for a single box. Follow the box directions for any purchased mix you use.

Cake mixes have been around since 1947 and have been so thoroughly tested that they are pretty foolproof. If you love baking cakes from scratch, then more power to you! We have included a recipe for Basic Yellow Butter Cake on page 247. But you will find that making a cake from scratch is definitely not helping you save time, effort, or money. However, we do suggest you make a tasty buttercream frosting from scratch. We give you an easy, no-cook recipe that tastes divine and makes these cakes both delicious and memorable.

But first things first! Read through this chapter in it's entirety to make sure you have all the equipment, refrigerator and freezer space, and time that you'll need to create a beautiful wedding cake.

# EQUIPMENT AND SUPPLIES

You'll already have most of this equipment in your own kitchen. For those items you don't, you will need to borrow or buy them to ensure best results.

- **Oven thermometer:** Ovens often vary in range 10 or 20 degrees or more, which can have a huge impact on your finished cake. Cakes baked at a temperature that is too high will have a big lump in the center, while a too-low temperature can result in a cake that is not cooked through. Invest in a good thermometer; it will serve you well for years to come, regardless of what you're baking.

- **Stand mixer:** While a hand mixer can get the job done, a good stand mixer adds muscle to your kitchen. It makes buttercream frosting easily, up to three times more quickly than a hand mixer.

- **Cake pans:** If you already own cake pans, make sure they are free of dents and have straight, even sides, not curved or slanted. Good cake pans don't have to cost a lot. Skip the pricier nonstick pans, as well as dark metal or glass. Darker-colored pans, in particular, tend to cause baked goods to brown more significantly than we like. Stick with light-colored, weightier aluminum pans for best results.

- **Parchment paper:** Parchment paper is one of the most important secrets for even cooking and easy release of your cakes. You can use this high-density, heat-resistant paper in lieu of, or in conjunction with, greasing your pans.

- **Kitchen twine:** You will need kitchen twine to tie cake-insulating strips around the cake pans. Don't try to tape it. Learn from our experience — it won't work, only burn and fall off.

- **Spreading spatula:** A spreading spatula, also known as an icing spatula, has a flat, flexible metal blade and a rounded edge. The spatulas range in size from 4 to 14 inches and come with flat blades or offset blades. For a good, all-purpose start, we suggest an 8-inch offset spatula.

- **Long, sharp slicing knife:** A serrated bread knife will work if you don't have a serrated slicing knife, but a true slicing knife will give you a smoother cut surface, making the cake easier to frost. (A slicing knife has smaller teeth than a serrated knife.) The longer the knife the better; look for one at least 10 inches long.

- **Pastry bag and tips:** You can find sturdy, disposable plastic pastry bags and a couple of plastic or metal tips at most restaurant supply and all cake decorating supply stores. Plastic tips cost only about a dollar each and provide a much cleaner output than simply snipping the corner off a plastic bag. Use a large tip with a

Order a 3 or 4 tier wedding cake from a bakery or your local grocery store bakery. Have them put a crumb coat of frosting on each tier and freeze the tiers separately. Pick it up and put it in your freezer until you are ready to assemble and decorate it. Customize your cake by asking for each tier to have a different filling or that each tier be a different flavor of cake.

Or order a perfectly, frosted, plain, tiered cake. Have the baker deliver it and add your own fresh flowers at the reception after the cake is in place.

½-inch opening to apply frosting evenly. For last-minute touch-ups and adhering decorations to the cake, use a ⅛-inch round tip.

- **Cardboard baking rounds and squares:** Cardboard baking pieces will help support your cake tiers and make moving easier. You can find them at any baking supply store. Be sure to purchase them in the same sizes as your cake pans, and buy an extra one that's a few inches larger to hold the finished cake and make transport easier. For a nicer presentation, purchase the larger round or square covered in silver or gold foil, or cover it yourself.

- **Cake insulating strips:** Sold under the name "Magi-Cake" or "Bake Even Strips," these strips insulate the cake for more even cooking. Besides keeping the outer edge from overcooking or drying out, they also help the surface of the cake bake more flat and even. You can make your own if you like: Tear off a piece of aluminum foil a few inches longer than the circumference of each cake pan: 24 inches for a 6-inch tier, 30 inches for an 8-inch tier, and 36 inches for a 10-inch tier. Lay the foil flat on your work surface. Tear off several paper towels in one long strip to about the same length as each foil piece. Fold the paper towel length-wise to about 2 inches wide. Dampen with water and place along one long edge of the foil. Fold the foil up and over, until you have a long strip about 2 inches wide. Wrap the foil around the outside of the cake pan, overlap the ends, and tie with kitchen twine to secure.

- **Cake tier supports:** Do not underestimate the importance of support columns, which help hold up the successive tiers of the cake and keep the layers from sliding off. For the cakes shown in this chapter, plastic drinking straws cut to fit the depth of the cake will work fine. You can also use ¼-inch wooden dowels cut to fit.

- **Cake separators:** These decorative cake stands offer a great solution for less experienced bakers. With them, the tiers do not sit directly on top of each other, but instead are separated by pillars that stand about 2 to 5 inches tall. They allow you to decorate each tier separately and then assemble the finished cake onsite in minutes. The final result looks larger and sometimes more impressive, and the separate tiers make slicing a snap.

- **Wire cooling racks:** Resembling lightweight oven racks, cooling racks are essential to bringing your cakes to room temperature as quickly as possible as they allow air to circulate around your cake and disperse the heat.

# WEDDING CAKE TO-DO LIST

Whether you prefer simple cupcakes, an assortment of flavored cheesecakes, or a multi-tiered cake dripping with flowers, the steps are the same:

1. Envision
2. Make
3. Assemble
4. Decorate
5. Transport
6. Display
7. Cut

The order may change depending on your cake and your circumstances. Some cakes will be completed in the kitchen, while others may be assembled onsite. You may outsource some of the steps and handle the rest yourself. Regardless of the order or the person responsible, you'll need to consider each of these components in planning for your wedding day.

## Envisioning Your Cake

Most brides draw upon the colors and themes used throughout the wedding to drive their decisions for the cake. You can duplicate flowers used in your bouquet, pipe the cake the color of your bridesmaids' dresses, or use a lace overlay for the cake table that matches your veil. We've created a variety of truly doable cakes that coordinate with the menus and the decorating ideas in the book. Mix and match colors and ideas to fit with your dream wedding. If one of these cakes doesn't strike your fancy, cull through magazines and cake cookbooks for inspiration. Just remember: less is definitely more with do-it-for-less wedding cakes. Simple elegance almost always trumps intricate design, unless you have years of experience.

## Who Says It Has to Be Round?

Cake pans come in all variety of shapes and sizes these days. Though a little bit trickier to use, many brides love the modern look of square cakes. You could even do a glazed pound cake in petal-shaped bundt pans. Perhaps even more fun is the trend toward cupcakes. For easy decorating, purchase a sugar paste flower to top each one. You can display them on a tiered serving tray for a wedding-cake look or use the lighthearted look of a cupcake tree. If you like the idea of cupcakes, but still want a traditional wedding cake, you could serve them for the groom's cake instead or have coordinated cupcakes for any children attending the wedding.

## HOW MUCH FROSTING DO I NEED?

The frosting in these amounts will cover the cake size specified with a crumb coat, an outer coat, and simple decorations. Stacking cake tiers directly on top of one another will cut down on the amount of frosting used, so if you stack you may have some left over.

3 cups buttercream frosting = 6-inch round

4 cups buttercream frosting = 8-inch round

6 cups buttercream frosting = 10-inch round

8 cups buttercream frosting = 12-inch round

4 cups buttercream frosting = 6-inch square

5 cups buttercream frosting = 8-inch square

7 cups buttercream frosting = 10-inch square

8 cups buttercream frosting = 12-inch square

## How Much Cake Do I Need?

Once you've decided on the overall look of your cake, you need to estimate how many guests will be attending the wedding. Use the table below as a guide for 12, 25, 50, and 75 guests. To save time and money, make a small, but beautiful wedding cake of 2 or 3 tiers and have a minimally decorated 13 x 9-inch sheet cake in the kitchen to cut and serve. For even more efficiency, you can make the "hero" cake out of Styrofoam and serve only the sheet cake in the back. Believe it or not, some companies specialize in renting beautifully decorated wedding cakes made of Styrofoam. You get the visual wow of a professionally decorated cake for a fraction of the cost, and you can serve a delicious cake from the kitchen without worrying whether you piped the basketweave correctly. Visit www.cakerental.com or www.rentthecakeofyourdreams.com to see what some vendors are offering.

### CAKE PAN SIZE

| round cake (3-inch deep) | serving size |
|---|---|
| 6 inch | 8-10 |
| 8 inch | 12-16 |
| 10 inch | 20-34 |
| square cake (3-inch deep) | serving size |
| 6 inch | 8-12 |
| 8 inch | 12-20 |
| 10 inch | 20-30 |

### Do-It-Ahead Wedding Cake

With a bit of confidence in the kitchen, you can make your own wedding cake. But you'll have a much easier go of it if you prepare it in stages ahead of time instead of saving it for the day before the wedding. Most of it, in fact, can be made a month ahead. The result will taste just as good, and your sanity will stay intact for the big day.

If you are making your cake more than a few days ahead, you will need room in your freezer to store the layers. Even if not making ahead, you will still need space to freeze the crumb coat. If space is an issue, you can place frozen items in your refrigerator for the hour it will take to freeze the crumb coat.

You can freeze cake layers before or after applying the crumb coat. If freezing with a crumb coat, place cake layers in the freezer without wrapping until the frosting is hard to the touch, about 45 minutes. After the frosting is hard, wrap the cake tightly in plastic wrap and then with foil. Wrapped properly, the cake layers will keep for up to 1 month in the freezer. Thaw in the refrigerator for 24 hours, and then bring to room temperature before unwrapping from the foil and plastic wrap.

If making your cake the week of your wedding, be sure to allow ample time for each step. Don't skimp on the cooling time for the cake; frosting a warm cake is a recipe for disaster!

## Do-It-Ahead Frosting

You can also freeze buttercream frosting for up to 1 month. Place it in a heavy-duty, resealable plastic bag, and squeeze out all excess air before sealing. Double-bag to avoid freezer burn. Thaw it in the refrigerator for 24 hours, and then let it come to room temperature before using. Frosting will also keep in the refrigerator for up to 2 weeks if stored in an airtight container. Buttercream frosting must be brought to room temperature and beaten again with an electric mixer until soft and fluffy before use.

## Moving Beyond Vanilla: Cake Flavorings for All Tastes

You can easily alter the flavor of the cakes in the book to suit your taste. Or, if using box mix, feel free to choose a flavor that suits your taste and bake the cake according to package directions.

To further personalize the flavor, consider these additions for your wedding cake. The amounts are based on the butter cake on page 247, replace the vanilla called for in the recipe with the same amount of liquid extract or flavoring of your choice. If using a box mix, follow the package directions and add any of these ingredients.

- ¼ cup shredded coconut
- ¼ cup white chocolate chips
- ¼ cup mini chocolate chips
- 2 tablespoons lemon zest
- 2 tablespoons orange zest
- 2 tablespoons poppy seeds
- 1½ teaspoons anise extract
- 1½ teaspoons almond extract
- 1½ teaspoons brandy flavoring
- 1½ teaspoons coffee flavoring
- 1½ teaspoons hazelnut flavoring
- 1½ teaspoons rum flavoring

## TYPES OF FROSTING

**Buttercream:** rich and flavorful, made mainly from butter, powdered sugar, and flavorings. Good in all weather.

**Cooked frosting:** a mixture of egg whites, sugar, and flavorings cooked and beaten over a double-boiler resulting in a meringue, which makes this frosting very stable. Good choice for warm weather weddings.

**Whipped cream frosting:** cream whipped with powdered sugar and flavorings. Must be kept cool or it will melt. Not suitable for warm weather weddings.

**Ganache:** made from chocolate melted with heavy cream and a little butter. These have a beautiful glossy finish and are suitable for any season.

**Fondant:** made from powdered sugar, gelatin, and water, fondant has the texture of modeling clay. Wedding cakes covered with rolled-out fondant have a polished, formal look. Good in any weather. Your local cake decorating store will have pre-made fondant in beautiful pastel colors available for purchase. It's not difficult to work with. Drape and tuck the fondant over any cake.

## Assembling the Cake

The cakes in this book are all stacked, meaning that the tiers rest directly on top of each other. If not stacking your tiers, see page 222 for some creative ways to display your cake.

Stacked cakes rely on four things for stability. Without these components, a cake could slide apart or collapse under the weight of the top layers.

1. **Even layers**
   As we explained in the previous section, you will likely need to trim the domed tops of your layers to create a flat surface for stacking. A long, thin knife works best for this task.

2. **Cardboard cake base**
   Place each baked cake on a cardboard base the same size as the cake.

3. **Careful measurements**
   Using a clean ruler, measure in 2 inches from the diameter of each cake layer. For example, if placing a 6-inch round on top of an 8-inch round, you'd measure in 2 inches from the edge in 2 or 3 places. Then take an empty 6-inch cake pan and press lightly, rim-side down, into the frosting. You'll have exact guide lines for positioning your next tier.

4. **Tier supports**
   Insert plastic drinking straws straight down into the top of your tiers; cut them so they are the exact height of the cake layer. If they're too short, they won't provide adequate support. If too tall, the layer above will be balancing on the straws instead of spreading its weight over the entire tier. For extra support, use wooden dowels instead of plastic straws.

## BETTER BAKING HINTS

- Make sure your oven baking racks are level. Don't just eyeball it — use a carpenter's level to make sure your cakes have the best chance for coming out with even tops.

- Preheat the oven until your oven thermometer registers the correct temperature for baking.

- Always use parchment paper to line your pans. You'll find no better way to keep them from sticking.

- Resist the impulse to fill the cake pans to the top with batter. Instead, stop short of the top by 1 inch to keep the batter from spilling over.

- Is it done yet? As a cake finishes cooking, it will begin to shrink away from the edge of the pan and the center will spring back when lightly pressed. To check for doneness, insert a wooden toothpick in the center of the cake. If the toothpick has wet bits stuck to it when you remove it, the cake is not done. A few moist crumbs are okay.

- After baking, remove the pans to wire racks and let them cool before turning out.

- A stacked cake depends on even tiers, and nearly all cakes will require a little surgery to level out the top surface. Wait until the cake is completely cool, and use a long, thin knife to slice off any uneven pieces.

## Flavorful Fillings

Besides injecting extra flavor into your cake with extracts and other additions, you can add moisture and taste with store-bought fillings. Little effort; large return. You can make extra frosting and flavor it with liqueur or fruit jam, or you can use jams, fruit spreads, and fruit curds straight from the jar. Allow about 1 cup for each tier. You'll want a relatively thin layer of filling; any more, and it will squish out the sides from the weight of the layer above. Make sure your filling has as much body as the frosting.

To add a filling to any of the recipes in the book, cut each tier horizontally into 2 even layers with a long, thin knife. Spread the filling on one of the cut sides, and top with the remaining half. Assemble the rest of the cake as instructed in the recipe.

- Lemon curd
- Raspberry or strawberry jam
- Apricot jam
- Black cherry jam
- Orange marmalade
- Creamy jam: Mix 1 part jam or curd with 1 part frosting
- Coconut: Combine 1 part sweetened, flaked coconut with 4 parts frosting
- Nutella
- Nutella frosting: Mix 1 part Nutella with 1 part frosting
- Candied fruit: Combine 1 part finely chopped candied fruit (like cherries, pineapple, ginger) to 4 parts frosting
- Toasted nuts: Combine 1 part finely chopped toasted almonds, pecans, or hazelnuts with 4 parts frosting

## Frosting

Have you ever made a delicious cake, only to have crumbs end up in your fluffy frosting? It's not attractive, but it's easy to fix. Professional bakers know they have to apply a crumb coat for a clean finish. For these cakes, you can use the basic buttercream frosting and thin it slightly with corn syrup. Working with cooled and evenly trimmed cake layers, apply a thin layer of frosting evenly over each tier to capture all the crumbs. Place the cake in the freezer, uncovered, until the frosting is hard. The outer layer of frosting will glide easily over the frozen frosting, which will have captured all the loose crumbs in the crumb coat. If baking the cakes in advance, let the crumb coat harden, and then wrap well in plastic wrap and aluminum foil. Thaw in the refrigerator for 24 hours before frosting.

When applying the final frosting to your cake, you need to be working with room temperature, freshly whipped frosting. The cake should

### FLAVORFUL FROSTINGS

Customize your wedding cake by flavoring the frosting. Simply replace half or all of the vanilla extract with any other extract flavor that you like. Extracts have a much stronger flavor than liqueurs, which makes them the better choice to flavor frostings as less is needed, keeping the frosting from becoming too soft. Here are some popular choices:

- almond
- apple
- apricot
- bourbon
- brandy
- butter pecan
- cherry
- cinnamon
- coconut
- coffee
- hazelnut
- honey
- Irish cream
- key lime
- lemon
- maple
- orange
- passion fruit
- peach
- peppermint
- raspberry
- rose
- rum
- spearmint
- strawberry
- violet

**LUSTER DUST**

Luster dust is a fine, edible powder, similar in look to glimmering eye shadow. It comes in many colors, but some of the best colors for wedding cakes include gold, silver, or pearlized white. You can paint the dust directly onto dried fruit, whole nuts, or decorations with a small, soft paintbrush for a gilded, sparkly look.

be thawed and the crumb coat should be chilled.

If you froze your buttercream ahead of time, thaw it in the refrigerator for 24 hours, bring to room temperature, and beat until soft and creamy. If the buttercream is too soft to hold its shape on the cake, you can stiffen it by beating in sifted powdered sugar, a quarter cup at a time. If the frosting is too stiff to spread easily, beat in corn syrup 1 tablespoon at at time, until the desired consistency.

To apply frosting, spread it on top of the crumb coat on the sides of the cake, and then smooth. Next add frosting to the top and smooth. You'll need to go back and forth between the sides and the top a few times for a nice finish. For a flat, finished look, place the spatula under hot running water and wipe dry. The warmed spatula will slightly melt the frosting and allow you to smooth it beautifully. Rewarm the spatula as needed.

For an even smoother finish, let the icing "crust" for 3 to 5 minutes, or until it's just hardened. If your frosting is particularly soft, you can place it in the refrigerator or freezer for several minutes. Make sure your cake is adequately crusted by touching it gently with your fingers; the icing may move or press slightly, but it shouldn't stick to your fingers. Place a piece of parchment paper, waxed paper, or nonpatterned paper towel over the frosting and press lightly, rubbing in even motions with your fingers or a spatula to smooth out your cake.

For a swirly finish instead of a flat finish, frost the cake with the crumb coat and then again with the frosting, creating a smooth surface. Let the smooth surface "crust" or set, and then use a clean spatula to add swirls of icing on the top and sides. Using a toothpick or skewer and a light hand, draw tight figure eights in the frosting to form peaks and valleys.

## DECORATING IDEAS

Resist the impulse to overdecorate. Remember: this is a wedding cake, not a parade float. Look at wedding cake photos in bridal magazines and cookbooks. Find simple designs that appeal to you and won't overwhelm you and your sous-chefs.

Mix different sizes of decorations to complement your theme. For example, if you're planning a vineyard-inspired reception, use fresh grapes. Clusters of tiny red champagne grapes, medium-sized green grapes, and a few large, dark purple grapes look stunning together. Add some grape leaves and tendrils or other greenery for contrast, et voila! — you have a  beautiful cake to match your reception theme.

### Fresh Flowers, Greenery, and Herbs

Keep fresh flowers and other greenery in water and in the refrigerator until you are ready to use them. Always place fresh flowers on your cake at the last moment. Also, it may seem obvious, but you should avoid toxic and poisonous plants.  (See sidebar on page 221.)

Stay away from anything that wilts quickly. Test your choices before you decide to use them. Cut a stem or leaf and leave it out for 8 hours. Does it still look quite fresh, or is it shriveled and brown? Consider using a flower spike to keep the blossoms fresh. A flower spike is a hollow plastic tube that holds water. You place the stems into the plastic holder and push the spike into the cake. This will lengthen the life of delicate flowers and keep the stems away from the cake.

   If you're less confident in your flower decorating abilities, order a small nosegay from a florist to use as a cake topper. A nosegay (literally, a pleasant-smelling item for keeping the "nose gay") is a small, tightly packed bouquet. If you have separated cake tiers, order nosegays in graduated sizes to top each tier.

- **Fresh flowers**
  The blossoms of such flowers as roses, pansies, Johnny-jump-ups, nasturtiums, lilacs, honeysuckle, geraniums, and violets make lovely embellishments to any wedding cake. Also consider using fuchsias, cymbidium orchids, chrysanthemum, calendula, orange blossoms, and marigolds.

- **Herbs**
  Flowering herbs look beautiful on wedding cakes and add a certain outdoorsy, garden look to your décor, while being wilt-resistant. Rosemary and lavender have beautiful foliage and flowers, as does lemon verbena. Use only the pretty blue flower of the borage plant, as the greenery is not attractive. Fresh bay leaves look beautiful in their natural green color or gilded with luster dust.

- **Greenery**
  Many plants have beautiful nontoxic leaves and stems that make lovely additions to your wedding cake decorations. These include bamboo, Boston fern, camellia, grape ivy, honeysuckle, geranium, and passionflower (whose curling tendrils are fun).

- **Fresh fruit**
  Fresh fruit is a wonderful cake decoration. Purchase fruit at the last moment for optimum life and freshness. Add fresh leaves for interest and a contrasting splash of green. Strawberries, raspberries, black-berries, blueberries, gooseberries, champagne grapes, green and red grapes, and currants are all beautiful decorations.

- **Sugared fruits or flowers**
  Brush pasteurized egg whites lightly on fruit or flowers and sprinkle with sanding sugar or glitter sugar, which are both available at cake decorating or restaurant supply stores. Let your sugared trimmings dry for at least an hour before using. (You can sugar dried fruit up to 2 days in advance; fresh fruit and flowers 1 day in advance.) Berries and grapes, with their  diminutive sizes and rich colors, look particularly beautiful sugared. Roses and rose petals also work very well, as do pansies, Johnny-jump-ups, violets, and geraniums.

Sugared flowers for your cake look like candy to guests, so make doubly sure you have chosen edible, pesticide-free blossoms.

- Marzipan
Almond paste mixed with sugar creates an edible modeling clay called marzipan. With a little practice, you can mold it into most any decorative item. Reasonably priced and readily available, pre-decorated marzipan comes in many shapes and sizes. Among the best for wedding cakes are the strawberries, persimmons, and cherries. Marzipan roses and leaves can also be purchased and are a good deal less expensive than sugar and gum paste flowers. For extra flourish, decorate your cake with a combination of marzipan and fresh leaves gilded with luster dust.

- Nuts
For a fall wedding, the use of whole or shelled almonds, hazelnuts, and pistachios, or walnut and pecan halves creates a lovely autumnal effect. You can use the nuts as is, candied, or brushed with luster dust. The results are beautiful! Add fresh bay laurel leaves for green accents.

- Silver-coated chocolate and almonds
Silver Jordan almonds make simple, elegant, and easy decorations — plus they're addictive to eat. You can also find silver-coated chocolate hearts to use for decoration or brush real gold or silver leaf onto molded chocolates for high-end elegance.

- Dragées
Dragées are small sugar beads or gum paste balls coated with metallic gold or silver. They also come in pearlized white, as well as many pastel colors. Silver-coated dragées are not available in and cannot be shipped to California due to state regulations, but they are available almost everywhere else.

- Sugar paste and gum paste flowers
Purchase gorgeous sugar or gum paste flowers from some finer cake decorating supply stores or one of many online resources. They look very much like real flowers, and you can choose from hundreds of them. If you want the look of a traditional wedding cake and are willing to spend $30 to $130 for the sugar flowers, then this is for you. One spectacular sugar or gum paste flower arrangement on the top of your cake will make a huge impact on any wedding cake. CakesBySam.com has many beautiful flowers to choose from.

• Fondant

Fondant is sugar paste that has not yet hardened. It is basically an edible modeling "clay" that you roll out and cut with fondant cutters. These look like small plastic cookie cutters and come in all different shapes and sizes. When working with fondant, always keep unused pieces sealed in plastic bags to prevent drying. Cut fondant decorations should be allowed to dry overnight before using them to decorate. Wilton makes fondant in many different colors including pastels, primary colors, bright colors, and white.

## CHOOSING SAFE PLANTS

When using fresh flowers, greenery, stems, leaves, berries, or any other part of a plant to decorate your cake, be sure to confirm that you've chosen a nontoxic decoration. And even if using a nontoxic plant, always rinse with water to remove any pesticides, dirt, bugs, or otherwise unwanted nature from your cake decoration.

Often, just one part of a plant is toxic, such as the berries or the stems. The plants on this list (which is by no means comprehensive) have at least some level of toxicity. If you simply cannot live without lilies on your cake, consult your nursery, a botanist, or other reliable resource to see if you can do so without endangering your guests.

- Amaryllis
- Azalea
- Bird of paradise
- Calla lily
- Clematis
- Creeping Charlie
- Cyclamen
- Daffodil
- Daylily
- Delphinium
- Easter lily
- Elderberry
- English ivy
- Foxglove
- Gladiolas
- Ground ivy
- Holly
- Hyacinth
- Hydrangea
- Iris
- Jack-in-the-pulpit
- Lantana
- Larkspur
- Lily of the valley
- Lupine
- Mexican poppy
- Morning glory
- Narcissus
- Oleander
- Poinsettia
- Poppy
- Rhododendron
- Star of Bethlehem
- Sweetheart ivy
- Tiger lily
- Tulip
- Wisteria

## DISPLAYING YOUR CAKE

Choose carefully when deciding on a display surface for your cake. You've worked hard to create a beautiful dessert, and you'll want the display to reflect the same attention to detail. First, make sure the piece has a large, flat, stable plane for displaying your cake. A too-small dish or a tray with a raised edge can cause your cake to shift and sag. Look, too, for something with at least 2 inches of overhang beyond the base of the cake to allow room for additional flowers or decorations.

Flat platters, mirrors, glass, marble, silver trays or stands, and simple white china all work very well.  If your china cabinet's lacking and your friends don't have any pieces that would work either, rental companies usually have a variety of reasonably priced options.

You may want to also consider a cake drum, available from cake decorating supply stores and online. This heavy-duty cardboard stand comes covered in silver or gold foil and elevates the cake for a professional finish. You can tie a ribbon around the bottom to coordinate with your colors and give the base a clean look. You can also find ruffle boards at cake decorating suppliers. Its frilly effect may not work with many of today's weddings, but in the right situation, it can look perfect.

The most expensive but possibly easiest way to display your cake is with a tiered cake stand. You'll avoid the work of stacking your tiers, while still presenting the look of one cake. Cutting is a breeze with separate tiers, and you'll find stands of all variety of styles to fit your taste. The stands are pricey to purchase, but reasonable to rent.

For brides wanting the ease of separate tiers without the traditional look of a tiered stand, you can bake separate cakes and arrange them on such unexpected displays as antique glass cake stands of different heights, metal cupcake "trees," a stepped display of colorfully wrapped boxes, or even rustic tree stumps.

### CAKE DISPLAY SURFACE

Glass is highly customizable, and you probably already have a glass-topped piece of furniture in your home. If not, look for previously owned glass from a glass shop. Make sure to use a piece with smooth edges to avoid any cuts. You can paint the underside of the glass to match your wedding or complement your cake. (And you can scrape the paint off the glass afterwards if needed.) You can also leave it clear and decorate underneath to great effect. See how these items might look underneath the glass:

- Pressed flowers
- Fresh-cut greenery, rich-colored autumn leaves, or large banana leaves
- Old photographs of the bride and groom
- Wide ribbons

- Photos from weddings past of parents and grandparents
- Grass skirts or reed placements
- Fabric
- Handmade paper
- Tulle or organza over table linens

# TRANSPORTING YOUR CAKE

Now that you've made the perfect cake, you've got to get it to the reception site, preferably in perfect condition. Make sure you or someone you know has a flat space in her vehicle large enough and tall enough for your cake to travel securely. An SUV or minivan tends to work better for this than a typical car. To keep the cake from sliding, use a soft rubber shelf liner or damp kitchen towel between the bottom of the cake platter and the floor for traction. If possible, find a sturdy cardboard box with short enough sides to hold the cake. Line the bottom of the box with a shelf liner in addition to the shelf liner between the box and the vehicle. Remove anything from the car that could fall on the cake or cause it to shift while driving. If the weather is warm, be sure to pre-chill your vehicle well to protect the icing from softening or melting en route.

### Last-Minute Fixes
Pack a touch-up bag for your cake, including a small spreading spatula and a pastry bag fitted with a small pastry tip and filled with your frosting, as well as a few extra decorations in case of mishaps. After you've transported the cake and put it into position on the display table, you'll likely need to repair a few nicks and smudges that occurred during transport and set-up. With steady hand and a bit of piping, most any blemish can be camouflaged quickly.

# CUTTING THE CAKE

Unless the cake is being cut out of sight of your guests, make sure you have an attractive cake knife and cake server. Silver-plated sets can be rented from party supply stores. Or maybe someone would like to buy you a set for your wedding present.

For the first piece of cake — the bride and groom's piece — cut a piece from the bottom tier. After the first piece is served, separate the cake tiers and remove the plastic straws or supporting dowels before continuing. Many couples like to save the top tier of their cake to share on their first anniversary. Let the designated cake cutter know this ahead of time so your guests aren't fed your anniversary dessert. Because the slicing process can get a bit messy, we recommend moving the cake into the kitchen or somewhere else out of the view of guests.

To make slicing easier, use a long, thin blade and have a damp kitchen towel handy to wipe the blade clean between slices. For 6-inch rounds, slice the cake in half, and then in half again, perpendicular to the first cut. You can get 2 to 3 slices from each quarter of the cake, for 8 to 12 slices total. For larger cakes, cut a circle 2 inches in from the outer edge of the cake. If a smaller cake was positioned atop the larger tier, use the indentation it made in the frosting as a guide for cutting. Slice 1½-inch pieces until you've cut around the entire cake. Cut the interior circle into wedges as you would a 6-inch tier.

# sunrise floral cupcakes

| ingredients | 24 cupcakes | 50 cupcakes | 75 cupcakes |
|---|---|---|---|
| Vanilla cake mix, plus ingredients specified on package | 1 (18.25-ounce) box | 2 (18.25-ounce) boxes | 3 (18.25-ounce) boxes |
| Shortening | ½ cup | 1 cup | 2 cups |
| Unsalted butter, softened | 4 ounces (1 stick) | 8 ounces (2 sticks) | 1 pound (4 sticks) |
| Vanilla extract | 1½ teaspoons | 1 tablespoon | 2 tablespoons |
| Confectioners' sugar | 4 cups | 8 cups | 16 cups |
| Milk | 2 tablespoons | ¼ cup | ½ cup |
| Wilton ready-to-use rolled fondant, pastel colors pack | 1 (17.6-ounce) package | 1 (17.6-ounce) package | 2 (17.6-ounce) packages |
| Wilton ready-to-use rolled fondant, white | 1 (24-ounce) package | 1 (24-ounce) package | 1 (24-ounce) package |
| Pearl-white dragées (optional) | ½ cup | 1 cup | 2 cups |

**helpful hint:**
Make both mini and regular-sized cupcakes for a varied appearance.

**do it for less time:**
Purchase gum paste flowers and leaves from a craft or cake decorating store to make decorating a snap.

**do it for less money:**
Marzipan flowers and leaves are an inexpensive alternative to gum paste decorations.

**do it ahead:**
You can make the cupcakes up to 1 month in advance and freeze. Wrap tightly in plastic wrap and then again in foil. At least 1 day before serving, remove from the freezer and decorate. (They can be decorated while still frozen.) Alternatively, you can bake the cupcakes up to 3 days ahead of serving if they are wrapped in plastic, stored in resealable plastic bags, and kept at room temperature until ready to frost.

## directions:

### to make the cupcakes:

1. Preheat the oven to 350 degrees. Place foil muffin tin liners into muffin tins.

2. Make the cake batter according to package directions. Fill the muffin liners two-thirds full of batter. Bake 18 to 20 minutes, or until a toothpick inserted into the center of a cupcake comes out clean.

3. Remove from the oven and allow the pans to cool on wire racks for 20 minutes. Remove the cupcakes from the muffin tins and let cool completely. The cupcakes can be frozen at this point up to 1 month if wrapped in plastic wrap and then in foil.

### to make the buttercream frosting:

1. In a large bowl with an electric mixer, beat the shortening and butter together until light and fluffy. Add the vanilla and beat well. Sprinkle in the confectioners' sugar, 1 cup at a time, beating well after each addition. The frosting may appear dry at this point. Add milk a tablespoon at a time, beating after each addition, until soft and fluffy but still firm enough to hold its shape. Do not overbeat.

2. To store before using, press plastic wrap directly onto the surface of the frosting, and refrigerate in an airtight container for up to 2 weeks or freeze for up to 1 month. If frozen, thaw first in the refrigerator for 24 hours. Bring refrigerated frosting to room temperature before using and beat again with an electric mixture to fluff and soften.

## directions: (continued)

### to make the fondant flowers:

1. Place a piece of fondant (about 2 tablespoons) on a sheet of waxed paper. Using a rolling pin, roll out to about ⅛ inch thick. Use fondant cutters to cut out flower and leaf shapes. Place the shapes on a paper towel and allow to dry, uncovered, overnight.

### to decorate:

1. Spread an even layer of frosting on the top of each fresh, frozen, or thawed cupcake to cover completely, smoothing the surface with a small spreading spatula. Reserve any leftover frosting.

2. Take a piece of fondant (about 2 tablespoons) in your desired color and place on a piece of waxed paper. Roll out to ⅙ inch thick with a rolling pin. Using a 3¼- to 3½-inch circle cutter, cut out 1 circle per cupcake. Keep the cut circles covered with waxed paper while you work to prevent them from drying. Place a fondant circle on each cupcake, pressing slightly at the sides to create a slight ruffled edge, as illustrated in the picture.

3. Using the extra frosting as glue, affix the fondant flowers and leaves to the tops of the cupcakes. The cupcakes can be stored at a very cool room temperature in an airtight container for up to 2 days.

### do it ahead:

The frosting can be made up to 1 month in advance and frozen or 2 weeks in advance if refrigerated. Press plastic wrap directly into the frosting and cover tightly with an airtight lid. If frozen, thaw first in the refrigerator for 24 hours. Bring refrigerated frosting to room temperature before using and beat again with an electric mixture to fluff and soften.

### equipment:

- Muffin tins
- Silver foil muffin tin liners
- Toothpicks
- Wire cooling racks
- Small spreading spatula
- Rolling pin
- Fondant cutters, flower and leaf shapes in assorted small sizes
- Circle cutter, 3¼ to 3½ inches across
- Large mixing bowl
- Electric mixer

# in full bloom pink flower cupcakes

| ingredients | 24 cupcakes | 50 cupcakes | 75 cupcakes |
|---|---|---|---|
| Yellow cake mix, plus ingredients specified on package | 1 (18.25-ounce) box | 2 (18.25-ounce) boxes | 3 (18.25-ounce) boxes |
| Shortening | 1 cup | 2 cups | 3 cups |
| Unsalted butter, softened | 8 ounces (2 sticks) | 1 pound (4 sticks) | 1½ pounds (6 sticks) |
| Vanilla extract | 1½ teaspoons | 1 tablespoon | 2 tablespoons |
| Confectioners' sugar | 8 cups | 16 cups | 24 cups |
| Milk | ¼ cup | ½ cup | ¾ cup |
| Pink gel food coloring | as needed | as needed | as needed |
| Wilton ready-to-use rolled fondant, pastel colors pack | 1 (17.6-ounce) package | 1 (17.6-ounce) package | 2 (17.6-ounce) packages |
| Wilton ready-to-use rolled fondant, neon colors pack | 1 (17.6-ounce) package | 1 (17.6-ounce) package | 2 (17.6-ounce) packages |

**do it ahead:**
Make the fondant cut-outs a day ahead of preparing and frosting the cupcakes.

## directions:

### to make the cupcakes:

1. Preheat the oven to 350 degrees. Place foil muffin tin liners in muffin tins.

2. Make the cake batter according to package directions. Fill the muffin liners two-thirds full of batter. Bake 18 to 20 minutes, or until a toothpick inserted into the center of a cupcake comes out clean.

3. Remove from the oven and allow the pans to cool on wire racks for 20 minutes. Remove the cupcakes from the muffin tins and let cool completely. The cupcakes can be frozen at this point up to 1 month if wrapped in plastic wrap and then in foil.

### to make the buttercream frosting:

1. In a large bowl with an electric mixer, beat the shortening and butter together until light and fluffy. Add the vanilla and beat well. Sprinkle in the confectioners' sugar, 1 cup at a time, beating well after each addition. The frosting may appear dry at this point. Add milk a tablespoon at a time, beating after each addition, until soft and fluffy but still firm enough to hold its shape. Do not overbeat. Add pink gel food coloring, 1 drop at a time, beating between each addition, until the desired color is reached.

## directions: (continued)

2. To store before using, press plastic wrap directly onto the frosting, and refrigerate in an airtight container for up to 2 weeks or freeze for up to 1 month. If frozen, thaw first in the refrigerator for 24 hours. Bring refrigerated frosting to room temperature before using and beat again with an electric mixture to fluff and soften.

## to make fondant:

1. Using a rolling pin, separately roll out pieces (about 2 tablespoons at a time) of pastel pink and neon pink fondant on a sheet of waxed paper. Use fondant cutters to make flowers in light and dark pink. Place on a paper towel and allow to dry overnight.

## to decorate:

1. Apply generous amounts of frosting on each cupcake, swirling frosting with a small spreading spatula for a pretty surface. Arrange a few fondant flowers on top of each cupcake. Cupcakes can sit out at a cool room temperature for up to 2 days.

## equipment:

- Muffin tins
- Silver foil muffin tin liners
- Toothpicks
- Wire cooling racks
- Small spreading spatula
- Large mixing bowl
- Electric mixer
- Rolling pin
- Fondant cutters of flower and leaf shapes of assorted sizes

# cheesecake with sea star cookies and fresh flowers

| ingredients | **25** servings/2-tiered cake *(makes one 6-inch tier and one 8-inch tier)* | **50** servings/3-tiered cake *(makes one 6-inch, 8-inch, and 10-inch tier)* | **75** servings/4-tiered cake *(makes one 6-inch, 8-inch, 10-inch, and 12-inch tier)* |
|---|---|---|---|
| Graham cracker crumbs | 3 cups | 6 cups | 9 cups |
| Unsalted butter, melted, plus extra for greasing | 4 ounces (1 stick) | 8 ounces (2 sticks) | 12 ounces (3 sticks) |
| Sugar | ⅓ cup, plus 2 cups | ⅔ cup, plus 4 cups | 1 cup, plus 6 cups |
| Cream cheese, softened | 6 (8-ounce) packages | 12 (8-ounce) packages | 18 (8-ounce) packages |
| Sour cream | 2 cups (16 ounces) | 4 cups (32 ounces) | 6 cups (48 ounces) |
| Vanilla extract | 1 tablespoon | 2 tablespoons | 3 tablespoons |
| Large eggs | 6 | 12 | 18 |
| Prepared sugar cookie dough | 1 (16-ounce) package | 2 (16-ounce) packages | 3 (16-ounce) packages |
| Confectioners' sugar for garnish | ¼ cup | ⅓ cup | ½ cup |
| Fresh flowers, star- or bell-shaped, like fuchsias, forget-me-nots, freesias, jasmine, lily of the valley, or narcissus | as needed | as needed | as needed |

## do it ahead:

The cookies can be baked up to a month ahead of time if wrapped well in plastic and then in foil and frozen. The cookies can also be baked 5 days in advance and kept in an airtight container at room temperature.

The cheesecake tiers can be baked up to 2 months in advance if wrapped well in plastic and then in foil and frozen. Keep wrapped and thaw in the refrigerator for at least 24 hours before serving. The cheesecakes can also be baked 5 days in advance if wrapped well and refrigerated. Plastic wrap is extremely important for cheesecakes, as they can easily absorb the odors of your refrigerator.

## directions:

### to make the cheesecake:

1. Preheat the oven to 350 degrees. Grease the springform pans on the sides and bottoms. Cut a piece of parchment the same size as the bottom of each springform pan and press into the bottoms of the pans. Combine the graham cracker crumbs, butter, and the smaller amount of the sugar in a bowl and crumble with your fingers. Press firmly into the bottom and sides of the prepared pans.

2. Beat the cream cheese and the remaining sugar in large bowl with an electric mixer until fluffy. Add the sour cream and vanilla and mix well. Add the eggs one at a time, beating well after each addition. Divide the batter among the springform pans.

3. Bake for 1 hour, or until the centers are almost set. Turn the heat off and let the cheesecakes sit in the oven for another hour. Remove the cheesecakes from the oven and set on wire racks to cool completely. Refrigerate at least 4 hours or overnight. Alternatively, wrap the cooled cheesecakes tightly (you can leave them in their springform pans for protection) in plastic wrap and then in foil and freeze for up to 2 months at this point. Unwrap and thaw in the refrigerator at least 24 hours before serving.

## directions: (continued)

### to prepare the layers:

1. Loosen and remove the springform rims. Place each cheesecake on a cardboard round of the same size. Take the remaining cardboard cake round — it should be 2 inches larger than your largest tier — and cover with foil, dull-side out. (If the surfaces of your cakes aren't pretty, flip the cakes upside down and use the crumb crust as the top!) Find the center of each cheesecake layer (except for the top layer). Insert 4 straws, dowels, or cake pins into each layer, 2 inches from the center, to support the upper tiers of cake. Refrigerate the layers until ready to assemble the cake.

### to make the starfish cookies:

1. Preheat the oven to 350 degrees. Roll out the cookie dough to ⅛ inch thick on a lightly floured work surface. Cut out various sizes using starfish or star-shaped cookie cutters. Place cookies on a greased baking sheet at least 1 inch apart. Bake for 8 to 10 minutes, or until just golden. Allow to cool on the baking sheets for 10 minutes before transferring to a cooling rack. When completely cool, the cookies can be stored for up to 5 days at room temperature in an airtight container, or frozen for up to 1 month if tightly wrapped in plastic wrap and then in foil.

### to assemble and decorate:

1. For easy transport, place the largest cake layer on the reserved cake round covered in foil or on your final display surface. Add the next layer,

resting it on the plastic straws, dowels, or cake pins to support the weight of the tiers. Repeat until you have assembled the entire cake.

2. Place the confectioners' sugar in a sieve or sifter and shake it over the cheesecake to cover the top surface. Arrange the starfish cookies and flowers on cake as desired.

### helpful hint:

This cake comes together very quickly, which makes it perfect for a destination wedding. Pack the tiers separately and place in a cooler, then assemble on-site. In place of the fuchsias pictured here, you can use any non-toxic and unsprayed flower in your color scheme that is star-shaped.

fyi

### equipment:

- 6-inch springform pan, 3 inches deep
- 8-inch springform pan, 3 inches deep
- 10-inch springform pan, 3 inches deep
- 12-inch springform pan, 3 inches deep
- Parchment paper
- Cardboard cake rounds: 6-, 8-,10-, 12-, and 14-inch sizes
- Wire cooling racks
- 3-inch-long ¼-inch plastic drinking straws, wooden dowels, or cake pins to support tiers
- Rolling pin
- Starfish cookie cutters in 2 or 3 sizes
- Fine mesh sieve or sifter
- Large mixing bowl
- Electric mixer

# sunset polka dot cake

| ingredients | 25 servings/2-tiered cake (makes one 6-inch tier and one 8-inch tier) | 50 servings/3-tiered cake (makes one 6-inch, 8-inch, and 10-inch tier) | 75 servings/4-tiered cake (makes one 6-inch, 8-inch, 10-inch, and 12-inch tier) |
|---|---|---|---|
| Yellow cake mix, plus ingredients specified on package | 2 (18.25-ounce) boxes | 3 (18.25-ounce) boxes | 4 (18.25-ounce) boxes |
| Shortening | ½ cup, plus more for greasing pans | 1 cup, plus more for greasing pans | 1½ cups, plus more for greasing pans |
| Unsalted butter, softened | 4 ounces (1 stick) | 8 ounces (2 sticks) | 12 ounces (3 sticks) |
| Vanilla extract | 1 teaspoon | 2 teaspoons | 1 tablespoon |
| Confectioners' sugar | 5 cups | 8 cups | 12 cups |
| Milk | 2 tablespoons | ¼ cup | ⅓ cup |
| Light corn syrup | ½ tablespoon | 1 tablespoon | 1½ tablespoons |
| Wilton rolled ready-to-use fondant, neon color pack | 1 (17.6-ounce) package | 1 (17.6-ounce) package | 2 (17.6-ounce) packages |
| Wilton rolled ready-to-use fondant, white | 1 (24-ounce) package | 1 (24-ounce) package | 1 (24-ounce) package |
| Cornstarch for dusting | as needed | as needed | as needed |

## do it ahead:

Make the fondant polka dots and balls anywhere from 2 days to 2 months ahead of time. After they are completely dry, they can be stored in an airtight container.

You can bake the layers up to 1 month in advance and freeze. Apply the crumb coat to the cake, let freeze to harden, and then cover tightly in plastic wrap and again in foil to protect from freezer burn. Alternatively, you can bake the layers 3 days in advance of serving. Wrap in plastic wrap and store in resealable plastic bags at a cool room temperature until ready to decorate. The frosting can be made up to 1 month in advance and frozen or 2 weeks in advance and refrigerated. Press plastic wrap directly into the frosting and cover tightly with an airtight lid. If frozen, thaw first in the refrigerator for 24 hours. Bring refrigerated frosting to room temperature before using and beat again with an electric mixture to fluff and soften.

## directions:

### to make the cake layers:

1. Preheat the oven to 350 degrees. Generously grease the bottoms and sides of the cake pans. Cut circles of parchment paper to fit into the bottom of each cake pan and grease the surface of the parchment paper. Add a small amount of flour to the pans and shake to coat the bottoms and sides, then tap out the excess flour.

2. Make the cake batter according to package directions. Divide the batter among the cake pans, filling pans to within an inch of the top.

3. Wrap the cake pans in insulating strips (see page 212). Bake the cakes 50 to 60 minutes for the largest size, 35 to 45 minutes for the smaller sizes, or until a toothpick inserted into the center of the cakes comes out clean.

4. Remove the cakes from the oven and allow the pans to cool on wire racks for 30 to 45 minutes. Carefully run a knife around the sides to loosen, then remove the cakes from the pans, removing the parchment from bottoms, and place each on a cardboard cake round of the same size. Take the remaining cardboard cake round — it should be 2 inches larger than your largest tier — and cover with foil, dull-side out. Let the cakes cool completely.

## directions: (continued)

5. Using a long serrated knife, carefully slice across the top of each cake layer to make a level surface. The layers can be frozen at this point for up to 1 month if wrapped tightly in plastic wrap and then in foil, though we recommend applying the crumb coat and supporting plastic straws before freezing.

### to make the buttercream frosting:

1. In a large bowl with an electric mixer, beat the shortening and butter together until light and fluffy. Add the vanilla and beat well. Sprinkle in the confectioners' sugar, 1 cup at a time, beating well after each addition. The frosting may appear dry at this point. Add milk a tablespoon at a time, beating after each addition, until soft and fluffy but still firm enough to hold its shape. Do not overbeat.

2. To make a thinner frosting for a crumb coat, place about a fourth of the frosting in a separate bowl and beat in the light corn syrup. Press plastic wrap down onto the remaining frosting and store in an airtight container until ready to use. It can be frozen up to 1 month in advance or refrigerated up to 2 weeks in advance. If frozen, thaw first in the refrigerator for 24 hours. Bring refrigerated frosting to room temperature before using and beat again with an electric mixture to fluff and soften.

### helpful hint:

Roll out the fondant for the tops and sides of the tiers just at the time that you are ready to decorate, as the fondant will dry out and crack quickly. Always keep unused fondant wrapped in plastic. Use leftover frosting as the glue to adhere the polka dots to the cake.

### equipment:

- 6-inch round cake pan, 3 inches deep
- 8-inch round cake pan, 3 inches deep
- 10-inch round cake pan, 3 inches deep
- 12-inch round cake pan, 3 inches deep
- Insulating strips
- Parchment paper
- Cardboard cake rounds: 6-, 8-,10-, 12-, and 14-inch sizes
- Spreading spatula
- 3-inch-long ¼-inch plastic drinking straws, wooden dowels, or cake pins to support tiers
- Toothpicks
- Wire cooling racks
- Round fondant cutters in various small sizes up to 1½ inches in diameter
- Pastry bag
- Small round pastry tip
- Cocktail stirrers or thin red straws
- Bamboo skewers
- Large mixing bowl
- Electric mixer
- Paint brush
- Rolling pin
- Long serrated knife

## directions: (continued)

### to add the crumb coat:

1. Brush off any extra crumbs from the cake with a pastry brush. Dole out small spoonfuls of the thinner crumb-coat frosting all over the top of the fresh or frozen cakes. Smooth across the top and around the sides with a spreading spatula. You will have crumbs in the frosting; do not worry, as this is the precise purpose of a crumb coat. It will keep the final layer of frosting crumb-free. Spread the crumb coat as smoothly as possible.

2. Find the centers of all the cake layers, except for the top tier. Insert 4 plastic straws, dowels, or cake pins into each, 2 inches from the center, to support the upper tiers of cake.

3. Place the cake layers in the freezer until the frosting is hard to the touch, at least 45 minutes. Continue frosting or, if decorating later, wrap tightly in plastic wrap and then in foil, and store in the freezer. The layers will keep for up to 1 month at this point if frozen.

### to make fondant polka dots:

1. Break off a piece of fondant about the size of a golf ball, and keep the remaining fondant covered to avoid drying out. Working on a piece of waxed paper, place bamboo skewers around the fondant to keep the rolling pin at an even height above the work surface. This will keep your fondant pieces of an even thickness. Roll out the fondant and cut out a variety of polka dots. Place the circles on a paper towel, and leave uncovered to dry overnight.

### to make fondant toppers:

1. Break off small pieces of each color fondant and roll each color into balls ¼-inch, ½-inch, and ¾-inch wide. Insert a cocktail stirrer into the bottom of each ball. Place them on paper towels, and leave uncovered to dry overnight.

### to make fondant strips and tops:

1. Break off a piece of white fondant about the size of a tangerine. Working on a piece of waxed paper, place bamboo skewers around the fondant to keep the rolling pin at an even height above the work surface. Roll the fondant into a strip 3 inches wide and long enough to go around each tier of the cake. The exact length will differ depending upon how thick the frosting is, but the approximate lengths are: 19½ inches for the 6-inch tier, 25 inches for the 8-inch tier, and 32¾ inches for the 10-inch tier. Cover with plastic wrap until ready to use.

2. To make the tops for each tier, break off another piece of fondant about the size of a tangerine. Working on a piece of paper, roll out the

## directions: (continued)

fondant into a circle about ⅛ inch thick. You'll need a finished circle that's about ¼-inch larger than the size of your tier's diameter. So, for a 6-inch tier, you'll need a 6¼-inch circle; for an 8-inch tier, you'll need a 8¼-inch circle. For easy measuring, use the cake pan you baked in or a cardboard cake round. Cover with plastic wrap until ready to use.

### to make fondant rope:

1. Break off a piece of white fondant about the size of a golf ball. Working on a piece of waxed paper, roll out into a long thin rope at least ⅛ inch thick. Cover with plastic wrap until ready to use. Do not allow to dry.

### to decorate:

1. Bring the frosting to room temperature if necessary. Beat with an electric mixer until soft and fluffy. Remove the cake layers from the freezer and unwrap. You can decorate the frozen cake directly.

2. Spread the frosting about ¼ inch thick over the crumb coat with the small spreading spatula. Run hot water over the spatula and wipe it dry. Run the warm spatula over surface of frosting to smooth, rewarming the spatula as needed.

3. Dust hands lightly with cornstarch. Place the prepared strips of fondant around the sides of the cake, pressing lightly with a clean spatula so that they stick to the frosting. Place fondant tops on top of cake tiers, pressing lightly with a spatula to flatten. Trim the edges if it overhangs slightly. (If a little frosting oozes out between the top and the sides don't worry about it; the fondant rope will hide it.)

4. Place the remaining frosting in a pastry bag fitted with a small round tip and pipe a thin line (about the thickness of spaghetti) along the joint between the top edge and the sides. Place a length of the fondant rope around the edge, using the frosting as glue, and press lightly to adhere.

5. Using frosting as glue, decorate the top and sides with various sizes of fondant polka dots. Place the largest layer on the reserved cake round covered in foil or on a display surface. Add the next layer, resting it on the dowels or cake pins and using the frosting as glue. Repeat until you have assembled the entire cake.

6. Insert the fondant balls on cocktail stirrers into the top of cake. If any cornstarch shows on cake, brush off with a small, soft brush.

7. The finished cake can stand, covered, at a cool room temperature for up to 2 days before serving.

# lemon cake with vanilla frosting and fresh flowers

| ingredients | 25 servings/2-tiered cake (makes one 6-inch tier and one 8-inch tier) | 50 servings/3-tiered cake (makes one 6-inch, 8-inch, and 10-inch tier) | 75 servings/4-tiered cake (makes one 6-inch, 8-inch, 10-inch, and 12-inch tier) |
|---|---|---|---|
| Lemon cake mix, plus ingredients specified on package | 2 (18.25-ounce) boxes | 3 (18.25-ounce) boxes | 4 (18.25-ounce) boxes |
| Shortening | 1 cup, plus more for greasing pans | 2 cups, plus more for greasing pans | 3 cups, plus more for greasing pans |
| Unsalted butter, softened | 8 ounces (2 sticks) | 1 pound (4 sticks) | 1½ pounds (6 sticks) |
| Vanilla extract | ½ tablespoon | 1 tablespoon | 2 tablespoons |
| Confectioners' sugar | 8 cups | 16 cups | 24 cups |
| Milk | ¼ cup | ½ cup | ¾ cup |
| Light corn syrup | 1 tablespoon | 2 tablespoons | 3 tablespoons |
| Edible purple flowers and leaves like lavender, sweet pea, citrus leaves | as needed | as needed | as needed |

**fyi helpful hint:**
To keep flowers looking fresh, purchase flower spikes from a floral supply store. These are tubes with a pointed, closed end for inserting into cake. Fill flower spikes with a little water and insert flower stems into spikes.

## directions:

### to make the cake layers:

1. Preheat the oven to 350 degrees. Generously grease the bottoms and sides of the cake pans. Cut circles of parchment paper to fit into the bottom of each cake pan and grease the surface of the parchment paper. Add a small amount of flour to the pans and shake to coat the bottoms and sides, then tap out the excess flour.

2. Make the cake batter according to package directions. Divide the batter among the cake pans, filling pans to within an inch of the top.

3. Wrap the cake pans in insulating strips (see page 212). Bake the cakes 50 to 60 minutes for the largest size, 35 to 45 minutes for the smaller sizes, or until a toothpick inserted into the center of the cakes comes out clean.

4. Remove the cakes from the oven and allow the pans to cool on wire racks for 30 to 45 minutes. Carefully run a knife around the cakes to loosen, then remove the cakes from the pans, removing the parchment from bottoms, and place each on a cardboard cake round of the same size. Take the remaining cardboard cake round — it should be 2 inches larger than your largest tier — and cover with foil, dull-side out. Let the cakes cool completely.

5. Using a long serrated knife, carefully slice across the top of each cake layer to make a level surface. The layers can be frozen at this point for up to 1 month if wrapped tightly in plastic wrap and then in foil, though we recommend applying the crumb coat and supporting plastic straws before freezing.

## directions: (continued)

### to make the buttercream frosting:

1. In a large bowl with an electric mixer, beat the shortening and butter together until light and fluffy. Add the vanilla and beat well. Sprinkle in the confectioners' sugar, 1 cup at a time, beating well after each addition. The frosting may appear dry at this point. Add milk a tablespoon at a time, beating after each addition, until soft and fluffy but still firm enough to hold its shape. Do not overbeat.

2. To make a thinner frosting for a crumb coat, place about a fourth of the frosting in a separate bowl and beat in the light corn syrup. Press plastic wrap down onto the remaining frosting and store in an airtight container until ready to use. It can be frozen up to 1 month in advance or refrigerated up to 2 weeks in advance. If frozen, thaw first in the refrigerator for 24 hours. Bring refrigerated frosting to room temperature before using and beat again with an electric mixture to fluff and soften.

### to add the crumb coat:

1. Brush off any extra crumbs from the cake with a pastry brush. Dole out small spoonfuls of the thinner crumb-coat frosting all over the top of the fresh or frozen cakes. Smooth across the top and around the sides with a spreading spatula. You will have crumbs in the frosting; do not worry, as this is the precise purpose of a crumb coat. It will keep the final layer of frosting crumb free. Spread the crumb coat as smoothly as possible.

2. Find the centers of all the cake layers, except for the top tier. Insert 4 plastic straws, dowels, or cake pins into each, 2 inches from the center, to support the upper tiers of cake.

3. Place the cake layers in the freezer until the frosting is hard to the touch, at least 45 minutes. Continue frosting or, if decorating later, wrap tightly in plastic wrap and then in foil, and store in the freezer. The layers will keep for up to 1 month at this point if frozen.

### to decorate:

1. Bring the frosting to room temperature if necessary. Beat with an electric mixer until soft and fluffy. Remove the cake layers from the freezer and unwrap. (You can decorate the frozen cake directly.) Place the largest layer on the reserved cake round covered in foil or on a display surface. Add the next layer, resting it on the plastic straws, dowels, or cake pins and using the frosting as glue. Repeat until you have assembled the entire cake.

2. Spread the frosting about ¼ inch thick over the surface of the cake. Using a wooden skewer or toothpick, draw figure eights all in the surface of the frosting to create a subtly elegant design.

3. The cake can stand, covered, at a very cool room temperature for up to two days at this point.

4. A few hours before serving, decorate the cake with purple flowers and greenery.

## equipment:

- 6-inch round cake pan, 3 inches deep
- 8-inch round cake pan, 3 inches deep
- 10-inch round cake pan, 3 inches deep
- 12-inch round cake pan, 3 inches deep
- Parchment paper
- Cardboard cake rounds: 6-, 8-, 10-, 12-, and 14-inch sizes
- Toothpicks
- Wire cooling racks
- Small spreading spatula
- 3-inch-long ¼-inch plastic drinking straws, wooden dowels, or cake pins to support tiers
- Insulating strips
- Long serrated knife
- Large mixing bowl
- Pastry brush

# butter cake with sugared fruit and mocha amaretto frosting

| ingredients | **25** servings/2-tiered cake *(makes one 6-inch tier and one 8-inch tier)* | **50** servings/3-tiered cake *(makes one 6-inch, 8-inch, and 10-inch tier)* | **75** servings/4-tiered cake *(makes one 6-inch, 8-inch, 10-inch, and 12-inch tier)* |
|---|---|---|---|
| Golden butter cake mix, plus ingredients specified on package | 2 (18.25-ounce) boxes | 3 (18.25-ounce) boxes | 4 (18.25-ounce) boxes |
| Shortening | 1 cup, plus more for greasing pans | 2 cups, plus more for greasing pans | 3 cups, plus more for greasing pans |
| Unsalted butter, softened | 8 ounces (2 sticks) | 1 pound (4 sticks) | 24 ounces (6 sticks) |
| Almond extract | ½ tablespoon | 1 tablespoon | 2 tablespoons |
| Confectioners' sugar | 8 cups | 16 cups | 24 cups |
| Cocoa powder | ¼ cup | ½ cup | ¾ cup |
| Instant espresso powder | 1 tablespoon | 2 tablespoons | 3 tablespoons |
| Hot water | 2 tablespoons | ¼ cup | ⅓ cup |
| Light corn syrup | 1 tablespoon | 2 tablespoons | 3 tablespoons |
| Green grapes | 1 small bunch | 1 large bunch | 2 large bunches |
| Red grapes | 1 small bunch | 1 large bunch | 2 large bunches |
| Dried apricots, cut in half | 6 ounces | 12 ounces | 16 ounces |
| Pasteurized egg whites | ½ cup | 1 cup | 1½ cups |
| White or gold sanding sugar | ⅓ cup | ⅔ cup | 1 cup |

## helpful hint:

Butter cake mixes vary by brand. We use Duncan Hines Butter Recipe Golden Cake Mix. Whichever brand you use, follow the instructions on the back of the box closely and use the ingredients and amounts listed there to ensure that your cake comes out correctly.

Bunches of champagne grapes or fresh currants also make beautiful sugared fruit decorations. Any dried fruit that you can easily cut, such as mango or pineapple, also works well.

## directions:

### to make the cake layers:

1. Preheat the oven to 350 degrees. Generously grease the bottoms and sides of the cake pans. Cut circles of parchment paper to fit into the bottom of each cake pan and grease the surface of the parchment paper. Add a small amount of flour to the pans and shake to coat the bottoms and sides, then tap out the excess flour.

2. Make the cake batter according to package directions. Divide the batter among the cake pans, filling pans to within an inch of the top.

3. Wrap the cake pans in insulating strips (see page 212). Bake the cakes 50 to 60 minutes for the largest size, 35 to 45 minutes for the smaller sizes, or until a toothpick inserted into the center of the cakes comes out clean.

## directions: (continued)

4. Remove the cakes from the oven and allow the pans to cool on wire racks for 30 to 45 minutes. Carefully run a knife around the sides to loosen, then remove the cakes from the pans, removing the parchment from bottoms, and place each on a cardboard cake round of the same size. Take the remaining cardboard cake round — it should be 2 inches larger than your largest tier — and cover with foil, dull-side out. Let the cakes cool completely.

5. Using a long serrated knife, carefully slice across the top of each cake layer to make a level surface. The layers can be frozen at this point for up to 1 month if wrapped tightly in plastic wrap and then in foil, though we recommend applying the crumb coat and supporting plastic straws before freezing.

## equipment:

- 6-inch round cake pan, 3 inches deep
- 8-inch round cake pan, 3 inches deep
- 10-inch round cake pan, 3 inches deep
- 12-inch round cake pan, 3 inches deep
- Parchment paper
- Cardboard cake rounds: 6-, 8-, 10-, 12-, and 14-inch sizes
- Toothpicks
- Wire cooling racks
- Small spreading spatula
- 3-inch-long ¼-inch plastic drinking straws, wooden dowels, or cake pins to support tiers
- Pastry brush
- Insulating strips
- Long serrated knife
- Large mixing bowl
- Electric mixer

## directions: (continued)

### to make the buttercream frosting:

1. Dissolve the espresso powder in the water and set aside.

2. In a large bowl with an electric mixer, beat the shortening and butter together until light and fluffy. Add the almond extract and beat well. Sprinkle in the confectioners' sugar, 1 cup at a time, beating well after each addition. Beat in the cocoa powder a little at a time until the desired color is reached. The frosting may appear dry at this point. Add the espresso mixture a tablespoon at a time, beating between each addition until soft and fluffy but still firm enough to hold its shape. Do not overbeat. If necessary, add a little extra water.

3. To make a thinner frosting for a crumb coat, place about a fourth of the frosting in a separate bowl and beat in the light corn syrup. Press plastic wrap down onto the remaining frosting and store in an airtight container until ready to use. It can be frozen up to 1 month in advance or refrigerated up to 2 weeks in advance. If frozen, thaw first in the refrigerator for 24 hours. Bring refrigerated frosting to room temperature before using and beat again with an electric mixture to fluff and soften.

### to add the crumb coat:

1. Brush off any extra crumbs from the cake with a pastry brush. Dole out small spoonfuls of the thinner crumb-coat frosting all over the top of the fresh or frozen cakes. Smooth across the top and around the sides with a spreading spatula. You will have crumbs in the frosting; do not worry, as this is the precise purpose of a crumb coat. It will keep the final layer of frosting crumb-free. Spread the crumb coat as smoothly as possible.

2. Find the centers of all the cake layers, except for the top tier. Insert 4 plastic straws, dowels, or cake pins into each, 2 inches from the center, to support the upper tiers of cake.

3. Place the cake tiers in the freezer until the frosting is hard to the touch, at least 45 minutes. Continue frosting or, if decorating later, wrap tightly in plastic wrap and then in foil, and store in the freezer. The layers will keep for up to 1 month at this point if frozen.

## directions: (continued)

### to make the sugared fruit:

1. Using a small pastry brush, brush the egg whites onto the surfaces of the fresh and dried fruit. Working over paper towels to catch the excess sugar, sprinkle sanding sugar over the fruit while the egg glaze is still wet. Place on waxed paper to dry for about 1 hour.

### to decorate:

1. Bring the frosting to room temperature if necessary. Beat with an electric mixer until soft and fluffy. Remove the cake tiers from the freezer and unwrap. (You can decorate the frozen cake directly.) Place the largest layer on the reserved cake round covered in foil or on a display surface. Add the next layer, resting it on the plastic straws, dowels, or cake pins and using the frosting as glue. Repeat until you have assembled the entire cake.

2. Spread the frosting about ¼ inch thick over the crumb coat with the small spreading spatula. To create fluted sides, place the flat edge of the spreading spatula against base of the tier and drag up, repeating all around the base of each tier.

3. The cake can stand, covered, at a very cool room temperature for up to 2 days at this point.

4. Before serving, decorate with sugared fruit as desired.

# white rose cake

| ingredients | 25 servings/2-tiered cake (makes one 6-inch tier and one 8-inch tier) | 50 servings/3-tiered cake (makes one 6-inch, 8-inch, and 10-inch tier) | 75 servings/4-tiered cake (makes one 6-inch, 8-inch, 10-inch, and 12-inch tier) |
|---|---|---|---|
| White or vanilla cake mix, plus ingredients specified on package | 2 (18.25-ounce) boxes | 3 (18.25-ounce) boxes | 4 (18.25-ounce) boxes |
| Shortening | 1 cup, plus more for greasing pans | 2 cups, plus more for greasing pans | 3 cups, plus more for greasing pans |
| Unsalted butter, softened | 8 ounces (2 sticks) | 1 pound (4 sticks) | 1½ pounds (6 sticks) |
| Vanilla extract | ½ tablespoon | 1 tablespoon | 2 tablespoons |
| Confectioners' sugar | 8 cups | 16 cups | 24 cups |
| Milk | ¼ cup | ½ cup | ¾ cup |
| Light corn syrup | 1 tablespoon | 2 tablespoons | 3 tablespoons |
| Unsprayed medium white roses, stems trimmed to 2 inches | 2 dozen | 2 dozen | 2 dozen |

 **helpful hint:**
This cake can be made for any wedding theme using different colored roses.

## directions:

### to make the cake layers:

1. Preheat the oven to 350 degrees. Generously grease the bottoms and sides of the cake pans. Cut circles of parchment paper to fit into the bottom of each cake pan and grease the surface of the parchment paper. Add a small amount of flour to the pans and shake to coat the bottoms and sides, then tap out the excess flour.

2. Make the cake batter according to package directions. Divide the batter among the cake pans, filling pans to within an inch of the top.

3. Wrap the cake pans in insulating strips (see page 212). Bake the cakes 50 to 60 minutes for the largest size, 35 to 45 minutes for the smaller sizes, or until a toothpick inserted into the center of the cakes comes out clean.

4. Remove the cakes from the oven and allow the pans to cool on wire racks for 30 to 45 minutes. Carefully run a knife around the sides to loosen, then remove the cakes from the pans, removing the parchment from bottoms, and place each on a cardboard cake square of the same size. Take the remaining cardboard cake square — it should be 2 inches larger than your largest tier — and cover with foil, dull-side out. Let the cakes cool completely.

5. Using a long serrated knife, carefully slice across the top of each cake layer to make a level surface. The layers can be frozen at this point for up to 1 month if wrapped tightly in plastic wrap and then in foil, though we recommend applying the crumb coat and supporting plastic straws before freezing.

## directions: (continued)

### to make the buttercream frosting:

1. In a large bowl with an electric mixer, beat the shortening and butter together until light and fluffy. Add the vanilla and beat well. Sprinkle in the confectioners' sugar, 1 cup at a time, beating well after each addition. The frosting may appear dry at this point. Add milk a tablespoon at a time, beating after each addition, until soft and fluffy but still firm enough to hold its shape. Do not overbeat.

2. To make a thinner frosting for a crumb coat, place about a fourth of the frosting in a separate bowl and beat in the light corn syrup. Press plastic wrap down onto the remaining frosting and store in an airtight container until ready to use. It can be frozen up to 1 month in advance or refrigerated up to 2 weeks in advance. If frozen, thaw first in the refrigerator for 24 hours. Bring refrigerated frosting to room temperature before using and beat again with an electric mixture to fluff and soften.

## equipment:

- 6-inch square cake pan, 3 inches deep
- 8-inch square cake pan, 3 inches deep
- 10-inch square cake pan, 3 inches deep
- 12-inch square cake pan, 3 inches deep
- Parchment paper
- Cardboard cake squares: 6-, 8-, 10-, 12-, and 14-inch sizes
- Toothpicks
- Wire cooling racks
- Small spreading spatula
- 3-inch-long ¼-inch plastic drinking straws, wooden dowels, or cake pins to support tiers
- 4 x 4 x 2-inch piece of white Styrofoam
- T-pins
- White, ivory, or silver ribbon, 2-inches wide
- Pastry brush
- Long serrated knife
- Large bowl
- Electric mixer
- Insulating strips

## directions: (continued)

### to add the crumb coat:

1. Brush off any extra crumbs from the cake with a pastry brush. Dole out small spoonfuls of the thinner crumb-coat frosting all over the top of the fresh or frozen cakes. Smooth across the top and around the sides with a spreading spatula. You will have crumbs in the frosting; do not worry, as this is the precise purpose of a crumb coat. It will keep the final layer of frosting crumb-free. Spread the crumb coat as smoothly as possible.

2. Find the centers of all the cakes layers, except for the top tier. Insert 4 plastic straws, dowels, or cake pins into each, 2 inches from the center, to support the upper tiers of cake.

3. Place the cake tiers in the freezer until the frosting is hard to the touch, at least 45 minutes. Continue frosting or, if decorating later, wrap tightly in plastic wrap and then in foil, and store in the freezer. The layers will keep for up to 1 month at this point if frozen.

### to decorate:

1. Bring the frosting to room temperature if necessary. Beat with an electric mixer until soft and fluffy. Remove the cake tiers from the freezer and unwrap. (You can decorate the frozen cake directly.) Place the largest layer on the reserved cake square covered in foil or on a display surface. Add the next layer, resting it on the dowels or cake pins and using the frosting as glue. Repeat until you have assembled the entire cake.

2. Spread the frosting about ¼ inch thick over the crumb coat with the small spreading spatula. Using a wooden skewer or toothpick, draw figure eights all in the surface of the frosting for a subtly elegant design. The cake can stand, covered, at a very cool room temperature for up to 2 days at this point.

## directions: (continued)

### to make the rose square:

1. No more than several hours before serving the cake, pick over the roses and choose the best, discarding any withered outer petals. Wrap the Styrofoam in parchment or waxed paper, securing the ends with T-pins. Place ribbon around the outside edge of Styrofoam for a finished look, and secure the ends with T-pins. Make holes for the rose stems by punching holes in the Styrofoam with a toothpick. Pack the roses very close together and refrigerate. The roses will hold several hours before beginning to wilt.

2. Add the rose square to the frosted top just before displaying the cake.

# spice cake with gilded pineapple flowers and star anise

island spice

| ingredients | 25 servings/2-tiered cake (makes one 6-inch tier and one 8-inch tier) | 50 servings/3-tiered cake (makes one 6-inch, 8-inch, and 10-inch tier) | 75 servings/4-tiered cake (makes one 6-inch, 8-inch, 10-inch, and 12-inch tier) |
|---|---|---|---|
| Spice cake mix, plus ingredients specified on package | 2 (18.25-ounce) boxes | 3 (18.25-ounce) boxes | 4 (18.25-ounce) boxes |
| Shortening | 1 cup, plus more for greasing pans | 2 cups, plus more for greasing pans | 3 cups, plus more for greasing pans |
| Unsalted butter, softened | 8 ounces (2 sticks) | 1 pound (4 sticks) | 1½ pounds (6 sticks) |
| Vanilla extract | 1½ teaspoons | 1 tablespoon | 2 tablespoons |
| Confectioners' sugar | 8 cups | 16 cups | 24 cups |
| Milk | ¼ cup | ½ cup | ¾ cup |
| Light corn syrup | 1 tablespoon | 2 tablespoons | 3 tablespoons |
| Sweetened shredded coconut | 2 cups | 4 cups | 5 cups |
| Whole star anise | ½ cup (20 to 24 pods) | 1 cup (40 to 50 whole pods) | 1 cup (40 to 50 whole pods) |
| Dried pineapple rings | 1 pound | 24 ounces | 24 ounces |
| Edible gold luster dust | 1 small jar | 1 small jar | 1 small jar |

## helpful hint:

Gold luster is an edible shimmer dust that can be used on homemade chocolates, baked goods, or on garnishes, as it is here. Look for it at baking supply stores. Brush whole shelled nuts with gold luster dust to use in place of the star anise. Add a few well-placed citrus leaves for a green accent.

## directions:

### to make the cake layers:

1. Preheat the oven to 350 degrees. Generously grease the bottoms and sides of the cake pans. Cut circles of parchment paper to fit into the bottom of each cake pan and grease the surface of the parchment paper. Add a small amount of flour to the pans and shake to coat the bottoms and sides, then tap out the excess flour.

2. Make the cake batter according to package directions. Divide the batter among the cake pans, filling pans to within an inch of the top.

3. Wrap the cake pans in insulating strips (see page 212). Bake the cakes 50 to 60 minutes for the largest size, 35 to 45 minutes for the smaller sizes, or until a toothpick inserted into the center of the cakes comes out clean.

4. Remove the cakes from the oven and allow the pans to cool on wire racks for 30 to 45 minutes. Carefully run a knife around the sides to loosen, then remove the cakes from the pans, removing the parchment from bottoms, and place each on a cardboard cake round of the same size. Take the remaining cardboard cake round — it should be 2 inches larger than your largest tier — and cover with foil, dull-side out. Let the cakes cool completely.

## directions: (continued)

5. Using a long serrated knife, carefully slice across the top of each cake layer to make a level surface. The layers can be frozen at this point for up to 1 month if wrapped tightly in plastic wrap and then in foil, though we recommend applying the crumb coat and supporting plastic straws before freezing.

### to make the buttercream frosting:

1. In a large bowl with an electric mixer, beat the shortening and butter together until light and fluffy. Add the vanilla and beat well. Sprinkle in the confectioners' sugar, 1 cup at a time, beating well after each addition. The frosting may appear dry at this point. Add milk a tablespoon at a time, beating after each addition, until soft and fluffy but still firm enough to hold its shape. Do not overbeat.

2. To make a thinner frosting for a crumb coat, place about a fourth of the frosting in a separate bowl and beat in the light corn syrup. Press plastic wrap down onto the remaining frosting and store in an airtight container until ready to use. It can be frozen up to 1 month in advance or refrigerated up to 2 weeks in advance. If frozen, thaw first in the refrigerator for 24 hours. Bring refrigerated frosting to room temperature before using and beat again with an electric mixture to fluff and soften.

## equipment:

- 6-inch round cake pan, 3 inches deep
- 8-inch round cake pan, 3 inches deep
- 10-inch round cake pan, 3 inches deep
- 12-inch round cake pan, 3 inches deep
- Parchment paper
- Cardboard cake rounds: 6-, 8-,10-, 12-, and 14-inch sizes
- Toothpicks
- Wire cooling racks
- Small spreading spatula
- 3-inch-long ¼-inch plastic drinking straws, wooden dowels, or cake pins to support tiers
- Small soft paintbrush
- Insulating strips
- Long serrated knife
- Pastry brush
- Electric mixer

## directions: (continued)

### to add the crumb coat:

1. Brush off any extra crumbs from the cake with a pastry brush. Dole out small spoonfuls of the thinner crumb-coat frosting all over the top of the fresh or frozen cakes. Smooth across the top and around the sides with a spreading spatula. You will have crumbs in the frosting; do not worry, as this is the precise purpose of a crumb coat. It will keep the final layer of frosting crumb-free. Spread the crumb coat as smoothly as possible.

2. Find the centers of all the cake layers, except for the top tier. Insert 4 plastic straws, dowels, or cake pins into each, 2 inches from the center, to support the upper tiers of cake.

3. Place the cake tiers in the freezer until the frosting is hard to the touch, at least 45 minutes. Continue frosting or, if decorating later, wrap tightly in plastic wrap and then in foil, and store in the freezer. The layers will keep for up to 1 month at this point if frozen.

### to decorate:

1. Using the small paintbrush, paint luster dust all over the pineapple slices and on the star anise. Set aside on waxed paper.

2. Bring the frosting to room temperature if necessary. Beat with an electric mixer until soft and fluffy. Remove the cake layers from the freezer and unwrap. (You can decorate the frozen cake directly.) Place the largest layer on the reserved cake round covered in foil or on a display surface. Add the next layer, resting it on the plastic straws, dowels, or cake pins and using the frosting as glue. Repeat until you have assembled the entire cake.

3. Spread the frosting about ¼ inch thick over the crumb coat with the small spreading spatula. Carefully press the coconut into the top and sides of the cake. Curl the pineapple slices into flower shapes and place on the cake. Place the star anise on the cake for decoration. Touch up the gold luster dust if necessary.

4. The decorated cake can stand, covered, at a very cool room temperature for up to 2 days.

# basic yellow butter cake

| ingredients | to replace **1** box of cake mix | to replace **2** boxes of cake mix | to replace **3** boxes of cake mix | to replace **4** boxes of cake mix |
|---|---|---|---|---|
| Unsalted butter, softened | 8 ounces (2 sticks), plus more for greasing pans | 1 pound (4 sticks), plus more for greasing pans | 1½ pounds (6 sticks), plus more for greasing pans | 2 pounds (8 sticks), plus more for greasing pans |
| Castor or superfine sugar | 1¾ cups | 2½ cups | 3¾ cups | 5 cups |
| Vanilla extract | 2 teaspoons | 1 tablespoon | 1½ tablespoons | 2 tablespoons |
| Large eggs | 4 | 8 | 12 | 16 |
| Cake flour | 2¾ cups | 5½ cups | 8¼ cups | 11 cups |
| Baking powder | 2 teaspoons | 1 tablespoon | 1½ tablespoons | 2 tablespoons |
| Salt | ⅛ teaspoon | ¼ teaspoon | ⅓ teaspoon | ½ teaspoon |
| Milk | 1 cup | 2 cups | 3 cups | 4 cups |

## directions:

1. Preheat the oven to 325 degrees. Generously grease the bottoms and sides of the cake pans. Cut circles of parchment paper to fit into the bottom of each cake pan and grease the surface of the parchment paper. Add a small amount of flour to the pans and shake to coat the bottoms and sides, then tap out the excess flour.

2. Using an electric mixer with a paddle attachment, cream the butter and sugar until light and fluffy, about 5 minutes. Beat in the vanilla extract. Add the eggs 1 at a time, beating well between each addition.

3. In another bowl, sift together the flour, baking powder, and salt. With the mixer on a low speed, add the flour mixture into the batter, 1 cup at a time, alternating with ⅓ cup of milk. Beat well between each addition.

4. Pour the batter into cake pans of desired sizes. Wrap the cake pans in insulating strips (see page 212). Bake the cakes 50 to 60 minutes for a 10-inch round cake, 35 to 45 minutes for 8-inch to 6-inch round cakes, or until a toothpick inserted into the center of the cakes comes out clean.

5. Remove the cakes from the oven and allow the pans to cool on wire racks for 30 to 45 minutes. Carefully run a knife around the sides to loosen, then remove the cakes from the pans and peel off the parchment. Let the cakes cool completely before continuing.

## helpful hint:

It is best to make this cake in batches, as the finished cakes will not rise as high if the batter sits for any length of time before baking. Use the ingredient list as your shopping guide, but make only what you have room in your oven to bake at one time.

**fyi**

## equipment:

- Electric mixer with paddle attachment
- Cake pans in desired sizes
- Parchment paper
- Toothpicks
- Wire cooling racks
- Insulating strips

## chapter 9
# beverages: a toast to a smooth-flowing bar

When it comes to alcohol, even the most experienced planners have bouts of uncertainty. Should you buy more red wine than white wine? How do you make a Singapore Sling? Should you use real or plastic glasses? This chapter will help you successfully plan your beverage needs.

Don't forget to look at the drink recipes on pages 94 and 95. While those drink recommendations and recipes are suggested for the specific seasonal, themed weddings in chapter 7 of this book, they make excellent choices for weddings of all types.

# SERVING ALCOHOL

First and foremost: SAFETY. Be aware of how much alcohol is being consumed and by whom. Hiring a trained bartender and/or waiters can alleviate this pressure. If you anticipate a rowdy party, you may want to hire a few drivers to shuttle the guests from the hotel to the ceremony, and then to the reception, and back to the hotel at the end of the wedding. It might make a dent in your budget, but it will be worth every penny to ensure your peace of mind.

What and how much to buy really depends on the make-up of the guest list. At a small family wedding in the morning, one might assume that alcohol will play a lesser role. But if you've envisioned a classic cocktail hour with your guests mingling and holding elegant drinks, followed by a three-course dinner with three different wines, plus champagne or sparkling wine for toasting, you'll need to buy much more.

Alcohol is usually one of the biggest party expenses, so consider your budget. For larger groups, serving hard liquor can be less expensive than wine. A 750-ml bottle of wine will yield about five drinks, whereas a 750-ml bottle of spirits (rum, vodka, gin, etc.) will yield about sixteen cocktails.

If you anticipate all of your guests arriving at the same time or if you have a large number of guests, split the bar into two areas, or place glasses of pre-poured wine on an entry table. This way guests can help themselves and alleviate bar-traffic congestion.

## Barware Options

Budget plays an important role in choosing the glasses for a party. The tone of an elegant cocktail party can be dashed when the perfectly chilled Chardonnay is served in plastic glasses that screw together at the stem. Renting all-purpose, 10-ounce glasses can be a great way to go if budget permits. If money is limited, start the event with real glasses and switch to disposable glasses for the latter part of the evening. Most rental companies request that glasses need only be rinsed and returned in the original boxes. A good quality plastic glass can be used for informal outdoor events.

## Chilling

How many times have you had to run out mid-party to the local liquor store for extra ice? You don't want anyone to have to tackle this chore at your wedding. Ice is an inexpensive part of the bar set-up, so opt for more rather than less. Estimate 1½ to 2 pounds per person. "Chilling tubs" are large, heavy-duty plastic containers that cost about $5 each from club or discount stores.

Fill them with ice and a little water to chill white wine and other drinks. This takes about 30 minutes and leaves your refrigerator (and bathtub) free. It takes about 40 to 50 pounds of ice to fill one chilling tub. A great do-it-for-less tip is to fill your empty washing machine with ice and chill bottles in it. As the ice melts, the water drains away. You can set this up the morning of the wedding, and then have the caterers or hired waitstaff shuttle the beverages over to the reception site.

# BAR BASICS

## Beverage consumption guides

For a cocktail hour, assume 2 drinks per person per hour. For the remainder of the reception, allow for 1 drink per person for each hour thereafter.

For instance, if you have 50 guests attending a 4-hour reception, you should plan on serving 250 drinks:

- 50 guests x 2 drinks (per person for the first hour) = 100 servings
- 50 guests x 3 drinks (1 drink per hour for 3 hours) = 150 servings

> 100 servings for the first hour
> + 150 servings for the next 3 hours
> 250 servings total for a 4-hour event

## Tending Bar

Inevitably someone will ask for a "sex on the beach" or a "monkey's uncle" cocktail. Unless you are serving from a fully stocked bar and have a whiz of a bartender, avoid this by instructing the bartenders to ask your guests, "Would you like a drink?" followed by, "We have wine, beer, or soda."

## BOTTLE YIELDS

| bottle size | beverage type | yield | serving size |
|---|---|---|---|
| 750 milliliters | Champagne | 6 servings | 4 ounces |
| 750 milliliters | Wine | 5 servings | 5 ounces |
| 750 milliliters | Spirits | 16 cocktails | 1½ ounces |
| 1 liter | Spirits | 22 cocktails | 1½ ounces |
| 1½ liters | Spirits | 33 cocktails | 1½ ounces |
| 1 liter | Mineral water | 4 servings | 8 ounces |
| 2 liter | Soda | 8 servings | 8 ounces |
| 12 ounces | Beer | 1 serving | 12 ounces |

## PARTIAL BAR (CHART IS BASED ON A 3 TO 3½-HOUR-LONG EVENT)

| ingredients | 12 guests | 25 guests | 50 guests | 75 guests |
|---|---|---|---|---|
| White wine | 7 (750-ml) bottles | 15 (750-ml) bottles | 30 (750-ml) bottles | 45 (750-ml) bottles |
| Red wine | 4 (750-ml) bottles | 8 (750-ml) bottles | 16 (750-ml) bottles | 24 (750-ml) bottles |
| Beer | 18 (12-ounce) bottles | 32 (12-ounce) bottles | 64 (12-ounce) bottles | 96 (12-ounce) bottles |
| Mineral water | 3 (1-liter) bottles | 5 (1-liter) bottles | 10 (1-liter) bottles | 15 (1-liter) bottles |
| 7-Up or Sprite | 1 (2-liter) bottle | 3 (2-liter) bottles | 6 (2-liter) bottles | 9 (2-liter) bottles |
| Cola | 2 (2-liter) bottles | 4 (2-liter) bottles | 8 (2-liter) bottles | 12 (2-liter) bottles |
| Diet cola | 2 (2-liter) bottles | 4 (2-liter) bottles | 8 (2-liter) bottles | 12 (2-liter) bottles |
| Glasses | 30 (10-ounce) glasses | 75 (10-ounce) glasses | 150 (10-ounce) glasses | 225 (10-ounce) glasses |
| Ice | 18 pounds | 38 pounds | 75 pounds | 115 pounds |

## FULL BAR (CHART IS BASED ON A 3 TO 3½-HOUR-LONG EVENT)

| ingredients | 12 guests | 25 guests | 50 guests | 75 guests |
|---|---|---|---|---|
| White wine | 4 (750-ml) bottles | 9 (750-ml) bottles | 18 (750-ml) bottles | 27 (750-ml) bottles |
| Red wine | 3 (750-ml) bottles | 7 (750-ml) bottles | 14 (750-ml) bottles | 21 (750-ml) bottles |
| Beer | 5 (12-ounce) bottles | 12 (12-ounce) bottles | 24 (12-ounce) bottles | 36 (12-ounce) bottles |
| Gin | 1 (750-ml) bottle | 2 (750-ml) bottles | 4 (750-ml) bottles | 6 (750-ml) bottles |
| Rum | 1 (750-ml) bottle | 2 (750-ml) bottles | 4 (750-ml) bottles | 6 (750-ml) bottles |
| Vodka | 1 (750-ml) bottle | 3 (750-ml) bottles | 6 (750-ml) bottles | 9 (750-ml) bottles |
| Scotch | 1 (750-ml) bottle | 1 (750-ml) bottle | 2 (750-ml) bottles | 3 (750-ml) bottles |
| Bourbon | 1 (750-ml) bottle | 1 (750-ml) bottle | 2 (750-ml) bottles | 3 (750-ml) bottles |
| Mineral water | 4 (1-liter) bottles | 6 (1-liter) bottles | 12 (1-liter) bottles | 18 (1-liter) bottles |
| 7-Up or Sprite | 1 (2-liter) bottle | 2 (2-liter) bottles | 4 (2-liter) bottles | 6 (2-liter) bottles |
| Cola | 1 (2-liter) bottle | 3 (2-liter) bottles | 6 (2-liter) bottles | 9 (2-liter) bottles |
| Diet cola | 1 (2-liter) bottle | 3 (2-liter) bottles | 6 (2-liter) bottles | 9 (2-liter) bottles |
| Tonic | 1 (2-liter) bottle | 3 (2-liter) bottles | 6 (2-liter) bottles | 9 (2-liter) bottles |
| Glasses | 30 (10-ounce) glasses | 75 (10-ounce) glasses | 150 (10-ounce) glasses | 225 (10-ounce) glasses |
| Ice | 24 pounds | 50 pounds | 100 pounds | 150 pounds |

### Coffee Service

If you are serving coffee, stock up on half-and-half, sugar, and sugar substitutes. Consider adding flavored syrups or liqueurs such as Irish cream and Kahlúa to the selection, or offer chocolate mint sticks as stirrers. You can make an elegant presentation at a coffee station in an out-of-the-way location.

The measurements below allow for 1 5-ounce cup of coffee, 2 teaspoons of cream and sugar, and 1½ packets of sugar substitute per person. If you are using large coffee mugs or expect your guests to drink two cups of coffee each, double the recipe. Party-size coffee pots often have measurements included on the inside.

## COFFEE SERVICE

| ingredients | 12 (5-ounce) cups | 25 (5-ounce) cups | 50 (5-ounce) cups | 75 (5-ounce) cups |
|---|---|---|---|---|
| Ground coffee | 4 ounces (1¼ cups) | 8 ounces (2½ cups) | 1 pound (5 cups) | 1½ pounds (7½ cups) |
| Bottled or filtered water | 2 quarts, plus 1 cup | 1 gallon, plus 1 pint | 2 gallons, plus 1 quart | 3½ gallons |
| Half-and-half or cream | ½ cup (4 ounces) | 1 cup (8 ounces) | 2 cups (16 ounces) | 3 cups (24 ounces) |
| Sugar | ½ cup (3½ ounces) | 1 cup (7 ounces) | 2 cups (14 ounces) | 3 cups (21 ounces) |
| Sugar substitute | 18 packets | 36 packets | 72 packets | 108 packets |

## WINE-BUYING GUIDE

Trying to choose a wine from the thousands of bottles on display can be overwhelming. Unless you know exactly what your guests like, ask the wine manager to recommend a good selection that fits your budget. (For more information on champagne, see page 96.)

**• Season**
Low-alcohol wines are best in summer. Choose light, refreshing whites and rosés, or even some light reds in warm weather. Choose more robust wines in cooler weather.

**• Extending your dollar**
If serving large numbers, combine wine with chilled fruit juices. Hot punches, mulled wine, and sangria make good use of inexpensive wines as well.

**• Temperature**
Champagne should be served from 45 to 50 degrees, white wine from 50 to 55 degrees, and red wine from 55 to 65 degrees. If you are chilling fairly expensive bottles of wine or champagne in ice buckets, slip the bottle into a clear plastic bag to protect the label.

## Wine Glossary

- **Barbera.** Light and fruity Italian red wine.

- **Cabernet Sauvignon.** Rich and full-bodied red wine, often tasting of black currant and sometimes mint and eucalyptus. Improves with age. Best served with red meat.

- **Chardonnay.** Depending upon how it's aged (in oak or not), this white wine is either dry and light or full-bodied and buttery. Excellent served with creamy sauces.

- **Chenin Blanc.** Can be dry to sweet. Sweet Chenin Blanc generally tastes of honey. Dry Chenin Blanc is fresh and fruity. Dry versions are excellent with shellfish.

- **Gamay.** Also know as Beaujolais. Most are light, fruity reds that are meant to be consumed while the wine is young. The taste of pears, bananas, and raspberries can often be detected in Gamays. Great for summer picnics.

- **Gewürztraminer.** Spicy, full-bodied white wine that can be dry or sweet. With its rose perfume and litchi flavor, Gewürztraminer is one of the few wines to go well with spicy foods.

- **Merlot.** Rich and smooth red wine.

- **Muscat.** Musky white wine, often very sweet. Sweet varieties make excellent dessert wines. Tastes of peaches and apricots, and sometimes pineapple. Excellent with fresh fruit.

- **Pinot Grigio.** An Italian white wine that's aromatic, light, and smooth. Excellent served with fish dishes.

- **Pinot Noir.** Light to medium-bodied red wine with a strawberry aroma and hints of red currants and cherries.

- **Riesling.** White wine that can vary from bone-dry to extremely sweet. Light in body, yet strongly flavored. The high acidity balances the richness of this wine. Wonderful paired with spicy foods.

- **Sangiovese.** Also known as Chianti, an Italian red wine.

- **Sauvignon Blanc.** Also known as Pouilly Fumé or Fumé Blanc. Very dry, fresh white wine. Tastes of green grass and gooseberries. Good with fish and with salads dressed with vinaigrettes.

- **Sémillon.** Dry to very sweet white wine. Makes some of the best sweet dessert wines. Serve with fruit.

- **Syrah.** Also known as Shiraz, depending on its origin. Dark, full-bodied red wines that are less tannic when aged. Aromas of black currant, raspberry, cedar, black pepper, and spice.

- **Viognier.** A perfumed and full-bodied white wine.

- **Zinfandel.** Can be a light white or rosé wine, or a massive and tannic red. Always with a berry-like flavor.

## How much?

For water, fill the glass almost full. For wine, fill the glass one-third to one-half full. This allows guests to aerate their wine.

reds, bordeaux

water

burgundy

whites, sauvignon blanc

champagne flute

# appendices

## INGREDIENT EQUIVALENTS

| dry goods | quantity | equivalent |
|---|---|---|
| Chocolate chips | 5 ounces | about 1 cup |
| Chocolate chips | 1 (12-ounce) bag | about 2½ cups |
| Chocolate, unsweetened | 1 ounce | 1 square |
| Cocoa powder | 3 ounces | 1 cup |
| Coconut, shredded | 1 (14-ounce) bag | 5⅓ cups |
| Flour, all-purpose | 1 pound | 3 cups sifted or 3½ to 4 cups unsifted |
| Flour, cake | 1 pound | 4½ to 5 cups sifted or 3¾ cups unsifted |
| Flour, whole wheat | 1 pound | 3½ to 3¾ cups unsifted |
| Rolled oats | 1 pound | 5⅓ cups |
| Shortening | 1 pound | 2 cups |
| Sugar, brown | 1 pound | 2¼ cups packed or 3½ cups not packed |
| Sugar, granulated | 1 pound | 2¼ cups |
| Sugar, powdered | 1 pound | 4½ cups sifted or 3¾ cups unsifted |
| Sugar, superfine | 1 pound | 2 cups |

| meat and poultry | quantity (uncooked) | equivalent (cooked) |
|---|---|---|
| Bacon | 1 pound (16 to 20 slices) | 3 cups cooked and crumbled |
| Chicken breast | 1 large | 2 cups cooked and diced |
| Chicken (bone-in) | 3 to 4 pounds | 4 cups cooked and shredded |

| legumes, pasta, and rice | quantity (uncooked) | equivalent (cooked) |
|---|---|---|
| Beans, dried | 1 pound (2½ cups) | 6 cups |
| Lentils or split peas | 1 pound (2¼ cups) | 5 cups cooked or 6 to 7 cups puréed |
| Macaroni | 1 pound | 8 to 9 cups |
| Spaghetti | 1 pound | 7 to 8 cups |
| Rice, regular white long-grain | 1 cup | 3 cups |
| Rice, brown | 1 cup | 3 to 4 cups |

## INGREDIENT EQUIVALENTS (CONTINUED)

| herbs and vegetables | quantity (uncooked, fresh produce) | equivalent |
|---|---|---|
| Beets | 1 pound | 2 cups cooked and diced |
| Bell pepper | 1 large | 1 cup chopped |
| Broccoli | 1 medium-size (9-ounce) bunch | 3½ cups florets |
| Cabbage | ½ small head | 3 to 4 cups shredded |
| Carrots | 6 to 8 medium-size (1 pound) | 3 cups shredded |
| Celery | 2 medium-size stalks | 1 cup diced |
| Eggplant | 1 medium-size (14 ounces) | 5 cups cubed or 3½ cups diced |
| Green onion | 1 onion | 2 tablespoons sliced |
| Herbs, fresh | ½ ounce | ¼ cup loose or 2 tablespoons chopped |
| Lettuce | 1 (6-ounce) bag pre-washed lettuce | about 3 cups |
| Mushrooms | ½ pound | 2 cups sliced |
| Onion | 1 large (5 to 6-ounce) | 1 generous cup chopped |
| Onions | 1 pound | 3 to 4 cups chopped |
| Potato | 1 medium-size | ½ cup mashed |
| Pumpkin | 1 pound | 1 generous cup cooked and mashed |
| Spinach | 1 pound | 8 cups uncooked or 1½ cups cooked |
| Sweet potatoes | 1 pound | 1½ cups cooked |
| Tomatoes | 1 pound | 1½ cups peeled, seeded, and diced |
| Zucchini | 1 pound | 3½ cups sliced or 2 cups grated |

| nuts | quantity | equivalent |
|---|---|---|
| Almonds, peanuts, pistachios, or pine nuts (shelled) | 1 pound | 3 cups |
| Pecans or walnuts (shelled) | 1 pound | 3½ to 4 cups |
| Pecans or walnuts | 1 pound in shell | 1¾ to 2 cups shelled |

## INGREDIENT EQUIVALENTS (CONTINUED)

| dairy | quantity | equivalent |
|---|---|---|
| Butter | 1 pound | 2 cups |
| Cheese | 1 pound | 4½ cups grated |
| Cream cheese | 3 ounces | 6 tablespoons |
| Cream cheese | 8 ounces | 1 cup |
| Egg whites | 8 to 10 large eggs | 1 cup |
| Egg yolks | 12 to 14 large eggs | 1 cup |
| Heavy whipping cream | 1 cup | 2 cups whipped |
| Parmesan cheese | 3 ounces | 1 cup grated |

| fruit | quantity (fresh) | equivalent |
|---|---|---|
| Apple | 1 medium-size (5 to 6-ounce) | 1 cup diced |
| Apples | 2 medium-size (1 pound) | 1¼ cups applesauce |
| Bananas | 3 medium-size | 1 cup mashed |
| Berries | 1 quart | 3½ cups |
| Cherries | 1 pound | 2½ cups pitted |
| Cranberries | 1 pound | 3 cups sauce |
| Cranberries | 1 (12-ounce) bag | 2½ cups sauce |
| Lemon juice | 1 medium-size lemon | 2 to 4 teaspoons juice |
| Lemon zest | 1 medium-size lemon | 1 teaspoon grated rind |
| Lime juice | 1 medium-size lime | 1½ to 2 teaspoons juice |
| Lime zest | 1 medium-size lime | ¾ teaspoon grated rind |
| Orange juice | 1 medium-size orange | 4 to 5 tablespoons juice |
| Orange zest | 1 medium-size orange | 3 to 4 teaspoons grated rind |

| dried fruit | quantity | equivalent |
|---|---|---|
| Candied fruit or peel | ½ pound | 1½ cups |
| Dates (pitted) | 1 pound | 2⅔ cups |
| Dates (with pit) | 1 pound | 3½ cups |
| Raisins, cranberries, or cherries | 1 pound | 3 cups |

## INGREDIENT EQUIVALENTS (CONTINUED)

| miscellaneous | quantity | yields |
|---|---|---|
| Bread | 4 slices | 1 cup crumbs |
| Coffee | 1 pound beans | 80 tablespoons ground |
| Graham crackers | 14 crackers | 1 cup crumbs |
| Popcorn | ¼ cup uncooked kernels | 5 cups popped |
| Vanilla wafers | 20 wafers | 1 cup crumbs |

## SUBSTITUTIONS

| ingredient | quantity | substitution |
|---|---|---|
| Chocolate | 1 oz unsweetened | 3 tablespoons unsweetened cocoa plus 1 tablespoon butter |
| Herbs | 1 tablespoon fresh | 1 teaspoon dried |
| Garlic | 1 clove fresh | ⅛ teaspoon garlic powder |
| Mustard | 1 tablespoon Dijon | 1 teaspoon dry mustard |

## BUTTER EQUIVALENTS TABLE

| sticks | tablespoons | cups | ounces |
|---|---|---|---|
| ½ | 4 | ¼ | 2 |
| 1 | 8 | ½ | 4 |
| 1½ | 12 | ¾ | 6 |
| 2 | 16 | 1 | 8 |

# APPENDIX B: U.S. AND METRIC CONVERSION TABLES

## COMMON U.S. MEASUREMENTS EQUIVALENTS

| teaspoons | tablespoons | fluid ounces | cups | pints | quarts | gallons |
|---|---|---|---|---|---|---|
| 1 teaspoon | ⅓ tablespoon | | | | | |
| 1½ teaspoons | ½ tablespoon | | | | | |
| 2 teaspoons | ⅔ tablespoon | | | | | |
| 3 teaspoons | 1 tablespoon | ½ ounce | | | | |
| | 2 tablespoons | 1 ounce | ⅛ cup | | | |
| | 3 tablespoons | 1½ ounces | | | | |
| | 4 tablespoons | 2 ounces | ¼ cup | | | |
| | 5⅓ tablespoons | | ⅓ cup | | | |
| | 6 tablespoons | 3 ounces | | | | |
| | 8 tablespoons | 4 ounces | ½ cup | | | |
| | 10 tablespoons | 5 ounces | | | | |
| | 10⅔ tablespoons | | ⅔ cup | | | |
| | 12 tablespoons | 6 ounces | ¾ cup | | | |
| | 16 tablespoons | 8 ounces | 1 cup | ½ pint | | |
| | | 16 ounces | 2 cups | 1 pint | | |
| | | 32 ounces | 4 cups | 2 pints | 1 quart | |
| | | 128 ounces | 16 cups | 8 pints | 4 quarts | 1 gallon |

## QUICK U.S. WEIGHT CONVERSIONS

| ounces | pounds |
|---|---|
| 4 ounces | ¼ pound |
| 8 ounces | ½ pound |
| 12 ounces | ¾ pound |
| 16 ounces | 1 pound |
| 24 ounces | 1½ pounds |
| 32 ounces | 2 pounds |
| 40 ounces | 2½ pounds |
| 48 ounces | 3 pounds |
| 56 ounces | 3½ pounds |
| 64 ounces | 4 pounds |
| 72 ounces | 4½ pounds |
| 80 ounces | 5 pounds |
| 160 ounces | 10 pounds |

## DRY MEASUREMENTS

| u.s. measurements | metric |
|---|---|
| 1/16 ounce | 1 gram |
| 1/3 ounce | 10 grams |
| 1/2 ounce | 15 grams |
| 1 ounce | 28.35 grams (30 grams for cooking purposes) |
| 3 1/2 ounces | 100 grams |
| 4 ounces (1/4 pound) | 114 grams |
| 5 ounces | 140 grams |
| 8 ounces (1/2 pound) | 227 grams |
| 9 ounces | 250 grams or 1/4 kilogram |
| 16 ounces (1 pound) | 453.6 grams (450 grams for cooking purposes) |
| 18 ounces (1 1/8 pounds) | 500 grams or 1/2 kilogram |
| 32 ounces (2 pounds) | 900 grams |
| 36 ounces (2 1/4 pounds) | 1,000 grams or 1 kilogram |
| 3 pounds | 1,350 grams or 1 1/3 kilograms |
| 4 pounds | 2,800 grams or 1 3/4 kilograms |

## LIQUID MEASUREMENTS

| u.s. measurements | metric |
|---|---|
| 1 teaspoon | 5 milliliters |
| 1 tablespoon | 15 milliliters |
| 1 fluid ounce (2 tablespoons) | 30 milliliters |
| 2 fluid ounces (1/4 cup) | 60 milliliters |
| 8 fluid ounces (1 cup) | 240 milliliters |
| 16 fluid ounces (2 cups/1 pint) | 480 milliliters |
| 32 fluid ounces (2 pints/1 quart) | 950 milliliters |
| 128 fluid ounces (4 quarts/1 gallon) | 3.75 liters |

# resource guide

## DIY RESOURCES

- The Bride's Year Ahead: The Ultimate Month-by-Month Wedding Planner, Marguerite Smolen ($22.95)
- The Bride's Year Ahead, Deluxe Edition: The Ultimate Month-by-Month Wedding Planner, Marguerite Smolen and Andrea Feld ($29.95)
- Wedding Papercraft: Create Your Own Invitations, Decorations, and Favors to Personalize Your Wedding, North Light Books ($19.95)
- Wedding Plans, Wedding Crafts: Organize, Personalize, Accessorize, Creative Publishing International ($19.95)
- Michael's Book of Wedding Craft, by Lark Books ($24.95)
- The DIY Bride: 40 Fun Projects for Your Ultimate One-of-a-Kind Wedding, Kris Cochran ($19.95)
- Creative Wedding Florals You Can Make, Terry L. Rye ($19.99)
- Wedding Flowers and Decorations Ideas Books on CD, ($19.95)
- The New Book of Wedding Flowers: Simple & Stylish Arrangements for the Creative Bride, Joanne O'Sullivan ($12.95)

## INTERNET RESOURCES

### General Wedding Resources

- **Bride.com** (www.bride.com) Excellent resource for finding wedding vendors and bridal shows in your area
- **Brides.com** (www.brides.com) The #1 source for wedding fashion, beauty, planning and style
- **The Knot** (www.theknot.com) Create a MyKnot account to keep track of amazing wedding ideas, checklists, and countdowns
- **WeddingChannel.com** (www.weddingchannel.com) Great resource for wedding ideas and advice, gift registry information, local vendors, and more

### Wedding Budget Resources

- **Wedding Wire** (www.weddingwire.com) Create a free account, plan out your wedding budget to perfection, and use other helpful applications
- **Brides.com** (www.brides.com) Create a free account and use the personalized wedding budget calculator to manage your money
- **Eventageous: the Planner's Advantage** (www.eventageous.com) Helpful resource with a suggested budget worksheet and calculator
- **OurDreamWedding.com** ( www.ourdreamwedding.com) Answer questions about your wedding and receive personalized help in budget calculation

## Gifts and Favors Resources

- **Gifts.com** (www.gifts.com) Find gifts for all your attendants
- **American Bridal** (www.americanbridal.com) Find a vast array of wedding gifts and favors
- **Hobby Lobby** (www.hobbylobby.com; find nearby location) Excellent resource for craft supplies if doing your gifts and favors yourself
- **Michael's** (www. michaels.com; find nearby location) Another great place for craft supplies
- **Groomstand.com** (www.groomstand.com) Groomsman gifts and accessories
- **SpaFinder.com** (www.spafinder.com) Find spa packages for bridesmaids; gift certificates can be used at any participating location

## Flowers and Decoration Resources

- **FlowerBud.com** (www.flowerbud.com) Offers excellent DIY wedding flower-arrangement information and sells flowers in bulk
- **ProFlowers.com** (www.proflowers.com) Find discount flower arrangements and search flowers by price range or occasion
- **WeddingDecor.com** (www.weddingdecor.com) Excellent source for wedding decoration ideas for all themes and color schemes
- **Paper Mart** (www.papermart.com) Offers favor boxes, fabric, ribbon, vases, balloons, and more for your wedding
- **Barn Loft Candles** (www.barnloftcandles.com) Find a wide variety of shapes, sizes, and colors of wedding candles for decoration

## Invitations and Stationery Resources

- **EnvelopeMan.com** (www.envelopeman.com) Great source for envelopes and stationery for your wedding
- **Jam Paper** (www.jampaper.com) Wonderful variety of paper, cardstock, and envelopes for making your own invitations
- **Olmsted-Kirk Paper Company** (www.okpaper.com) One of the most established and reputable sources for paper and stationary in the industry
- **XPEDX** (www.xpedxstores.com) Well-known for their paper and envelopes, paper crafting, and party products
- **Greenwich Letterpress** (www.greenwichletterpress.com) Beautiful but expensive resource for hand-pressed cards
- **The American Stationery Company** (www.theamericanwedding.com) Find and personalize stylish wedding invitations and other stationery
- **Wedding Paper Divas** (www.weddingpaperdivas.com) A happy medium for stylish invitations on a budget
- **Custom Paper** (www.custompaper.com) Beautiful, handmade papers
- **Invitation Box** (www.invitationbox.com) Invitations, stationery, save-the-date cards, and other wedding papery

## Location Resources

- UniqueVenues.com (www.uniquevenues.com) Search engine for wedding venues all over the United States, Canada, and the UK
- Party Pop (www.partypop.com) Find wedding locations by type all over the United States, Canada, and the UK
- WeddingMapper.com (www.weddingmapper.com) Explore local wedding areas and create a personalized wedding map for your guests

## Music and Entertainment Resources

- GigMasters.com (www.gigmasters.com) Excellent resource for finding wedding bands, DJs, soloists, and ensembles
- ForeverWed.com (www.foreverwed.com/music) Find articles addressing wedding music issues and browse wonderful wedding song lists
- OurWeddingSongs.com (www.ourweddingsongs.com) Lists of wedding songs grouped by wedding and reception activities
- MyPartyPlanner.com (www.mypartyplanner.com) Find wedding bands and DJs
- American Disc Jockey Association (www.adja.org) Find a DJ anywhere in the United States

## Personal Wedding Web site Resources

- MyWedding.com (www.mywedding.com) Free wedding Web site that allows for wedding story, photos, gift registry, and wedding party information
- WeddingWindow.com (www.weddingwindow.com) $29.95 yearlong wedding Web site subscription with unlimited uploading content
- WedQuarters.com (www.wedquarters.com) Rated #1 Wedding Web site Provider Overall by The Wall Street Journal
- TheWeddingTracker.com (www.theweddingtracker.com) $60.00 yearlong wedding Web site subscription with many different content options

## Photography & Videography Resources

- YouShoot.com (www.youshoot.com) Rent digital cameras for your wedding
- Professional Photographers of America (www.ppa.com) Find professional photographers all across the country
- Wedding and Event Videographers Association International (www.weva.com) Locate a videographer to capture your wedding day

## Wedding Attire

- Like.com (www.like.com) Excellent resource for men's and women's wedding attire accessories
- EBay (www.ebay.com) Find discount wedding, bridesmaid, and flower girl attire
- Target (www.target.com) Sells inexpensive wedding dresses
- Lane Bryant (www.lanebryant.com) Sells inexpensive wedding attire and

accessories for women sizes 14-28

- **Jessica McClintock** (www.jessicamcclintock.com) Find beautiful, moderately priced wedding attire for brides and flower girls
- **Ann Taylor** (www.anntaylor.com) Find average priced wedding dresses, bridesmaid dresses, and groom accessories
- **David's Bridal** (www.davidsbridal.com) One of the best resources for wedding attire and matching accessories for brides and bridesmaids
- **Group USA** (www.groupusa.com) Sells moderately priced wedding attire for brides and bridesmaids and often has discounts
- **Priscilla of Boston** (www.priscillaofboston.com) Find expensive, high-end wedding attire for brides
- **J. Crew** (www.jcrew.com) Sells beautiful bridesmaid dresses
- **Watters and Watters** (www.watters.com) Find moderately priced and fashion-forward bridesmaid gowns
- **Wtoo** (www.watters.com) Find casual and less-expensive bridesmaid gowns
- **Bill Levkoff** (www.billlevkoff.com) Sells elegant and fashionable bridesmaid dresses

## DIY CATERING AND COOKING EQUIPMENT RESOURCES

- **Ace Mart** (www.acemart.com) Over four thousand cooking equipment items with competitive pricing
- **Big Tray** (www.bigtray.com) Great prices on restaurant-grade supplies
- **Cooking.com** (www.cooking.com) Find recipes, menus, and a buying guide for new and classic kitchen essentials
- **Costco** (www.costco.com) Excellent source for buying food in bulk
- **Restaurant Supply Solutions** (www.restaurantsupplysolutions.com) Sells all items wholesale to the public with many great bargains
- **Sur La Table** (www.surlatable.com) Sells a great variety of items for all aspects of cooking
- **Surfas** (www.surfasonline.com) Los Angeles-based "chef's paradise" for specialty and quantity cooking needs

# index

# acknowledgments

The reason you see a lengthy thank-you page in most cookbooks is simple: it takes many people to create, work through, and complete a cookbook.

I may have had the idea, but without the incredible cast of characters I'm about to thank, there would be no *Do-It-for-Less! Weddings*.

My sincere appreciation and admiration starts with Cindie Flannigan and Martha Hopkins. These two women do more for me than I have time to write. They are smart, beautiful, and talented. I am lucky to count them as friends. They act as writers, editors, recipe testers, and style mavens. They are my support group and my sounding boards, and they make my life rich. Thank you, ladies.

My next thanks go to my agents Lisa Ekus and Jane Falla of The Lisa Ekus Group, who sold this book to Robin Haywood, Executive Editor of Sellers Publishing. I am lucky enough to have two agents who are honest, hard working, and tireless cheerleaders and who laugh at my jokes. They refuse to give up even when I have. Thank you.

At Seller's Publishing, I'd like to thank Robin, Megan Hiller, Mary Baldwin, and Charlotte Smith. These professional women have been incredibly supportive of the process of writing. An author cannot ask for more than that.

From Martha's office, my thanks to her partner Randall Lockridge, who designed *Do-It-for-Less! Parties* on which this wedding book is modeled. He created a classic, user-friendly book for home caterers. Thank you, Randall, for your wonderful design sense.

To Kristen Green Wiewora, who worked on our party book and helped us again with this wedding book. Kristen, I truly thank you for your continued, dependable involvement with our series. Revekah Kim, Rachel O'Neal, and Linda Asher — every page you researched or proofed or corrected, I appreciate it.

Many of the beautiful food photos in this book were shot by Matt Armendariz Photography. Matt, I hope you know how much Cindie, Martha, and I appreciate you and your talent.

Other photographs were contributed by generous clients of Jon Edwards Photography. Jon makes a picture of food taste and smell good. He's a lighting god. I adore you, Jonnie.

And last but not least, a hearty thank you to our recipe testers. Cindie and I designed menus, tested them, and then sent them to chef friends to test them again and give us their input. So much work, time, and sweat goes into recipes testing — especially on quantity recipes. I know for a fact that there are no more generous people in the entire world than those that cook. Our thanks go to Paty Winters, Lynley Fleak, Adam Pearson, Marla Simon, and Betsy Rodgers.

This list would not be complete without mentioning my husband, Ken Meyer. He makes me believe I can do everything I want. My love, thanks, and appreciation to him.